Health
of the Human
Spirit

Other Books by
Brian Luke Seaward, PhD

A Beautiful World:
The Earth Songs Journals

Quiet Mind, Fearless Heart:
The Taoist Path of Stress and Spirituality

Hot Stones & Funny Bones:
Teens Helping Teens with Stress and Anger

Achieving the Mind–Body–Spirit Connection

The Art of Calm:
Relaxation Through the Five Senses

Stressed Is Desserts Spelled Backward:
Rising Above Life's Challenges with Humor, Hope, and Courage

Stand Like Mountain, Flow Like Water:
Reflections on Stress and Human Spirituality,
10th Anniversary Edition

Table for Two, Please:
Morsels of Inspiration and Wisdom over the Noon Hour

Health and Wellness Journal Workbook, 3rd Edition

Managing Stress:
A Creative Journal, 4th Edition

Managing Stress:
Principles and Strategies for Health and Well-Being,
7th Edition

Essentials of Managing Stress, 2nd Edition

Health
of the Human
Spirit *Second Edition*

Spiritual Dimensions for Personal Health

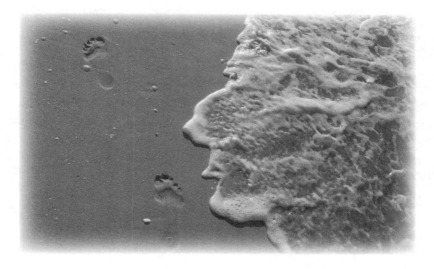

Brian Luke Seaward, PhD

Paramount Wellness Institute
Boulder, Colorado

JONES & BARTLETT
LEARNING

World Headquarters
Jones & Bartlett Learning
5 Wall Street
Burlington, MA 01803
978-443-5000
info@jblearning.com
www.jblearning.com

Jones & Bartlett Learning books and products are available through most bookstores and online booksellers. To contact Jones & Bartlett Learning directly, call 800-832-0034, fax 978-443-8000, or visit our website, www.jblearning.com.

Substantial discounts on bulk quantities of Jones & Bartlett Learning publications are available to corporations, professional associations, and other qualified organizations. For details and specific discount information, contact the special sales department at Jones & Bartlett Learning via the above contact information or send an email to specialsales@jblearning.com.

Production Credits

Executive Editor: Shoshanna Goldberg
Editorial Assistant: Agnes Burt
Editorial Assistant: Sean Coombs
Production Manager: Julie Champagne Bolduc
Production Assistant: Emma Krosschell
Marketing Manager: Jody Yeskey
V.P., Manufacturing and Inventory Control:
    Therese Connell
Composition: Laserwords Private Limited, Chennai, India
Cover Design: Scott Moden
Photo Researcher: Sarah Cebulski
Permissions and Photo Research Assistant: Gina Licata
Cover Image: © Brian Luke Seaward
Printing and Binding: Malloy, Inc.
Cover Printing: Malloy, Inc.

Unless otherwise indicated, all photographs and illustrations are under copyright of Jones & Bartlett Learning, or have been provided by the author.

Some images in this book feature models. These models do not necessarily endorse, represent, or participate in the activities represented in the images.

Library of Congress Cataloging-in-Publication Data

Seaward, Brian Luke.
    Health of the human spirit : spiritual dimensions for personal health / by Brian Luke Seaward.—2nd ed.
        p. cm.
    Includes bibliographical references and index.
    ISBN 978-1-4496-4845-9—ISBN 1-4496-4845-2
    1. Spiritual life. I. Title.
    BL624.S422 2013
    204—dc23

                                                                    2011049833

6048

Printed in the United States of America
16 15 14 13 12   10 9 8 7 6 5 4 3 2 1

*This book is dedicated to my dear friend and colleague
Michael York, who embodies integrity, humor, compassion, and all
the traits illuminated by the health of the human spirit!*

Contents

Foreword   xiii

Introduction   xv

Acknowledgments   xxi

About the Author   xxiii

CHAPTER **1** | 1
The Call to Spirit

The World in Crisis   2
A Spiritual Hunger?   5
A Turning Point in Consciousness   6
Spiritual Materialism   8
An Unhealthy Spirit?   9
I Don't Believe It!   9
The Winds of Change *Are* the Winds of Grace   10
Stress and Spirituality: Partners in the Dance of Life   12
Of Spirit and Character   12
Profiles of Human Spirituality   13
Keeping an Open Mind   16
Summary   16
Terms and Concepts   17
Soul-Searching Exercises   17
Exercise 1.1 Got The Spirit? Let's Hear It!   17
Exercise 1.2 Are You a Cultural Creative?   18
Exercise 1.3 Of Character and Spirit   19
Exercise 1.4 A Matter of Conscience   20
Endnotes   21
Additional References   22

CHAPTER **2** | 25
The Wellness Paradigm Revisited

A Closer Look at the Wellness Paradigm   26
Wellness in the Limelight and the Life Cycle   29
Human Spirituality: The Neglected Component of Well-Being
(If you cannot measure it, it is not real.)   30

The Legacy of Descartes: Division and Separation   32

New Common Ground Between Science and Religion   32

A Closing Story   34

Summary   34

Terms and Concepts   35

Exercise 2.1 The Mandala of Personal Wellness   35

Endnotes   37

Additional References   37

CHAPTER **3** | **39**

Theories of Human Spirituality: Perspectives from the Sages and Wisdom Keepers

Carl Gustav Jung: Divine Consciousness   42

Rachel Naomi Remen: To Be of Service   44

Abraham Maslow: To Be Self-Actualized   46

M. Scott Peck: The Four Stages of Spiritual Growth   48

Black Elk: Mother Earth Spirituality   52

Hildegard von Bingen: The Mystical Path   55

Joan Borysenko: The Feminine Path   57

Ken Carey: Divine Messages   59

The Dalai Lama: Compassion and Happiness   60

Joseph Campbell: The Hero's Journey   61

Barbara Marx Hubbard: Conscious Evolution   64

Deepak Chopra: Seven Spiritual Steps on the Divine Path   65

Larry Dossey: The Nonlocal Mind   68

Albert Einstein: Light and Energy   70

Matthew Fox: Creation Spirituality   72

Lao Tzu: Tao—The Balance of Life   74

Viktor Frankl: The Search for Life's Meaning   77

Jean Houston: Our Human Potential   80

Jesus of Nazareth: Unconditional Love   81

Paramahansa Yogananda: To Be Self-Realized   85

Ken Wilber: The Spectrum of Consciousness   86

Summary   89

Terms and Concepts   89

Exercise 3.1 High on a Mountaintop   90

Exercise 3.2 The Road Less Traveled: Stages of Spiritual Growth   92

Exercise 3.3 The Hero's Journey   93

References and Resources   95

Additional References   97

CHAPTER **4** | 99

The Nature of Human Spirituality

Definitions of Human Spirituality   100
Spirit: The Breath of Life   101
One Source, Many Names   103
Definitions of Religion   103
The Perennial Philosophy   104
Metaphor: The Language of Spirit   106
The Path and the Journey   106
Spirits on a Human Path   108
Of Spirit and Soul   109
What Is Stress?   110
What Is the Soul?   111
The Three Pillars of Human Spirituality   113
Desire + Commitment = Discipline   117
Summary   118
Terms and Concepts   118
Exercise 4.1 The Three Pillars of Human Spirituality   119
Exercise 4.2 Personal and Interpersonal Relationships   120
Exercise 4.3 Your Personal Value System   121
Exercise 4.4 Your Meaningful Purpose in Life   122
Exercise 4.5 Mandala of the Human Spirit   123
Endnotes   124
Additional References   125

CHAPTER **5** | 127

Mountains, Molehills, and Muscles of the Soul

The Metaphorical Mountain   128
Molehills: Roadblocks on the Spiritual Path   129
Distractions on the Spiritual Path   131
Muscles of the Soul   132
Spiritual Potential and Spiritual Health   136
Rainbows and the Yellow Brick Road   138
Seasons of the Soul   139
Summary   149
Terms and Concepts   149
Exercise 5.1 Roadblocks on the Spiritual Path   150

Exercise 5.2 Distractions on the Spiritual Path   151
Exercise 5.3 Muscles of the Soul   152
Exercise 5.4a Seasons of the Soul   153
Exercise 5.4b Your Seasons of the Soul   154
Endnotes   156
Additional References   156

CHAPTER **6** | **157**
Mind–Body–Spirit Healing

The Ghost in the Machine   160
A New Era of Medicine   162
The Human Energy Field: The Interface Between Body and Soul   165
Stress and Disease   166
Cellular Consciousness   167
Complementary Medicine/Energy Medicine   168
So Why Doesn't Everybody Get Healed?   170
Summary   173
Terms and Concepts   173
Exercise 6.1 Anatomy Energy Map   173
Exercise 6.2 When Your Biography Becomes Your Biology   175
Exercise 6.3 Energy System "Vitamins"   176
Exercise 6.4 Unresolved Anger or Fear?   177
Endnotes   179
Additional References   181

CHAPTER **7** | **183**
Embrace the Mystery

Be a Good Mystic!   185
No Short List of Mysteries Here!   186
The Mystery of DNA   189
The Kundalini Effect   190
Science's Blind Spot   192
Prayer, Distant Healing, and the Nonlocal Mind   192
Summary   193
Terms and Concepts   194
Exercise 7.1 On Being a Good Mystic   194
Exercise 7.2 More Than Just Intuition!   196
Exercise 7.3 One: A Holy Moment   197

Endnotes   198
Additional References   199

CHAPTER 8 | 201
The Art of Meditation

Cleansing the Mind   203
Of Ego and Soul   204
Domesticating the Ego   205
A Free Spirit Must Be Disciplined   205
Types of Meditation   206
Steps in Meditation   209
Summary   211
Terms and Concepts   212
Exercise 8.1 Meditation Checklist   212
Meditation Exercises   213
Exercise 8.2 Breathing Clouds Meditation   213
Exercise 8.3 Open Heart Meditation   214
Exercise 8.4 Crystal Cave Meditation   216
Exercise 8.5 Seven Veils Meditation (Lifting the Veils of Illusion to Be One with the Source)   217
Exercise 8.6 Body Colors and Healing Light Meditation   221
Exercise 8.7 The Rainbow Meditation   222
Exercise 8.8 Energy Ball Meditation   224
Exercise 8.9 DNA Meditation   226
Endnotes   227
Additional References   228

CHAPTER 9 | 229
Health of the Human Spirit

Medicine for the Soul   231
Keeping the Human Spirit Healthy   232
Summary   243
Terms and Concepts   244
Exercise 9.1 Health of the Human Spirit   244
Exercise 9.2 The Doors of Perception   246
Exercise 9.3 Sweet Forgiveness   248
Exercise 9.4 Creative Altruism: The Power of Unconditional Love   249
Exercise 9.5 The Divine Paradox   251

Endnotes   252
Additional References   252

CHAPTER **10** | 253
The End Is Just the Beginning

Index   259

Foreword

A Conversation with Elisabeth Kübler-Ross, MD

Author of *The Wheel of Life* and *On Death and Dying*

January 14, 2000

"Give me your finger," Elisabeth said softly with that undeniable Swiss-German accent. Her voice and body were weak from a series of debilitating strokes, but the gleam in her eyes showed her spirit was still vibrant.

"Like this," she said, pointing her index finger in the air toward my outstretched hand. We were sitting in a corner of her study, a room overflowing with books, letters, and hundreds of unread manuscripts. In hearing about this project, Elisabeth, one of the most renowned experts on death and dying, invited me down to Scottsdale, Arizona, to talk about the textbook. As in Steven Spielberg's movie *E.T.*, when the alien touches his index finger with little Elliot's hand, our fingers connected.

"This is how I hug now. My body is very weak," she explained, with a frail smile, "so this is how I hug." With her demonstration of affection, she taught me that the power of spirit is as subtle as it is dynamic.

"Do you have any words you would like to share about human spirituality with today's college students?" I asked. This was her response: "Each person has to get in touch with their own spirituality. Love is the most important thing I can say. It's all about love, unconditional love. Humor... you need humor to survive. Forgiveness is essential. Patience is hard to learn, but necessary. If you have enough love, you don't need all the others.

"It is important to count your blessings instead of your handicaps. This is very hard to do, but we must...

"Every human being has a soul, but most are not in touch with it. Some get confused with religion, but it has nothing to do with religion or dogma...

"My spiritual healer is Joseph. I was paralyzed for five months. My doctor said I could never move my left arm. Then Joseph came into my life and now look [she moves her left arm]—I can give karate chops with my paralyzed arm. First Joseph worked with my spiritual body, then my mental body, my emotional body, and then physical body. Look at me now. I can move my arm! My doctor came by to see me after Joseph worked with me. I said to her, 'Come closer, I have to show you something—what my healer did for me.' She came as close as possible and I gave her the biggest karate chop with my paralyzed arm. She was converted within two minutes. Now she sends all her hopeless patients to Joseph. Without spirituality, you cannot do healing...

"There is a greater acceptance of spirituality today, but there is much work to do. I am glad to hear about your book. It is about time!..." It's about time.

"Give me your finger again," she said, as I stood up to leave. And we hugged once more.

Introduction

The best and most beautiful things in the world cannot be seen, nor touched... but are felt in the heart.

—Helen Keller

IT IS A WEDNESDAY EVENING in Boulder, Colorado. I am sitting in a small room with about forty other people attending a workshop conducted by a Mayan shaman from Guatemala. His name is Martin Prechtel, and he has just spent the first hour talking about his initiation as a shaman. He is funny, witty, and very wise. For the next few hours, he describes various aspects of his spiritual traditions, and although he places them in the context of the Mayan culture, there are similarities to the traditions of other shamans, healers, and wisdom keepers from other cultures and religions I have heard speak over the years.

At the end of his presentation, Martin ends with a traditional indigenous prayer, closing with these last words: "Long life. Honey in the heart. No evil. Thirteen thank-yous." He then explains, "*Long life* means to live healthy over the years. *Honey in the heart* translates to mean may all your thoughts come through your heart and may they be sweet. May no evil befall you, nor may you take part in evil acts. *Thirteen thank-yous* means to hold an ever-present attitude of gratitude." And with that, he waves good-bye. His message is unique, but at the same time quite familiar.

The previous night I attended a presentation in Boulder by Larry Dossey, MD, on the topic of mind–body–spirit medicine. The premise of his talk was that a huge change was occurring in Western medicine, a change in which consciousness was finally being added to the human equation of healing. His message was new to a great many people there that night, but his words were a confirmation of what I have known for many years. The times, they are a-changing!

Boulder, Colorado, attracts many sages and mystics who come to the area to share their wisdom. But my travels have also taken me all over the world, to the Lapland of Norway, the Outback of Australia, the Vatican in Rome, the Islands of Hawaii, and the Reservations of the Lakota Sioux to study human spirituality. Over the past twenty-six years, I have attended workshops, seminars, conferences, and retreats, listening, conversing, praying, meditating, and studying with the wisdom keepers of the modern age. I have also read scores of books and manuscripts, all of which have led to a culmination of profound wisdom that I synthesized in the pages of this book.

I know I have been very fortunate to have had the time to listen, read, and study with the wisdom keepers of many cultures. With each lesson comes the obligation to pass along these insights to any and all who seek them. My path, which began as a young child, became clearly defined when I wrote my first book, *Managing Stress*, a textbook on the topic of stress management. I included a chapter on the topic of stress and human spirituality.

The book was and continues to be met with great success. This has led to several other books and articles, which I am told have helped thousands of people.

In 1993, I approached my editor about writing a textbook on human spirituality with a focus on health. He laughed and said I was ahead of my time—there are no courses on this topic. I placed the manuscript on a shelf, indefinitely. So you can imagine my surprise when in the summer of 1999, I received a phone call from him asking how long it would take to pull together a manuscript on the topic of human spirituality. Eager to do this project, I answered, "It's nearly finished!"

The following guide will help you navigate the contents of this material:

- Chapter 1: The Call to Spirit introduces you to a historical perspective of the receptivity of the spiritual dimension of health in various aspects of society.

- Chapter 2: The Wellness Paradigm Revisited presents a brief overview of the wellness paradigm as ageless wisdom, as described by Elisabeth Kübler-Ross, MD, a renowned figure in the wellness movement.

- Chapter 3: Theories of Human Spirituality explores a host of philosophies and tenets of human spirituality through the eyes of sages, mystics, psychologists, and theologians of all ages and cultures. Information from this chapter forms the premise for the content of the rest of the book.

- Chapter 4: The Nature of Human Spirituality outlines a model of human spirituality based on the pillars of relationships, values, and purpose in life.

- Chapter 5: Mountains, Molehills, and Muscles of the Soul looks at human spirituality through the language of metaphor and the relationship between stress and human spirituality.

- Chapter 6: Mind–Body–Spirit Healing explores the role of human spirituality in the healing process, from prayer to energy healing.

- Chapter 7: Embrace the Mystery ventures into the mystical side of human spirituality, with the premise that there are some things that cannot be explained scientifically; we all are mystics when we realize that we don't have to solve the mystery to enjoy it.

- Chapter 8: The Art of Meditation highlights aspects of meditation, a common practice among noted spiritual teachers of all traditions.

- Chapter 9: Health of the Human Spirit presents a program of ideas and suggestions to incorporate into your daily routine to fully integrate human spirituality as part of optimal wellness.
- Chapter 10: The End Is Just the Beginning is a very brief summary of the concepts presented in the book, concluding with a letter from a student who put these concepts to the test.

It's no secret that the world is in a very precarious position today. Many people frequently use the expression "a perfect storm" to describe the state of world affairs. Terrorism, global warming, famines, political unrest, economic collapse, environmental degradation and social upheaval—to name a few—all threaten the world's balance. But even in the darkest hour of recorded history, human nature has always found a way to rise to its highest potential. This time will be no different. Since *Health of the Human Spirit* was first published in 2001, the term *spiritual well-being* has taken on a greater comfort level in many circles, including in academic classrooms where health education is taught. This is not only a good thing; it is essential! As many spiritual luminaries shared with me when I first prepared this manuscript: without acknowledging the health of the human spirit in health education and health care, we are destined for mediocrity, if not annihilation.

This book is a collection of wisdom to remind us of our highest potential at a time when it is most needed.

In the time it has taken to pull these ideas together, revisit them for this new edition, and re-draft them into a presentable format, there have been several devastating earthquakes, hurricanes, and floods that have tested the mettle of hundreds of thousands of people. Currently, the economy is struggling, and signs of a dysfunctional and agitated society increase and show no signs of abating. Experts from many fields, including Martin Prechtel, Larry Dossey, science fiction writer Arthur C. Clark, and primatologist Jane Goodall, whose autobiography, *Reason for Hope*, I just reread, indicate that time is not on our side. If we are going to continue living comfortably on this planet, we are going to have to make some significant changes. The hope and future of the world lie with the current generations—in your hands. May this book help serve as a guide to your highest potential.

It is no exaggeration to say that this book has been a labor of love. It is one thing to read about theories, concepts, and ideas of life. It is quite another to experience them firsthand. By and large, human spirituality is experiential. It is my wish that this book becomes a stepping-stone for you to go out into the world and explore on your own the essence of human spirituality; one book cannot do this topic justice. There are only two items required for this journey: an open heart and an open mind. As you explore on your journey, may your insight, humbleness, and compassion help bring the world back into balance. So I would like to begin with a blessing:

Long life.

Honey in the heart.

No evil.

Thirteen thank-yous.

Acknowledgments

HEALTH OF THE HUMAN SPIRIT has found a new home at Jones & Bartlett Learning, where it was originally conceived. I am delighted to see it return to where it belongs and am ever so grateful to my editor, Shoshanna Goldberg, for her passion in making this possible.

Special thanks to my first textbook editor, Joe Burns, who saw the promise of this topic and made *Health of the Human Spirit* a reality in 2001. Thanks, Joe! You're the best!

A big bear hug and an E.T. touch to my mentor and friend Elisabeth Kübler-Ross, MD, who not only has been an inspirational force in my career but who also so graciously invited me into her home to make a contribution to this book. I love you, Elisabeth!

My world became wonderfully enriched in 1992 when I had the great pleasure to meet Larry Dossey, MD. Since that time, he has become a great mentor and friend. Thanks, Larry, you're a class act!

It may take a whole village to raise a child, but the same could be said for writing a book! My village includes Shoshanna Goldberg, Emma Krosschell, Julie Bolduc, and Jody Yeskey at Jones & Bartlett Learning.

Special thanks go to my colleagues across the country who not only have applauded my efforts to stand at the vanguard of human spirituality, but also in some cases have actually encouraged me take the next step and to continue to raise the level of consciousness higher as the hunger for a more complete picture of human spirituality increases. You know who you are, and I thank you a thousand times over.

There are many colleagues and friends outside of academia whose encouragement, advice, inspiration, and well-wishes are so greatly appreciated, including everyone at the Institute of Noetic Sciences, The International Society for the Study of Subtle Energy and Energy Medicine (ISSSEEM), and especially former Executive Director Linda Chapin and the staff of the National Wellness Institute in Stevens Point, Wisconsin.

A special word of gratitude to all my students over the years who have been wonderful teachers in their own right. Many thanks! As always, words of praise and gratitude go to my friends and family who epitomize love by giving their support in ways they don't even know, yet ask nothing in return.

Finally, a gracious bow goes out to all the shamans, sages, wisdom keepers, mystics, and healers who have so gracefully shared their ageless wisdom with me in one way or another, and to The Divine Spirit who makes all things possible. Peace be to all.

About the Author

BRIAN LUKE SEAWARD, PHD, is considered a pioneer in the field of health psychology, and he is internationally recognized for his contributions in the area of holistic stress management, human spirituality, and mind–body–spirit healing. The wisdom of Dr. Seaward can be found quoted in college lectures, medical seminars, boardroom meetings, church sermons, keynote addresses, PBS specials, and political speeches all over the world. As a TEDx speaker, he is respected throughout the international community as an accomplished teacher, consultant, lecturer, author, visionary, and mentor. Dr. Seaward has authored more than 12 books, many published in several languages. He is a faculty member at the University of Northern Colorado, and his books *Stand Like Mountain, Flow Like Water; Quiet Mind, Fearless Heart; Managing Stress: Principles and Strategies for Health and Well-Being, Seventh Edition;* and *Stressed Is Desserts Spelled Backward* have helped tens of thousands of people overcome personal life crises. He continues his work through relaxation CDs, including *A Change of Heart, Sweet Surrender,* and *A Wing and a Prayer,* and DVDs, including *Earth Songs* and *Seasons of the Heart,* both of which have been nominated for numerous awards. When not instructing or presenting stress management programs, Dr. Seaward relaxes back home in the Rocky Mountains of Colorado. He can be reached at http://www.brianlukeseaward.net.

CHAPTER

The Call to Spirit

Faith dares the soul to go farther than it can see or know.

—William Clark

WHAT COMES TO MIND WHEN you hear the word *spirit*? Whether you realize it or not, this word, or some derivation thereof, gets used a lot in everyday conversation. "He's got the spirit," we say at a sporting event. "She's so inspiring," we say of our mentor, role model, or hero. "He aspires to great heights," someone is overheard to say when goals, dreams, and wishes are the topic of conversation. And we often call those who march to the beat of their own drummers "free spirits." When a person dies in a hospital, no matter what the cause, it is written on her chart, "Mrs. Smith expired at 12:02 p.m." Quite literally, this means her spirit left her body. So, in truth, the word *spirit* and all its many inferences have a solid presence in the American vernacular.

Although the word *spirit* is not uncommon in everyday conversation, the words *spiritual* and *spirituality* have only recently entered the American lexicon with great regularity. Perhaps as a legacy of *The Oprah Winfrey Show*, these words are now used publicly with a higher degree of comfort. It is no longer uncommon to hear people discussing the spiritual aspect of their lives at various social functions, whether it's at a baseball game or in the frozen-food section of the grocery store. Years ago, people just didn't talk about their spirituality. It was a private matter.

In fact, it wasn't that long ago that public conversations about human spirituality were considered taboo or, at best, left in the recesses of one's own mind. For decades, if not centuries, the acknowledgment of human spirituality was relegated to the Sabbath or Sunday service: spirituality was observed purely in a religious context. And in academic circles, it is fair to say that one didn't dare mention the word *spirituality* in the same breath as *science*, because of an unspoken assumption that these two constructs were mutually exclusive. Moreover, the standard line in most academic circles is that *soul* is a four-letter word.[1]

It is now generally understood, at least in some disciplines, that the spiritual dimension is not only present in the human equation, but that it is an integral—if not essential—part of it. Furthermore, it is now recognized that to really understand the human journey, we must acknowledge and nurture these matters of the soul on a daily basis in all aspects of life. Although this belief is woven into the fabric of many global cultures, it is certainly a new revelation to a great many people standing at the horizon of Western thought and philosophy at the dawn of the new millennium.

The World in Crisis

IN THE ACCLAIMED BOOK *Waking Up in Time,* physicist and psychologist Peter Russell writes:

> We may be living through the most stimulating and exciting times in history; but our rapid development has brought with it unexpected dangers, not the least of which is humanity's ever-growing size. The winds of change are brewing into a storm of change, perhaps a hurricane of change. If we are to survive the accelerating changes that are coming our way, we need to be flexible. We need to let go of outdated assumptions and habits of thinking that no longer serve us.[2]

One of the primary outdated assumptions that Russell speaks of is the short-sighted exclusion of the spiritual dimension by various cultural institutions, from academia to the corporate world.

In the last decade of the twentieth century, and more so in the first two decades of the twenty-first, a time when the collective consciousness strives to deal with a host of issues ranging from global warming, gun control, and deforestation to genetic cloning and urban sprawl, the words *spiritual* and *spirituality* have entered the realm of everyday conversation. Dysfunction in the educational system, the political system, the healthcare system, the banking system, and in many other facets of our global society indicates that the neglect of the spiritual dimension in everyday life (from business ethics to political fear-mongering) has created many problems. Perhaps this is why the topic of human spirituality has emerged as part of the conventional wisdom shared in everyday conversation. Interestingly enough, as noted earlier, it wasn't always like this.

Years ago, it was theologians and religious leaders who closely held and cautiously shared the domain of spiritual thought. Today, however, it is not uncommon to hear people in all walks of life—from sports legend Magic Johnson and former Russian President Mikhail Gorbachev to singer-songwriter Naomi Judd and former South African President Nelson Mandela—address the issue of human spirituality not only in their own lives, but also in the lives of everyone on the planet. Perhaps there is a good reason for this, given that these luminaries and others like them travel the world and see the need to move beyond the confines of labels (e.g., Christian, Jew, Muslim) and the associated perceptions that may give a myopic perspective of life and thus limit our collective human potential.

Sociologists have added their two cents by suggesting that the rapid changes created by technology (e.g., smartphones, social networking, etc.) seem to have created an ever-growing abyss between people's hearts. Although people are connected in what Marshall McLuhan has nicknamed the "Global Village,"[3] the virtual feel of these communications leaves much to be desired without a humanistic (real face-to-face contact) approach to life. To put it bluntly, people may be communicating, but in isolation; they are not always connecting heart to heart. This fact, coupled with significant changes in family dynamics (e.g., single-parent issues, two-income household issues, day-care and elder-care issues, and telecommuting issues), have forced some people to reexamine their lives, only to find a disturbingly hollow foundation upon which their lives are built.

A general consensus exists among experts in virtually every academic discipline that we simply cannot keep living as we are without eventually putting ourselves at risk of extinction. World-renowned journalist Alistair Cooke, in a nationally broadcast interview, said that the state of the world today is dismal at best, and when compared to the Great Depression, noted that "there was no random violence as has become so commonplace today."[4] Actor and environmentalist Robert Redford notably stated, "We are the first generation to leave the world in worse shape than we received it. What does this say to our children and grandchildren?"[5] The World Health Organization often says that stress is "a global epidemic," and that the epidemic shows no signs of abating. In the words of eminent theologian Matthew Fox, "Living in a spiritual vacuum has its consequences, and we are seeing these played out on a daily basis all over the planet as other cultures adopt the American lifestyle."[6] French novelist and former Minister of Culture André Malraux added these sobering words, "The twenty-first century will be spiritual, or it will not be at all."[7]

We are living in stressful times on the planet Earth, and according to those sociologists with their finger on the pulse of humanity it doesn't seem to be getting better. The pace of life is fast, furious, and becoming more so in nearly every corner of the globe. As the world quickly spins into the new millennium, the topic of human spirituality is taking a prominent, if not urgent, role in various discussions, because an expanding community of people feel that the survival of the human race depends on it. There is a growing assumption from all corners of the globe that dire living conditions loom on the near horizon if consumeristic behaviors, which ultimately will eliminate natural resources and pollute the planet, persist.

Statistics compiled by the World Watch Institute sound a continuous alarm, which by and large seems to be ignored by multinational corporations and the governments they so strongly influence.[8] Deforestation of equatorial rain forests, ozone depletion, extinction of plant and animal species, leaking toxic waste dumps, and depletion of natural ocean fisheries are just some of the problems facing the human race, with greed as a primary underlying cause of this dysfunction. Greed is not a spiritual value!

Although greed is certainly part of the human landscape, altruism (selfless, compassionate service) is a noteworthy landmark as well. Under the worst situations and most horrible conditions, countless people open their hearts and extend a helping hand, often without asking for anything in return. In fact, it is fair to say that despite our shortcomings we can rise to any occasion when we put our hearts and minds to it. A healthy human spirit, however, responds not only in times of crisis but is also engaged in all of life's moments every day.

An anthropology survey conducted by Paul Ray in 1995 revealed a new phenomenon emerging in American culture, what Ray calls the "Great Divide." Ray explains this as a shift from modernism to transmodernism, a shift in which society is caught in a transition of "integral cultures" (e.g., Christian, Hindu, Buddhist, Scientist) greatly influenced by spiritual, ecological, and feminine values. With an estimated 50 million Americans being part of a group that Ray calls "Cultural Creatives" (see **Exercise 1.2**)—those people leading the movement of an evolved (spiritual) consciousness—the future of America, specifically, and humanity as a whole, may be transformed from our current volatile situation.[9]

Russell concludes his book *Waking Up in Time* by saying, "Whether or not this particular species on planet earth will be able to blossom into full consciousness is still an open question." He recites a now famous quote by Albert Einstein, "No problem can be solved from the same consciousness that created it."[10]

A Spiritual Hunger?

IN TIMES OF CRISIS, PEOPLE of every generation and every culture have been known to seek help from a divine source. In the past, people took spiritual refuge in their religious traditions. However, today some people seem a little disenchanted with their standard religious practices because they just don't seem to provide answers to the problems looming on the horizon of humanity, such as cloning, genetic engineering, and depletion of the rain forests.

According to a 2003 poll conducted by the George H. Gallup International Institute, 50% of Americans describe themselves as religious, whereas 33% describe themselves as spiritual but not religious (a 10% increase from 1998).[11] Similarly, a MacArthur Foundation survey revealed that seven out of ten Americans say they are religious and consider spirituality to be an important part of their lives, but that half attend religious services less than once a month or never. Church attendance is down, and current projections show a continued decline for the foreseeable future.[12]

In what is being referred to by some as the "postdenominational age," many people do not feel a loyalty to one particular religious upbringing but seek a host of sacred traditions, blending various practices to form their own spiritual path. There are Catholics who practice Buddhist meditation, Jews who participate in American Indian sweat lodges, and Methodists, Mormons, and members of the Greek Orthodox Church who participate in Sufi dancing.[13] Even hell has gotten a makeover, as the biblical conception of the most dreaded place in the universe moves from a literal to a figurative interpretation. Once described as eternal flames of death, hell is now described by the Vatican as "a state of those who freely and definitively separate themselves from God."[14] Many of those who claim to have already been to hell (on earth, that is) as well as those who have come close are seeking a better understanding of their relationship to God.

The expression used today is *spiritual hunger,* a term that describes a searching or longing for that which cannot solely be attained by traditional religious practices. Another term used in conjunction with spiritual hunger is *spiritual bankruptcy,* a concept that suggests a sense of moral decay, perhaps due to an emptiness that cannot be filled with material possessions. Yet a strong element of human nature (the ego) encourages us to try anyway. One only need reflect on the 1999 shootings at Columbine High School in Colorado or the 2011 Oslo massacre, or other events like them, to see that something is terribly amiss.

The Reverend Billy Graham, interviewed on the eve of the new millennium, stated, "I am afraid that people are losing their faith in God and replacing it with a faith in technology that will solve all our problems. They are being led down the wrong path. There must be a change in the human heart." The change he referred to is what is typically called a *spiritual awakening.*[15] A fourth phrase commonly heard today is *spiritual dormancy.* It refers to people who for one reason or another choose not to recognize the importance of the spiritual dimension of health and well-being at both the individual and societal levels. The result of such inaction often leads to a state of dysfunction (a term many now call the national adjective). Like hitting the snooze button on the alarm clock, falling asleep on the spiritual path can have real consequences, because one is ill-equipped to deal with the problems at hand as well as those down the road.

A Turning Point in Consciousness

A NUMBER OF FACTORS HAVE COME together to raise human consciousness to today's current level of awareness. They include, but are not limited to, the following:

- Vatican II, which in the 1960s changed its mass from Latin to various indigenous languages around the world, opened the doors to a wealth of knowledge about Christianity (which had pretty much remained known only to a chosen few because Latin is not a contemporary language). For the first time, Catholics were encouraged to read the Bible on their own. (Note: In 2011 the Vatican began changing parts of the mass back into Latin.)

- The invasion of Tibet by China in 1959 not only forced thousands of Tibetans into exile around the world, but also ultimately allowed for the sharing of their sacred knowledge that, until that time, had remained in seclusion for thousands of years.

- The Apollo Space Project, landing Americans on the moon in 1969, for the first time allowed people to see planet Earth as a whole, suspended in space, without national borders. This view altered many minds with regard to the future of the planet and her many inhabitants.

- The proliferation of self-help groups that use variations of the Twelve-Step program, as outlined in Alcoholics Anonymous, that asks members to relinquish control of addiction to a higher power. Such self-help groups are nondenominational.

- The American Indians, particularly the Lakota and Hopi, who for decades had been told by their elders *not* to share various aspects of their cultural heritage and spirituality because of lack of trust, have now been told that this is the time to reveal their sacred knowledge, and they have done so. The Lakota Sioux prophecy foretold of the age of the white buffalo, when a shift in consciousness would occur. A white buffalo named Miracle was born in Janesville, Wisconsin, on August 20, 1994.[16] Several more have been born since.

- The Kabbalah, the sect of Jewish mysticism revealed only to a chosen few for the past several millennia, has only recently been made available to anyone who has an interest in this topic.

- Since the early 1970s, near-death experiences (NDEs) have been studied in earnest to learn more about the recollections of these survivors. Research compiled by *U.S. News and World Report* in 1997 revealed that over 15 million documented NDEs had occurred in the previous 25 years, from every religious denomination. Those who recall their experiences often say that they have a new life mission to teach compassion and inner peace by their example. Children, many of whom have not been exposed to various spiritual matters, come back to consistently describe experiences of a divine, mystical nature.[17]

- In the 1990s, South American shamans for the first time shared their wisdom of healing with "their younger brothers" in the Northern Hemisphere.

- The telecommunications revolution opened the door to information to anyone with access to the Internet. Knowledge from around the world and from many sources suddenly became accessible without the censorship of intellectuals, religious leaders, or politicians, who for centuries played a major role in keeping people in the dark about a great many issues and facts. Access to information has become a major stepping-stone toward higher consciousness.

- The collaboration between media giant Oprah Winfrey and bestselling author Eckhart Tolle has helped spread Tolle's message of higher consciousness, explained in his acclaimed book *A New Earth,* via Winfrey's television show, website, online chat rooms, and podcasts, to millions of people around the world.

- Many have heard the disturbing wake-up call regarding the issue of global warming and climate change. The realization has come that all people need to work together to adapt to new, extreme conditions that no person can escape.

It is on the global stage where we see the dynamics of ego (stress) and human spirituality played out on a daily basis, whether it involves environmental factors, economic issues, or healthcare reform, because they are all related. Everything is connected. Before we begin to understand these dynamics on a national or global scale, perhaps it is best to first become reacquainted with some of the basics of stress at the individual level.

Spiritual Materialism

SIMPLY STATED, THE SPIRITUAL PATH is one of egolessness, yet reaching such a state is far easier said than done. To achieve emotional and material detachment is a daily challenge. Many Eastern spiritual leaders who have migrated West to share their perspectives on human spirituality and spiritual well-being, including Tibetan Buddhist leader Chogyam Trungpa Rimpoche, have encountered a phenomenon: an oxymoron they now call ***spiritual materialism***.[18] Spiritual materialism reveals itself among people with the best intentions but with egotistical trappings, people who pride themselves on attending countless spiritual retreats, workshops, or pilgrimages to distant holy lands. They drop the names of their yogis, spiritual teachers, healers, and ashrams like the names of popular movie stars. Nowhere is this is more prevalent than in the practice of hatha yoga (an egoless activity) that is now laden with certifications, competitions, wardrobes, and workout props. Spiritual materialism, a status of falsely claiming to be spiritual or enlightened, misses the boat when it comes to really understanding the balance of ego and soul.

An Unhealthy Spirit?

SPIRITUALITY IS AN INCLUSIVE TOPIC covering a wide magnitude of perspectives on the alchemy of humanity and divinity. However, many aspects of humanity seem anything *but* spiritual. Just as many words are used to convey the true essence of human spirituality, many words can be used to describe an **unhealthy spirit**. These include, but are not limited to, *laziness, greed, rudeness, sarcasm, prejudice,* and *hostility*. These and other traits do not foster a sense of greatness or human potential; in fact, they greatly detract from both.

A quick study of human spirituality eventually leads one to the front door of the ego, often cited as the greatest roadblock on the human journey. Left undisciplined, the ego promotes perpetual stress. Examples of a dis-spirited nature abound and constitute the majority of news headlines today, giving examples of greed, intolerance, hostile aggression, and prejudice. Most likely, the root of these everyday tragedies can be found in exaggerated ego-based fear itself. Ancient mystics from Eastern cultures often spoke of a "closed heart" as being responsible for poor spiritual health—the result of unresolved fear and anger. Today, many Western healthcare practitioners, including Dean Ornish, MD, concur with this idea.[19] As our world spins faster and faster into an age of information overload and high-paced technology that contains less personal and leisure time—the "24/7 lifestyle"— unresolved issues of anger and fear and all the many ways that these affect human behavior are likely to promote a greater prevalence of poor spiritual health. To quote a popular expression, "Trust the Universe."

I Don't Believe It!

SINCE HUMANS FIRST WALKED THE earth, the search for truth—the meaning of human existence, Divine Consciousness, creation, miracles, and so forth—has taken many roads. Until we actually experience something directly (and even then doubt may arise), it is hard to accept everything at face value, let alone on the faith of someone else's word. In fact, it is not uncommon to reject as fact some, if not all, of what we encounter. For some people, this rejection may be the result of a bad experience with church leaders or parents who try to limit or force a particular "truth." It is a consensus among those who study the field of human spirituality that Divine Truth comprises several paradoxes and ironies, all of which can make anyone scratch his or her head in confusion. Whether one claims to be an **agnostic** (someone who doesn't know if there is a higher power) or an **atheist** (someone who doesn't believe in a higher power), doubt and disbelief are actually part of the spiritual path as well. Doubts can certainly appear once a person leaves home and discovers other people with differing beliefs. As with a child who eventually grows up to leave home and discover the world on his or her own, questioning life's answers is part of the human journey, which is why a period of not knowing, or not believing, is considered a stage of spiritual development. But if a person finds him- or herself stuck in this phase out of fear (doubt) or anger (arrogance), this can lead to an unhealthy spirit. The inventor, philosopher, and global citizen Buckminster Fuller said it best: "God, to me, is a verb, not a noun (proper or improper)."[20] Implied in his message is that the verb is *love*, something we can (and perhaps should) all believe in.

The Winds of Change *Are* the Winds of Grace

THE ROOTS OF FEAR EXTEND deep into the heart of humanity. Fear of failure, fear of rejection, fear of the unknown, and perhaps the biggest anxiety—fear of death—all seem to lurk deep in the shadows of what psychologist Carl Gustav Jung called our "collective unconscious."[21] Yet if there is an articulate way to describe the proliferation of fear-based thinking, it can be summed up in the word *change.* It is no secret that we are living in a time of great change. Although it's true that change has always been part of the human landscape, the rate of change today is far greater than ever before. We don't seem to know how to fully adapt to it, as evidenced in the many social problems we see, such as alcoholism, clinical depression, and divorce.

Furthermore, as a rule, we don't like change because it forces us out of our comfort zones. In the words of educator Roy Blitzer, "The only person who likes change is a wet baby."[22] Comfort is another word for security, and change carries the potential to threaten our level of security. The desire for a sense of comfort is woven deep into the fabric of the human soul, not only for our physical living space but also for our abstract perceptions, ideas, and beliefs. When these are threatened by change, the defenses of the ego are activated as a means of protection. Unfortunately, the result is a closed heart. Like a storm wall on an oceanfront, the ego stands on guard, yet the waters of change seep through these walls quite easily. Nothing is spared from the tides of change. Some call upon faith in times of stressful crises. Others abandon it.

Sometimes what seemed like the worst disaster to occur in our lives over time turns out to be a blessing in disguise. Mark Twain was often quoted as saying, "I'm an old man now, and I have known a great many problems in my life, most of which never happened."[23] In hindsight, being moved, if not pushed, out of our comfort zones is not necessarily a bad thing, because this is often where real growth takes place. In talking to scores of people who have taken a trip to hell and back (e.g., those who have experienced terminal cancer, clinical depression, loss of a job, or the end of a twenty-year marriage), I hear a common response. They begin by saying that they thought this was the worst event in their lives. But looking back at the event, and all that was learned, they say that it was one of the best things that ever happened to them. What appeared to be the winds of change literally became the winds of grace. As Dumbledore told Harry Potter, "The greatest magic is love."

No matter how well we fortify our comfort zones with barriers of protection, change can afflict the most comfortable of all humans. For as discomforting as it may be, change is also an inevitable fact of life. We live in a dynamic world that is spinning in space at a rate of 66,000 mph in its ellipse around the sun. This fact alone creates change. Add to this equation a growing population of over seven billion people and a technological revolution, and it stands to reason that change is inevitable. Change keeps the world dynamic. In a dynamic universe, stagnation can only lead to toxicity and decay. With this in mind, the question that begs to be asked is, "How can we learn to become comfortable (adapt) with change?" The answer may sound simple, but its application is challenging. The fear of change must be faced diplomatically with an open heart—the premise of a healthy spirit. The choice is ours.

Our comfort zones may be in twilight in an ever-changing world, but proverbial wisdom suggests that after night comes the promise of a new day. In the cycle of life, day follows night, spring follows winter, and peace comes after the storm. No disaster lasts forever, unless we choose to live in a frame of mind grounded in the illusion of fear.

Stress and Spirituality: Partners in the Dance of Life

FOR AGES, IN A GREAT many cultures, aspects of human spirituality have been symbolically represented as light, whereas the forces against the spirit are depicted as darkness. One need only think of the characters in *Star Wars*—Luke Skywalker, dressed in a white robe, and Darth Vader, immortalized in black—to make the point clear. From medieval knights to cosmic Jedis, the universal story of good and evil has been played out symbolically like this many times throughout the ages in virtually all cultures across the globe. Although it may be difficult to pinpoint the source of evil, one place to start is to look within—specifically at our own egos and at the issues of unresolved fear and anger.

A brief look at the emotions of anger and fear indicates clearly how intertwined emotional and spiritual well-being really are. Both fear and anger are survival emotions. When recognized and utilized correctly (e.g., fear will indeed help you flee a burning building), they are an asset. However, when left unresolved for weeks, months, years—even decades—fear and anger literally choke the human spirit and ultimately wreak havoc on our bodies as well. In the Eastern culture, unresolved issues of fear and anger are described as the "veils of illusion," because they cloud our vision, making us feel cut off or separated from our divine source. And although nothing could be further from the truth—for we are never separated or disconnected from our divine source (whatever you conceive this to be)—misperceptions give strength to these veils and add layers and layers to the point where, metaphorically speaking, darkness overcomes light (this is typically how people describe states of depression). These veils of illusion are considered to be nothing less than blinding. In fact, studies show that when people are stressed their peripheral vision dramatically decreases.[24] Perhaps poet Maya Angelou said it best when she wrote, "I believe that Spirit is one and everywhere present. That it never leaves me. That in my ignorance I may withdraw from it, but I can realize its presence the instant I return to my senses. I cannot separate what I conceive as spirit from my concept of God."[25]

Of Spirit and Character

WE TEND TO THINK OF the human spirit as a force of energy, divinely endowed within each human being, that enables us to navigate the shoals of our earthly existence. A healthy spirit is synonymous with striving toward the heights of human potential, and we take delight in anyone who achieves a personal goal, as much as if it had been our own. The more remarkable the endeavor, the more amazed we become.

Feats of greatness, heroic deeds, or courageous acts take our breath away and make our own spirits soar. We call these people heroes, but as time passes their accomplishments become legends and sometimes they are nicknamed "gods." One only need think of cancer survivor Lance Armstrong, who not only made a remarkable recovery from his disease but then went on to win the Tour de France seven consecutive times (1999–2005).[26] Words like *courage, faith, optimism, persistence, forgiveness, patience,* and *compassion,* to name a few, come to mind when we search for ways to describe the power of the human spirit. Often these words never quite hit the mark, yet they come close enough to understand and, more specifically, appreciate the caliber of greatness that can be accomplished when our human spirit pushes us to a new level of our human potential.

People often use the words *character* and *integrity* synonymously, but they are not necessarily the same thing. In his book *The 7 Habits of Highly Effective People,* Stephen Covey addresses the issue of character. In what he calls the "Character Ethic," Covey describes the attributes of character as integrity, humility, fidelity, simplicity, modesty, courage, and patience. He notes that over the past 50 years a shift has occurred from character to personality, with a focus on skills and techniques that manipulate, intimidate, or deceive others for personal gain, particularly in the business world.[27] As such, character is eclipsed by personality and ego. **Character**, it is said, is who you are and what you do when no one is looking. What do you make of your character? (**Exercise 1.3** might give you some insights.)

It is a common belief that a challenging circumstance helps build character. Although character may be composed of more than just integrity, faith, humor, courage, honesty, and patience, it is these attributes we typically think of when the word *character* is mentioned. These are the same aspects that give definition to the profile of the human spirit as well.

Profiles of Human Spirituality

NEWSPAPERS, MAGAZINES, AND BOOKS ARE often filled with stories of remarkable human endeavors, achievements that speak to the nature of spiritual health, even when one's physical health is severely compromised. Take, for example, Marc Wellman, a man who became a paraplegic from a climbing accident in 1982. Casting aside this limitation, he set a goal to climb El Capitan Mountain in Yosemite National Park in 1989, and did it before a televised audience! In 1991 Wellman climbed another of Yosemite's peaks, Half Dome.[28]

In the 1990s Nelson Mandela became an international figure extraordinaire, not merely for overwhelmingly winning the election in South Africa to become the first black president of that country, but also for emerging from 26 years in jail as a political prisoner with no remorse or animosity toward his captors. He channeled his energy to work with the existing government to reform apartheid and make a peaceful transition to democracy in his country.[29]

The name Gabrielle Giffords has become synonymous with the word *resiliency*, and she has become the epitome of grace under pressure. On January 8, 2011, U.S. Representative Giffords survived an assassination attempt at a supermarket in Tucson, Arizona, in which several of her supporters and staff were killed. Taking a bullet to the head, clear through her brain, she spent months in a rehabilitation hospital in Houston, Texas, learning how to walk, speak, read, and write. On August 1, in the midst of a national showdown between Congress and President Obama, Giffords made her first appearance in the Capitol and the House of Representatives to cast her vote to raise the national debt ceiling, and in doing so brought tears to the eyes of everyone on Capitol Hill, as well as a standing ovation. She continues with her recovery, and in doing so has become a role model of the triumph of the human spirit.[30]

A similar, but no less remarkable, story is that of former model Gari Carter. While driving on a country road in Virginia one snowy afternoon, Carter was hit head-on by a car that lost control. Upon impact, her car spun unmercifully in circles, whereupon it smashed into a side rail. Carter crashed through the windshield, and metal and glass destroyed her face. Medics were astonished to see that she was still alive. Completely immobilized and grossly marred, she was told the damage to her facial structure was nearly irreparable. She was determined to come back strong, and that she did. With an incredible will and fortitude, she incorporated prayer, meditation, and a host of healing practices that have allowed her to return to a normal life.[31]

Once while flipping through *People* magazine, I came across a story of a little girl who survived a terrible fire. Her entire body was engulfed in flames; every inch was brutally burned. She was horribly disfigured, so much so that she didn't look human—more like an insect or an alien. But when you looked into her eyes, all doubt was removed, for within her eyes was a light, a sparkle of energy, an undeniable sense of the Divine Spirit within.

My father died of cancer in 1993. I flew to Florida to see him and stayed with him for days until his last breath. He had waited until I arrived to explain to me several last-minute items he wished to have attended to. They seemed rather trivial to me, but to him they were extremely important. Each day the hospice nurse would visit and administer her special care. One day

I walked her to her car and asked her point blank how much longer my dad had to live. He hadn't eaten in well over a week and, from what I could tell, had taken no fluids either. Everything in my educational training suggested that a person couldn't live for more than three days without water, yet here he was going on five.

"It's hard to say," she said with a faint smile. "I know the scientists say you cannot go more than a few days without water, but I can tell you I've seen more than a few people hang on for weeks without taking anything. They are waiting for that son or daughter, or perhaps special someone to walk through that door, so they can say good-bye before they take their last breath. I've seen it too many times to know it's very real." She gave me a hug, and then got in her car to drive to the next patient. Before she started the car engine, she rolled her window down and motioned her hand for me to come close.

"There is an undeniable strength of the human spirit," she said. "It defies everything we understand rationally," and with that she waved her hand and drove away.

Just as a healthy spirit can prolong life, an unhealthy spirit can hasten one's demise. Nazi concentration camp survivor Viktor Frankl spent three years in the worst camp, Auschwitz, only to live and witness the horrors known forever as the crimes against humanity. As a psychiatrist, Frankl realized early in his career that the cornerstone to human spirituality was a meaningful purpose in life. It was his belief that those who lost their meaning to live quickly succumbed to physical death. His time in Auschwitz proved his theory correct. As he noted in his book *Man's Search for Meaning,* several prisoners who escaped the gas chambers and crematoriums to work hard labor in the camp perished when an absence of meaning and purpose suffocated their will to live.[32]

No one who comes into this earthly existence can escape the trials and tribulations of the human journey. Although on the surface appearances can look quite different, the lives of a New York stockbroker, a Tibetan monk, a French sculptor, a Filipino housemaid, a Navajo school teacher, and a Peruvian farmer share more common human experiences than the differences that separate them.

As the world of six billion people transforms from a collection of several hundred independent nations to a global village ensconced in political commerce, economic trade, environmental toxins, and digital communications, the recognition of human spirituality and the evolution of human consciousness will take on a greater role in the human landscape. We will have to pool our human resources to help solve and resolve the problems that threaten the global village we have created.

Keeping an Open Mind

TEACHING, DISCUSSING, AND SHARING IDEAS about human spirituality is not without its challenges. For some, such a personal experience is difficult to articulate in conversation. For others, it has become merely a status symbol for egotistical or political gain. And for still others, the topic has been a nonissue, with very little if any thought given to the aspects and concerns that constitute the very essence of human spirituality in everyday life. As you read through these pages, I recommend that you travel light and keep an open mind. Some ideas may relate to and resonate with you completely, some concepts may appear new yet seem vaguely familiar, and still others may challenge your belief system. Unlike other textbooks, which present a fact-based style of writing, this text was specifically written in a conversational style to give you a greater comfort level as you read.

The concepts, philosophies, and ideas in this book are a synthesis of many different perspectives on human spirituality. The purpose of this information is not to intimidate you. Rather the intention is to show that despite our varied backgrounds and religious differences there are elements of truth common to all of us. I ask you to focus on these common aspects, not on the differences, as you read. Moreover, I recommend that you respect and be receptive to all ideas different from your own; because, as you will see, an open mind will ultimately strengthen your own beliefs, attitudes, and philosophies, and consequently will strengthen the integrity of your spiritual well-being.

The seeds of inspiration for this book began several years ago when the concept of holistic wellness gained a wider acceptance in the American culture, which seemed ready to change the status quo of health education beyond the belief that health was merely the absence of disease. But like a bottle of wine that must age before being served, the content that is found among the pages of this book was groomed and cultivated until the time was right to bring these ideas to a wider audience. Long ignored, sometimes shunned, and often avoided in health education, the topic of human spirituality has emerged today to take its rightful place in the wellness paradigm. Indeed, it is now accepted by more and more people that human spirituality is the cornerstone of that paradigm.

◀ SUMMARY

WHILE THE SUBJECT OF HUMAN spirituality has been largely ignored in the Western Hemisphere over the past several centuries, the topic emerged in the last decade of the twentieth century as a viable, if not essential, construct in all aspects of life, from health practices to environmental concerns. Experts from a great many backgrounds and disciplines suggest that humanity is at a turning point, where the recognition of human spirituality and the utilization of its components are vital to our future. Just as greed, laziness, fear, and anger—manifestations of ego-driven stress—lead to an unhealthy spirit; faith, courage, compassion, and love allow the spirit to soar.

◈ TERMS AND CONCEPTS

agnostic	spiritual dormancy
atheist	spiritual hunger
character	spiritual materialism
spiritual bankruptcy	unhealthy spirit

◈ SOUL-SEARCHING EXERCISES

THROUGHOUT THE TEXT, YOU WILL find exercises that include questionnaires, journal themes, and personal inventories to augment your understanding of the concepts presented and to expand your awareness. Various themes are explored through comments and questions to allow you to do some soul-searching so that you may enhance the health of your human spirit. Before you begin each exercise, read through the chapter's corresponding text. Then take your time to address the various comments and questions. Keep in mind that the spiritual journey is dynamic, and the answers you have today may differ greatly from those with which you might respond months or years later. For this reason, you might consider revisiting some of these questions down the road, should the need arise.

EXERCISE 1.1
GOT THE SPIRIT? LET'S HEAR IT!

This first exercise is provided to get you thinking about the topic of human spirituality and to hopefully increase your comfort level with it. As you will see with these introductory questions, there are no wrong answers, so take a moment to explore your thoughts and write down whatever comes to mind.

1. When you hear the word *spirituality*, what is your first thought? What does this word mean to you?

    _____

    _____

    _____

2. In your opinion, do you see any similarity between building character and cultivating a healthy spirit? If so, how? Can you describe one challenging situation in which you felt that some aspect of your character was enhanced?

    _____

    _____

    _____

3. Is the topic of human spirituality one that you feel you can talk freely about, or is it one that you reserve for a particular day of the week or for certain people? Explain.

    _____

    _____

    _____

4. Make a list of things that you feel stifle (limit) your sense of spirit (e.g., anxiety, impatience, apathy, intolerance). Then pick one item from your list and explain why it limits your sense of spirit.

    _____

    _____

    _____

EXERCISE 1.2
ARE YOU A CULTURAL CREATIVE?

The term *Cultural Creative* was coined several years ago by a team of sociologists (Paul Ray and Sherry Anderson) to describe a person who is spiritually savvy in a changing world. As mentioned earlier in the chapter, Ray and Anderson suggest that in America alone 50 million people fall into this new demographic. Many adjectives can be used to describe a Cultural Creative, including *authentic, independent, creative, altruistic, environmentally active*, and *curious*. Agreement with eight or more of the following statements suggests that you might be a Cultural Creative.

1. I have a love of nature and spend as much time as I can outdoors.

2. I am acutely aware of planetary issues, from global warming to the depletion of our ocean fisheries.

3. I make an effort to cultivate strong relationships with my friends and family.

4. I volunteer several hours a month for various causes to help others.

5. I have an intense interest in my spiritual growth and psychological development.

6. I believe in the equality of all people, including women and children.

7. I am unhappy about the extreme left and right in today's politics.

8. I see spirituality as an important aspect of life, but worry about religious fundamentalism.

9. I tend to like people, places, and things that are different or exotic.

10. I consider myself to be an authentic person; my actions are consistent with my words and beliefs.

11. I am willing to spend more money on goods and services to help protect the environment.

12. Despite all the world's problems, I am optimistic about the future.

EXERCISE 1.3
OF CHARACTER AND SPIRIT

Although the concept of the human spirit may be hard to define, let alone quantify, the concept of moral character is thought to be a bit easier to identify and is sometimes reduced to one word: integrity. The following statements are based on various aspects of what is considered by many to be the highest quality of one's character. Although there is no specific questionnaire or survey to see who has the best moral character, by reading through these statements you will get a pretty good idea of where you stand. If you agree with twelve of the following fourteen statements, consider yourself to be of good character.

1. I keep the promises I make to friends, family, and colleagues.

2. I am honest with my friends and family (the occasional white lie, notwithstanding).

3. I honor the concept of fidelity with my partner and don't cheat on him or her.

4. I am willing to compromise and find consensus with difficult issues rather than controlling people so that I can have my way.

5. Before I act, I take into consideration the thoughts and feelings of others who might be impacted by my actions.

6. I consider myself to be a patient person and am noted for being patient among my friends, family, and colleagues.

7. I respect the rights of others and am tolerant of opinions and attitudes that differ from my own.

8. Although I may not agree, I respect the rights and dignity of others to live the lives they choose.

9. I take responsibility for my actions rather than blaming others for things that appear to go wrong.

10. I respect myself and strive to maintain a reputation of high standing.

11. I treat others as I wish to be treated, seeing everyone as equal.

12. I consider myself to be self-reliant, drawing strength from within when needed.

13. I am able to stay calm and rational even under stressful conditions.

14. When I make decisions, I take into account how others will be impacted by my actions.

EXERCISE 1.4
A MATTER OF CONSCIENCE

The human voice can never reach the distance that is covered by the still small voice of conscience.

—Mohandas Gandhi

The word *conscience* was heard often several decades ago, but today one could argue that it is rarely heard. Your conscience is your moral compass. Some might say that it is another word for the soul. Your conscience is what helps you distinguish right from wrong, good from bad, and appropriate versus inappropriate behavior. In the words of Mohandas Gandhi, "There is a higher court than courts of justice and that is the court of conscience. It supersedes all other courts."

Spiritual luminaries believe that being in harmony with our conscience is the secret to happiness. Thomas Jefferson put it this way: "Our greatest happiness does not depend on the condition of life in which chance has placed us, but is always the result of a good conscience, good health, occupation, and freedom in all just pursuits."

Some suggest that it is the conscience that counterbalances the ego. (Those who have seen the Disney cartoon *Pinocchio* may remember that Jiminy Cricket was the personification of Pinocchio's conscience.) However, if one's ego is huge, the voice of the conscience is rarely heard.

When we act against our conscience, feelings of anxiety and guilt often surface. It is no secret that many people, including prison inmates and people on their deathbeds, wish to clear their consciences, revealing lifelong secrets, resolving issues, and making amends so that they may find inner peace. People often use the expression of "clearing one's conscience."

1. What does the word *conscience* mean to you? Describe it as best you can in a few sentences.

   _____

   _____

   _____

2. Is your conscience clear? Are there things you need to clear to find peace in your heart?

   _____

   _____

   _____

3. Do you hear the voice of your conscience, or is the voice of your ego drowning it out?

   _____

   _____

   _____

❦ ENDNOTES

1. Pert, C., as quoted in Bill Moyers' *Healing and the Mind*, PBS, 1993.
2. Russell, P., *Waking Up in Time.* Origin Press: Novato, CA, 1998.
3. McLuhan, M., Global Village term. Available: http://en.wikipedia.org/wiki/Marshall_McLuhan.
4. Cooke, A., as interviewed on NPR's *All Things Considered,* Sunday, October 3, 1999.
5. Redford, R., as cited in a presentation at Sundance, Utah, 1999.
6. Fox, M., Keynote Address, "The Greening of Spirituality." Voices of the Earth Conference, Boulder, Colorado, July 29–31, 1994.
7. Quoted by L. Dossey, presentation at the Boulder Bookstore, October 12, 1999.
8. *World Watch Institute Annual Report,* Washington, DC, 2011.
9. Ray, P., "The Rise of the Integral Culture." *Noetic Sciences Review,* No. 37, pp. 4–15, 1996.
10. Russell, P., *Waking Up in Time.* Origin Press: Novato, CA, 1998.
11. Gallup, G. H., "Americans' Spiritual Searches Turn Inward." February 11, 2003. Available: www.gallup.com/poll/7759/americans-spiritual-searches-turn-inward.aspx.
12. Cimino, R., and Lattin, D., "Choosing My Religion." *American Demographics,* pp. 60–65, April 1999.
13. Taylor, E. "Desperately Seeking Spirituality." *Psychology Today,* pp. 54+, November/December 1994.
14. Sheler, J. L., "Hell Hath No Fury." *U.S. News and World Report,* pp. 44–50, January 31, 2000.
15. Graham, B., as quoted on *Larry King Live.* CNN, December 31, 1999.
16. Engen, J., "White Buffalo Hailed as Omen." *Newsday,* September 19, 1994.

17. Atwater, P. M. H., *Children of the Millennium: Children's Near-Death Experiences and the Evolution of Humankind.* Three River Press: New York, 1999.
18. Trungpa, C., *Shambhala, The Sacred Path of the Warrior.* Shambhala Press, Boston, 1998.
19. Ornish, D., *Love and Survival.* HarperCollins: New York, 1998.
20. WikiQuote. Available: http://en.wikiquote.org/wiki/Buckminster_Fuller.
21. Jung, C. G., *Man and His Symbols.* Anchor Press: New York, 1964.
22. Blizter, R., as quoted in R. von Oech's *A Whack on the Side of the Head,* p. 71. Warner Books: New York, 1983.
23. Ayres, A., *The Wit and Wisdom of Mark Twain.* Harper & Row: New York, 1987.
24. Anderson, M. D., and Williams, J. M., "Seeing Too Straight: Stress and Vision." *Longevity,* August 1989.
25. Angelou, M., *Wouldn't Take Nothing for My Journey Now.* Bantam Books: New York, 1993.
26. Armstrong, L., *It's Not About the Bike: My Journey Back to Life.* Putnam: New York, 2000.
27. Covey, S., *The 7 Habits of Highly Effective People.* Fireside Books: New York, 1989.
28. Thompson, T., "Climbing with Ability." Available: www.gorp.com/gorp/activity/climb/ability.htm.
29. Mandela, N., *Long Walk to Freedom.* Back Bay Books: Boston, 1994.
30. "Gabrielle Giffords." Available: http://en.wikipedia.org/wiki/Gabrielle_Giffords.
31. Carter, G., *Healing Myself: A Hero's Primer for Recovery from Tragedy.* Hampton Roads Publishing Co.: Norfolk, VA, 1993.
32. Frankl, V., *Man's Search for Meaning.* Pocket Books: New York, 1963.

✦ ADDITIONAL REFERENCES

Banyacya, T., "Hopi Prophecies." Whole Life Expo, Denver, CO, October 20, 1996.

Elliot, W., *Tying Rocks to Clouds: Meetings and Conversations with Wise and Spiritual People.* Image Books: New York, 1996.

Fields, R., Taylor, P., Weyler, R., and Ingrasci, R., *Chop Wood, Carry Water: A Guide to Finding Spiritual Fulfillment in Everyday Life.* Tarcher Books: Los Angeles, 1984.

Gorbachev, M., "A Call for New Values." *Noetic Sciences Review,* No. 35(3), pp. 12–13, 1995.

Hammerschlag, C., *The Theft of the Spirit: A Journey to Spiritual Healing.* Fireside Books: New York, 1994.

Keck, R., *Sacred Eyes.* Synergy Associates: Boulder, CO, 1992.

Lee, S. C., *The Circle Is Sacred: A Medicine Book for Women.* Council Oak Books: Tulsa, OK, 1998.

Lerner, M., *Spirit Matters.* Walsh Books: Charlottesville, VA, 2000.

Lesser, E., *The New American Spirituality.* Random House: New York, 1999.

McGuire, M., "The New Spirituality: Healing Rituals Hit the Suburbs." *Psychology Today,* pp. 57–64, January/February 1989.

Norikuki, D., "Stories, Traditions and the Baby White Buffalo." *Los Angeles Times,* September 22, 1994.

O'Donohue, J., *Anam Cara: A Book of Celtic Wisdom.* HarperSanFrancisco: San Francisco, 1997.

Russell, P., *The Global Brain Awakens.* Atrium Publishers Group: San Francisco, 1995.

Ryan, M. J. (Editor), *Fabric of the Future: Women Visionaries Illuminate the Path of Tomorrow.* Conari Press: Berkeley, CA, 1999.

Seaward, B. L., *Quiet Mind, Fearless Heart: The Taoist Path of Stress and Human Spirituality.* John Wiley and Sons: New York, 2005.

Simone, C., and Vasudev, S.J., *Midnights with the Mystic.* Hampton Roads: Charlottesville, VA, 2008.

Skog, S., *Embracing Our Essence: Spiritual Conversations with Prominent Women.* Health Communications: Deerfield Beach, FL, 1995.

Wheatley, M., *Leadership and the New Science.* Berrett-Koehler Publishers: San Francisco, 1994.

The Wellness
Paradigm Revisited

A vast cosmos of the different forces of nature is tied together by God's directing power.
Everything works in mutual harmony with the Divine Plan.

—Paramahansa Yogananda

Y EARS AGO I HAD THE great privilege of hearing and meeting Dr. Elisabeth Kübler-Ross, a pioneer not only in the field of death and dying
but in the field of holistic wellness as well. She was the keynote speaker at
the American Holistic Medical Association Conference held in La Crosse,
Wisconsin.[1] The title of her talk was "Holistic Wellness." She began by saying
that although the word *wellness* is quite new to the American vernacular, the
concept of wellness is ageless and goes back thousands of years. The premise of holistic wellness is simple—the whole is greater the sum of its
parts. This ancient (ageless) wisdom is shared by Tibetan monks, Australian
aborigines, Peruvian shamans, American Indian healers, and scores of other
wisdom keepers around the globe.

As she reminded the audience of this premise, she drew a big circle
on a flip chart, a line going from top to bottom, and then a line going
from right to left, dividing the circle into four equal quarters. In the upper
right-hand corner, she wrote the words *emotional well-being*. In the lower
right-hand corner, she scribbled the words *physical well-being*. Moving
clockwise, she placed the magic marker in the lower left-hand quadrant
and wrote the words *mental well-being*. Then, she reached as high as
she could and wrote in the upper left-hand quadrant the capital letters
SPIRITUAL well-being.

Before she proceeded with an explanation of wellness throughout the
life cycle, she explained that the circle is a universal symbol of wholeness
that is found in Tibetan mandalas, American Indian medicine wheels,
Mayan calendars, full moons, and Roman architecture. "The circle is a symbol of wholeness," she reiterated. Then, drawing a breath, Kübler-Ross said,
"The word *health* comes from the Anglican word *hal*, which means to be
whole or holy. The minute you start talking about health, whether you know
it or not, you are inferring some sense of human spirituality." The audience,
packed into the standing room–only lecture hall, gave reassuring nods and
smiles, for the wisdom she shared validated what most people already knew
at a deep intuitive level.

A Closer Look at the Wellness Paradigm

L ET'S EXAMINE THE **wellness paradigm** more closely. Perhaps the most
accurate definition of *holistic wellness* is this one: wellness is the integration, balance, and harmony of mind, body, spirit, and emotions that lead
to optimal well-being, where the whole is greater than the sum of its parts.[2]
The words—*integration, balance,* and *harmony*—are not used poetically.
Each relates specifically to the inclusive nature of wellness. Integration

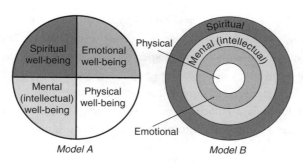

FIGURE 2.1 a. Mandala of Wellness Paradigm. b. Energetic Patterns of the Wellness Paradigm.

is the blending and coming together of all aspects of being—mind, body, spirit, and emotions. Balance suggests that no one component should eclipse or overshadow the other three, because each has equal weight. Harmony describes the energetic resonance between mind, body, spirit, and emotions that constitutes a healthy vibration. The lack of a healthy vibration leads to a disease state. Despite what might appear to be four separate components joined in a circle, no division or separation between any of these components exists. All is one.

In **Figure 2.1,** model A depicts the illustration that Kübler-Ross calls the ageless wisdom of optimal well-being, in which integration, balance, and harmony of mind, body, spirit, and emotions are essential. Model B shows the same components of wellness, depicted in the human energy field with the understanding that mind, body, spirit, and emotions are layers of consciousness, each at a different vibration. This, too, underscores the concept of harmony in wellness.

Indeed, the whole is greater than the sum of its parts. In fact, the lines that separate, for example, mind from body and emotions from spirit, really don't exist. They are just there for theoretical and academic purposes. In truth, there is no separation, because all parts come together as one. However, if we were to look at each component separately for a brief moment, just long enough to understand its essence, we would find the following.[3]

Emotional well-being is defined as the ability to feel and express the entire range of human emotions (everything from anger to love) and to control them, not to be controlled by them. This may sound like a tall order, but it is not an impossible one. This spectrum comprises all emotions, but a great many people (more men than women) do not allow themselves to feel a particular emotion (e.g., anger) or are conditioned to express an emotion in an unhealthy way, such as prolonged grief or guilt.

Physical well-being can best be described as the optimal functioning of all the body's physiological systems. Once thought to be independent from each other, the body's physiological systems include, but are not limited to, the respiratory system, the endocrine system, the cardiovascular system, and the immune system. All act as one system in the body's efforts to maintain homeostasis, or balance. It is because these systems are interconnected that a suppressed immune system ultimately affects all the other systems.

Mental well-being is the ability to gather, process, recall, and communicate information. If this sounds like a computer, you're right. The dynamics of a computer are designed to function like the human mind. Mental well-being also involves the balance of right-brain functions (e.g., intuition, imagination, receptivity, etc.) and left-brain functions (e.g., rationality, analysis, judgment, etc.) and also uses the wisdom found beneath in the waters of the unconscious mind (e.g., dream symbols, archetypes, etc.). This balance of the conscious and unconscious is what psychologist Carl Jung called *psychic equilibrium*. Mental well-being also means being able to quiet the mind through meditation, as well as to gather various sensory information.

Spiritual well-being is rather difficult to define. For starters, we can say that spiritual well-being is the maturation of higher consciousness that is developed through three factors: an insightful and nurturing relationship with oneself and others, a strong personal value system, and the fulfillment of a meaningful purpose in one's life.

It is interesting to note that despite the legacy of these four pillars of wellness, the (left-brained) American culture has attempted over the years to divide the wellness pie into smaller and smaller pieces, which only further fragments and separates the theoretical constructs that were never meant to be divided (keep in mind that there really is no separation at all). Social wellness, personal wellness, sexual wellness, financial wellness, and environmental wellness are just a few of the various components that have been teased from the original construct of mind, body, spirit, and emotions. For example, social well-being (relationships) is a core part of spiritual well-being. Environmental wellness demonstrates how tightly woven these four components really are and integrates both physical and spiritual well-being. This integration also can be seen with the other subdivisions. But rather than divide and separate, the new paradigm is to see the integration, balance, and harmony of mind, body, spirit, and emotions.

Wellness in the Limelight and the Life Cycle

BACK AT THE HOLISTIC WELLNESS conference, Kübler-Ross began an eloquent soliloquy on wellness.

> These lines which I drew to separate mind and body, spirit from mind, and so on, really don't exist. The reason I placed them here is to explain, as I see it, how we journey through the wellness paradigm. Keeping in mind that all four aspects are always present, we enter the life cycle with the limelight on the upper right-hand corner, emotional well-being. In the first few years of our lives we try on emotions, all of them. We laugh, we cry, we pout, we grieve, we go through the whole gamut, many times each to develop our emotional processing. This is a very important stage in our lives. What happens, though, is that we get cultured to act a certain way. "Big boys don't cry," boys are told. "Wipe that smile off your face." "Don't you ever talk back to me." These words can be very damaging to any child because they stifle our emotions. The result is that we carry emotional baggage around the rest of our lives, or until we learn to feel and express our emotions correctly. For some, this never really happens.

Next came a shift in the limelight as the focus moved in a clockwise direction to physical well-being:

> At puberty, we become our bodies. Now keep in mind that emotions are still present as is the mind and spirit, but the body has the limelight. Perhaps because of hormones, perhaps social pressures and the emergence of our sexuality, a greater emphasis is now placed on the physical body. It's in this period where kids spend hours in front of a mirror, and even more hours grooming themselves. Clothes, skin, muscles, weight, shoes, hair—all get top priority.

Although it might seem like some people continue this pattern of obsession of physical prowess for quite some time, at some point between high school and college the shift in focus turns to the mind—and to mental well-being. She explained that for the next several years, perhaps decades, we sharpen our mental acuity to gather, process, recall, and communicate information. What begins in high school and even more so in college continues into adulthood with conferences, workshops, continuing education, computers, and even leisure reading.

The last quadrant, spiritual well-being, is no less challenging than the first three. In fact, there are those who would say that it is the most challenging, which is perhaps why it is the last quadrant to hold the lime-light. Spiritual well-being involves a dynamic integration of relationships, values, and a meaningful purpose in life. The aspects of relationships (both personal and interpersonal), values (e.g., freedom versus responsibility), and a meaningful purpose in life (from choosing a college major to a full-blown midlife crisis) can all seem overwhelming, so much so that it was Kübler-Ross' opinion that the majority of people choose not to venture into that limelight. As if to say, "I'm not budging," they fold their arms across their chest in defiance, transforming themselves into spiritual couch potatoes. But if we are to complete the cycle of wellness, we must go into the spiritual quadrant.

Since the word *wellness* entered the American lexicon, there have been many theories of the wellness paradigm. Yet Kübler-Ross' particular expla-nation of wellness is not only charismatic in style but also dynamic in scope. No other models I have encountered discuss growth throughout the human life cycle. People who present concepts that are not mainstream are often said to be ahead of their time. Such was the case with this sage.

Kübler-Ross ended her presentation by inviting the audience to help her (and others like her) reintroduce the concepts of human spirituality back into the healthcare setting. When she was finished with her address, she closed her eyes for a moment, then waved her hand and blew a kiss to the crowd. The audience responded with a thunderous standing ovation.

Human Spirituality: The Neglected Component of Well-Being (If you cannot measure it, it is not real.)

IT IS SAD TO SAY that as important, even crucial, the spiritual aspect of our lives is, it often gets neglected. The result is some level of dysfunction, for optimal wellness is the integration, balance, and harmony of mind, body, spirit, and emotions, not just mind, body, and emotions. When one aspect of our being is denied, all parts suffer.

Why has the concept of human spirituality been neglected and ignored in virtually all aspects of society, including health care? Is there a cultural bias against human spirituality? The answer appears to be an unequivocal yes! For the most part, the answer can be traced back to one man, René Descartes.[4] During the European Renaissance, a time of fan-tastic intellectual freedom and discovery, Galileo confirmed Copernicus' finding that the Earth orbits the sun. Planet Earth, it turned out, was not the center of the universe. This bit of news didn't sit well with the pope, because it forced a different way of thinking, a change of paradigms. In an effort to hide the truth, the pope excommunicated Galileo and locked him in a tower for a full year. The Vatican did make a formal apology to Galileo in 1992.[5]

Enter René Descartes—scientist, philosopher, and consummate Renaissance man. Sensing the rift between science and religion over the quest for truth, Descartes met with the pope and, acting as a peace negotiator, proposed that the church keep to matters of the soul, which Descartes pointed out resided in the pineal gland of the brain. The church could have from the neck up, he proposed, and science could then have from the neck down. Thus an agreement was made to separate mind from body. Wielding great influence at the time, Descartes' philosophy practically became law in what today is commonly known as the **Cartesian principle** of science, the **mechanistic paradigm,** or the reductionistic theory.[6]

In simplest terms, the Cartesian principle states that for things to be real, for truth to become a scientific fact, observations must be made only by the five senses and must be measured repeatedly for accuracy. Western science is built on this foundation and often supported with mathematical equations. As scientific advances pushed our understanding of the world and as technology advanced life expectancy (through vaccinations) and leisure (with cars, microwave ovens, smartphones, and so on), a culture emerged in which science began to overshadow human spirituality. Issues of the soul and matters of spirit were left entirely to various religious organizations. Whenever aspects of the human spirit manifested, they were dismissed as nonsense because they could not be proved scientifically. For example, those cases of spontaneous cancer remission experienced by patients who prayed for a miracle are often denied in the medical community with a remark of this sort: "Oh well, you were misdiagnosed; you never really had cancer."

In her memoir, *Reason for Hope*, renowned primatologist Jane Goodall writes:

> I was taught as a scientist to think logically and empirically, rather than intuitively or spiritually. When I was at Cambridge University in the early 1960s most of the scientists and science students working in the Department of Zoology, so far as I could tell, were agnostic or even atheist . . . Fortunately, by the time I got to Cambridge I was 27 years old and my beliefs had already been molded so that I was not influenced by these opinions. I believed in a spiritual power that, as a Christian, I called God.[7]

The Legacy of Descartes: Division and Separation

THE LEGACY OF THE REDUCTIONISTIC theory, which created the lines of separation between mind and body, became superimposed over the spiritual domain as well. When people were looking for answers to life's difficult problems, they adopted a religious paradigm that separated God from Self. They perceived God as being a fixed external entity (one often depicted as an old man with gray hair and beard dressed in a toga, hanging out on a cloud, offering rewards and punishments based on various acts of human behavior).

Over the years, more emphasis has been placed on an external Divine Source with less and less emphasis being placed on the internal Divine Source, with the two being regarded as quite different. For example, during a presentation on the topic of mind–body–spirit healing, I shared with a group of physicians, nurses, and clergy a story of a man who healed himself of cancer through visualization, mental imagery, and meditation when all efforts by Western medicine had failed. A minister in the audience stood up to speak, apparently quite upset with the story. "The man didn't heal himself," he said. "Only God can heal," he stated emphatically, as if the man himself had absolutely nothing to do with his healing. The minister argued vehemently that God was a separate and distinct entity (as if riding high above on a cloud with a magic wand), denying any sense of Divine Presence within (or collaboration with) the mind or body of the man who was healed.[8]

The ancient proverb, "As above, so below," which implies that the Divine Force, however it is referred to, resides equally everywhere, was abandoned for a simpler black-and-white reality—not just in the minds of scientists, but apparently in the minds of some clergy as well. Passed down through the centuries, this idea resulted in a division and separation, either implicitly or explicitly, from our Divine Source. The matter gets even more complicated when turf issues arise between science and religion, as can best be illustrated with the never-ending debates on evolution and creationism or nature versus nurture.

New Common Ground Between Science and Religion

INTERESTINGLY ENOUGH, THE ABYSS BETWEEN science and religion is narrowing, and in some circles the span is close enough to jump across.

In a 1994 *Psychology Today* article entitled "Desperately Seeking Spiritual-ity," it was reported that in that same year the American Association for the Advancement of Science conducted a symposium on religion and science to a packed house. The article noted that this symposium was part of a much larger network of institutes sparking dialogue between science and religion.[9]

In the wake of scientific discoveries in the field of quantum physics, a bridge is forming to span the once humongous divide, and many people are quite excited about the connection being made. Common ground is being acknowledged, not ridiculed, between the disciplines of science and religion. However, in some cases, it is not science and religion that are forming an alliance, but rather science and spirituality. The common ground can best be described as an understanding of light (a term used in both camps) and energy and is described by Diarmuid Ó Murchú in his book *Quantum Theology*:[10]

> Light has been the subject of intense scientific pursuit for the past few hun-dred years. The ancient Greeks considered light to be a form of energy, but did not speculate about its essential nature. Newton, at the beginning of the sixteenth century, claimed that light consists of small, corpuscular bodies which travel in straight lines, and that within the light spectrum, sensation of color is determined by wave length. This became the new tantalizing question which was finally resolved (not to Einstein's satisfaction) by quan-tum theory and its acknowledgment of the dual particle–wave nature of light. Light features dominantly in how people tend to describe their mysti-cal experiences. Mystics, sages, and philosophers of all ages and cultures have sought enlightenment, not just intellectual understanding or esoteric knowledge.

Today, scientists, primarily physicists, make reference to the "God Particle," the first building block of the Universe, suggesting that science and spiritu-ality may be more closely linked than Descartes proposed.[11] As a physicist, Bernard Haisch took a stab at reconciling the differences between sci-ence and religion with his book, *The God Theory*, in which he explores the concept of light from both sides.[12] Adding scientific fact to the spiritual side of this equation is Dean Radin, lead researcher at the Institute of Noetic Science. In his book, *Entangled Minds*, Radin used the language of physics (the entanglement theory) to help explain consciousness as energy. Examin-ing data from numerous double-blind, peer-reviewed experiments, Radin outlines a rather strong case that the abyss between science and spirituality is quite small, and in fact may not exist at all.[13]

There is an expression that says the more things change, the more they remain the same. As the evolution of human consciousness slowly rises to a higher level with each succeeding generation, pieces of understanding fit together to bring greater clarity to a world vision. Some ideas that were passed over as ridiculous are now being revisited and appreciated for their true merit. Such is the case with the wellness paradigm, a golden nugget of ageless wisdom that has come back to center stage, not only in the context of health and well-being, but also in a great many other aspects of humanity. And with this appreciation of the wellness philosophy, where the whole is greater than the sum of its parts, so, too, is the recognition that spiritual well-being is the foundation upon which the other components rest.

A Closing Story

A RECENT ARTICLE IN *National Geographic* magazine explores the latest scientific discoveries of the universe through the lens of the Hubble Space Telescope, which give more credence to the Big Bang theory.[14] Speculation by several leading astronomers suggests that the universe is indeed expanding. Can the expansion go on forever? In his book *A Brief History of Time*, famed British physicist Stephen Hawking suggests that the expanding universe will someday reach a point at which movement halts—he calls this "the still point"—which is followed by a contraction of energy or implosion.[15] In a 1993 debate entitled "Physics and Metaphysics," renowned astronomer Richard Berendzen closed his presentation with this thought: "Several thousand years ago, Buddhist tradition explained that the universe expands and contracts ever so slowly with the breathing cycle of God. Perhaps science and spirituality have more in common than they know."[16]

⬩ SUMMARY

THE WELLNESS PARADIGM IS AGELESS wisdom based on the premise that the whole (mind, body, spirit, and emotions) is greater than the sum of its parts. Western science and academic knowledge are based on the Cartesian principle, or reductionistic theory, by which truth (fact) is determined by separating and examining various pieces that can be repeatedly measured through the five senses—the parts are valued more than the whole. Kübler-Ross' wellness model is based on ageless wisdom—the integration, balance, and harmony of mind, body, spirit, and emotions—and addresses how we move through each respective quadrant during the progression of our own life journey. Science and religion, which have been at odds over the search for truth since Galileo was excommunicated centuries ago, seem to be finding common ground today with regard to the aspects of light and energy in quantum physics.

❧ TERMS AND CONCEPTS

Cartesian principle

emotional well-being

mechanistic paradigm

mental well-being

physical well-being

spiritual well-being

wellness paradigm

EXERCISE 2.1
THE MANDALA OF PERSONAL WELLNESS

Consider the metaphor of a circle with four quadrants as one way to illustrate the concept of wellness. One of the tenets of wellness is "balance" among these four components: mind, body, spirit, and emotions. Perhaps because the body is so tangible and easy to measure, this quadrant gets most of the attention, leaving an imbalance with the other three. The spiritual component often gets the least attention. Take a moment to think about what activities you do in the course of each day that can be assigned to each of the four quadrants in the figure below. An example would be including weight training in the quadrant labeled BODY and meditation in the quadrant labeled SPIRIT. Write each activity on the lines provided in that quadrant to get an idea of the percentage you dedicate to each component (e.g., mind 75%, emotions 50%, body 89%, and spirit 25%). Upon completion, take a look at your wellness circle and ask yourself this question: If you were to gently roll this wheel, would it roll evenly, or would it stop on one quadrant and fall over due to being top heavy? Would it even roll at all? If you answered yes to any of these questions, the next question to answer is why.

Another tenet of holistic wellness is integration. Do you see or feel any integration—crossconnections between how the mind affects the body, how the body affects the spirit (hatha yoga comes to mind), or how emotions (perhaps stress in particular) affect the spirit? Take a moment to contemplate this aspect of integration and write down your thoughts.

_____

_____

_____

_____

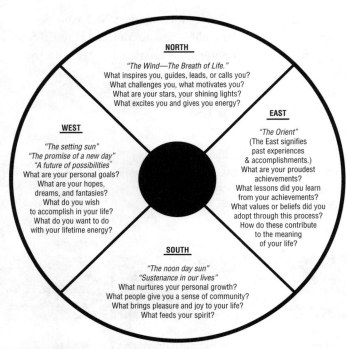

NORTH

"The Wind—The Breath of Life."
What inspires you, guides, leads, or calls you?
What challenges you, what motivates you?
What are your stars, your shining lights?
What excites you and gives you energy?

EAST

"The Orient"
(The East signifies
past experiences
& accomplishments.)
What are your proudest
achievements?
What lessons did you learn
from your achievements?
What values or beliefs did you
adopt through this process?
How do these contribute
to the meaning
of your life?

WEST

"The setting sun"
"The promise of a new day"
"A future of possibilities"
What are your personal goals?
What are your hopes,
dreams, and fantasies?
What do you wish
to accomplish in your life?
What do you want to do
with your lifetime energy?

SOUTH

"The noon day sun"
"Sustenance in our lives"
What nurtures your personal growth?
What people give you a sense of community?
What brings pleasure and joy to your life?
What feeds your spirit?

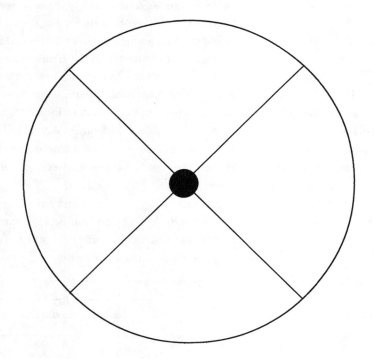

Last is the tenet of harmony. Is there harmony among these four components in your life, or does one component negate another (e.g., do you spend so much time studying that the health of the human spirit is neglected?). Does a healthy spirit give harmony to your emotional well-being? Please explain.

_____

_____

_____

_____

⚕ ENDNOTES

1. Kübler-Ross, E., Keynote Address, "Holistic Wellness." American Holistic Medical Association Conference, La Crosse, WI, April 19, 1981.
2. Seaward, B. L., *Managing Stress: Principles and Strategies for Health and Well-Being* (7th edition). Jones & Bartlett Learning: Burlington, MA, 2011.
3. Seaward, B. L., *Managing Stress: Principles and Strategies for Health and Well-Being* (7th edition). Jones & Bartlett Learning: Burlington, MA, 2011.
4. Pert, C., Interview with Bill Moyers, *Healing and the Mind*, PBS, 1993.
5. Cowell, A., "After 350 Years, Vatican Says Galileo Was Right." *New York Times*, October 31, 1992.
6. Damasio, A., *Descartes' Error*. HarperCollins: New York, 1995.
7. Goodall, J., *Reason for Hope: A Spiritual Journey.* Warner Books: New York, 1999.
8. Seaward, B. L., "Mind–Body–Spirit Healing." Health Promotion, Health Prevention Conference of the U.S. Army, Atlanta, GA, August 24–25, 1999.
9. Taylor, E., "Desperately Seeking Spirituality." *Psychology Today*, pp. 54+, November/December 1994.
10. Ó Murchú, D., *Quantum Theology*. Crossroad: New York, 1997.
11. The God Particle. Available: http://en.wikipedia.org/wiki/Higgs_boson.
12. Haoisch, B. *The God Theory*. Weiser Books: Berkeley, CA, 2009.
13. Radin, D. *Entangled Minds*. Paraview Pocket Books: New York, 2006.
14. Swerdlow, J., "Asking Infinite Questions." *National Geographic*, No. 196(4): 5–41, 1999.
15. Hawking, S., *A Brief History of Time*. Penguin Books: New York, 1993.
16. Berendzen, R., "Physics vs. Metaphysics—A Debate." The American University, Washington, DC, April 20, 1993.

⚕ ADDITIONAL REFERENCES

Benson, H., and Stewart, E., *The Wellness Book*. Simon & Schuster: New York, 1993.
Sams, J., *The Sacred Path*. HarperCollins: New York, 1990.
Travis, J., and Ryan, S., *Wellness Workbook* (second edition). Ten Speed Press: Berkeley, CA, 1988.
Yogananda, P., "Inner Reflections." Calendar, Self-Realization Fellowship, Los Angeles, CA, 1999.

CHAPTER 3

Theories of Human Spirituality:
Perspectives from the Sages and
Wisdom Keepers

Be careful not to become a prisoner of the thoughts of your own paradigm.

—Charles Tart, Ph.D.

God is not a person. God is the force. God is the essence of all life. God is pure and undefiled consciousness. God is eternal. To seek God, one need not go on a pilgrimage or light lamps and burn incense before an altar. For God resides in our hearts. If we could completely obliterate fear in the consciousness of our body, we would see God face to face.

—Mohandas Gandhi

EVERY AGE, EVERY EPOCH, AND perhaps at times every community has a wisdom keeper. Someone—either male or female—who spends a great amount of time soul-searching, talking to God, making sense of life, accruing experiences, gaining knowledge, and distilling all of this into an elixir of truth, which he or she then gratefully shares with anyone who approaches seeking an upper hand on the sojourn of life.

The journey of a wisdom keeper is not an easy one. Actually, it is extremely difficult. Like the explorers who bushwhack an uncharted path toward the top of a mountain only to get cut and bruised, wisdom keepers are often shunned for expressing their views which, to some, seem radical. Sometimes they even become outcasts because their ideas conflict with the conventional thought paradigm, making true the expression, "You cannot be a prophet in your own hometown." But as has been repeated so many times, the wisdom shared by these sages and mystics proves itself true over the years, and their insights remain an invaluable resource of wisdom for generations.

Imagine, if you will, that human spirituality is like a majestic mountain, reaching to the heights of the Earth's stratosphere. This universal symbol of human spirituality is as beautiful from the plains as it is from the peak, a mountain so compelling that it begs to be explored. We climb mountains because of the promise of the view—clear visibility for miles and miles, all the while thinking that we have touched a layer of heaven or the face of God. It's no secret that the lure of the mountain vista provides us with insights into new passages in our lives. We seek the mountain journey because we crave the wisdom.

Since the dawn of humanity there have been hundreds, if not thousands, of luminaries with remarkable insights of truth and wisdom. These people are those who have taken the bold step to explore the heights of the divine mystery through introspection and service. As bushwhackers and explorers who head toward the mountain's summit, they are seekers of truth, and they gladly share their perspectives with any and all who wish to listen.

If indeed spirituality can be compared to a mountain, then these people are mountain hikers who have taken the bold step to climb uncharted territory. Like any mountain on any one of the Earth's seven continents that hosts several paths to the top, so, too, the mountain of human spirituality offers numerous paths with views and perspectives shared by those luminaries who have hiked and reached the summit. And so they share with all who listen the beauty of the vista upon which they have gazed.

My aim in this chapter is to present a balance of insights and perspectives from both men and women around the globe, those with contemporary knowledge as well as ageless wisdom, so as to provide the widest perspective possible. Metaphorically speaking, this chapter presents an aerial view of "The Mountain," with each wisdom keeper highlighting the view of human spirituality from the path he or she has chosen to take.

To avoid René Descartes' mistake of reductionism, these theories and philosophies have not been divided into groups, nor have they been categorized by belief. Rather, the individuals are listed randomly, signifying the equal contribution of each to the whole. You might take note as you read through this chapter that whereas some individuals focus on one particular aspect of the human spirit, such as love, others offer a series of steps to reach a higher point of consciousness. Because of the universal wisdom of the themes presented throughout this chapter, most, if not all, will surface again throughout the rest of the text.

It is interesting to note that while we gather nuggets of information from various masters and sages, our left brain needs validity of the source. For this reason, a brief background of each person is woven through his or her insights to round out the context of their message. It is also interesting to note that many people who come upon a sage, a teacher, or a guru tend to place him or her on a pedestal (a metaphorical mountain, so to speak) when they feel moved by the message. If there is a cautionary note to this chapter (and life itself), perhaps it is this: focus on the message rather than the messenger. And if your favorite wisdom keeper is not found within these pages, please don't feel slighted, for no text can possibly contain all that there is to this subject. This is merely a starting point to begin a discussion, a juncture of thoughts for more soul-searching to occur.

Rest assured, there is more wisdom on this topic of human spirituality than any book or series of books can embody. This chapter contains only a small handful of such views collected from those who have hiked and climbed their respective paths. Throughout these pages you will see names of people from all corners of the globe, from various backgrounds, languages, and experiences, all speaking about the perennial philosophy of human spirituality.

Some additional words of caution to note as you hike vicariously on the paths these wisdom keepers have traveled. Because our experiences of human spirituality are so personal, it is easy to pass judgment and to think that our path is superior to others. Nothing could be further from the truth. Once again comes the reminder to keep an open mind and focus on the message rather than the messenger. In the words of the famous Chinese philosopher Lao Tzu, the start of each journey begins with the first step. So let us begin.

Carl Gustav Jung: Divine Consciousness

TYPICALLY, WHEN INDIVIDUALS FIRST CONSIDER the source of the human spirit, their search leads them externally to nature and the heavens above. It was the work of psychiatrist Carl Jung who, as a pioneer in the field of psychology, turned the search inward to an exploration of the depths of the human mind, or psyche, as a means to understand the spiritual nature of humankind. Jung was fascinated with the realm of the human psyche and the relationship between the conscious and the unconscious mind. With an unyielding search for clues to better understand the mind, Jung spent much time learning about intuition, clairvoyants (people whose dreams foretold future events that actually happened), seemingly bizarre coincidences, and supernatural occurrences. This fascination led him to explore the mystical side of the mind, and for this reason he was ridiculed by many of his contemporaries. Yet, with time, perceptions have changed. Although Jung is still considered ahead of his time by many, today his theories are recognized as the cornerstones not only of mental and emotional well-being but of spiritual well-being as well. Although Jung was not an advocate of any particular religion, his work is studied, taught, and cited by psychologists, theologians, and spiritual leaders around the world. Moreover, his work has given impetus to a new discipline of healing called *transpersonal psychology* or *psychospirituality*, the relationship between the mind and the soul.

Unlike his mentor Freud, an atheist who hypothesized that humans functioned at an instinctual level, Jung proposed a spiritual element to human nature—a spiritual drive located in the realm of the unconscious mind that manifests when it bubbles to the conscious level. A man who studied the myths and belief systems of many cultures on virtually every continent, Jung observed similarities of dream symbols and artwork between various groups of people who had no possible way of communicating with one another. From research gathered during his professional experiences, as well as his own intensive self-reflection, Jung theorized that these similarities are often represented in symbolic forms that he called "archetypes." Archetypes are primordial images or concepts that originate from the unconscious mind at a level so profound that there appears to be a common element among all humankind: an element of unity. Jung theorized that there are two levels that constitute the unconscious mind. The first level he called the "personal unconscious," the memories, repressed thoughts, feelings, and any information no longer needed by the individual's conscious mind. At a deeper level, however, is what he called the "collective unconscious," which he described as a universal consciousness: a unifying force within all individuals, or a collective soul, a **divine consciousness.** He believed that the collective unconscious had a divine nature, the essence of God within us all. According to Jung, this divine essence manifests in the conscious mind through several cognitive functions, including intuition, creativity, and the interpretation of dreams.

In the exploration of dream analysis, Jung discovered several people who dreamed of events that they had no possible knowledge of at a conscious level, only to discover that these events emerged as crystal-clear predictions of events to come. Moreover, in his counseling sessions, Jung would sometimes find himself in awe of coincidences that unfolded right in front of him. One example included listening to a client's dream about a fox, in which he and his patient walked on a dirt road, only to have a wild fox appear seconds after the animal was mentioned. Pondering the concept of coincidences and then studying this phenomenon more closely, Jung found that when two seemingly unrelated events happen at once, there is a reason and a purpose, no matter how significant or banal, a purpose that cannot be rationally explained by cause and effect. He coined the term *synchronicity* to explain this phenomenon and hypothesized that, in reality, there is no such thing as coincidence. Rather, everything is connected, and specific events unfold simultaneously for a reason. His study of Taoism and the I Ching led him to believe that there is a connectedness that extends beyond the individual throughout the entire universe, a concept not well accepted in the West during his lifetime.

Jung was once quoted as saying that "every crisis a person experiences over the age of 30 is spiritual in nature." Although some have credited Jung with addressing the midlife-crisis phenomenon, Jungian psychologists have maintained the spiritual importance of each individual. With regard to this spiritual crisis, Jung further elaborated that fertile ground for life's stressors is caused by the inability of modern men and women to get in touch with their inner selves. He added that sickness is a result of the individual not being whole; that is, never connecting with the divine qualities of the unconscious mind to clarify values and gain a focus of one's life meaning. One of Jung's theories, "**the shadow**," is based on the concept that there are ego-based characteristics of our personality that we keep hidden, even from ourselves, but usually project onto other people. Confronting the shadow of the soul, a profound self-awareness process, allows us to come to terms with several issues that generate the undercurrents for stress in our own lives and to become whole.

In a story described in his autobiography *Memories, Dreams, Reflections*, Jung tells of a young boy who asked an old wise man why no one in this day and age ever sees the face or hears the voice of God. The wise old sage replied that man no longer lowers himself enough to God's level. Jung tells this story to reinforce the concept that people of civilized cultures have become distant from the depth and the knowledge seated in the fathoms of the unconscious mind. Instead, they see God primarily as an external force or Supreme Being in the clouds. Jung suggested that God is a unifying force that resides in all of us, in the depths of our unconscious mind. Like the ancient Asian mystics he studied who practiced meditation to attain spiritual enlightenment, Jung advocated a personal responsibility to examine the conscious and unconscious mind and to find what he called "psychic equilibrium." In the book *Modern Man in Search of a Soul,* he warned that the advancement of technology and materialism, elements now accepted by many to be stressors, would further widen the gap between the conscious and the unconscious mind.

Jung believed that as technology and materialism increased, people would spend less and less time cultivating their inner selves. This 1933 observation had come to pass toward the end of the twentieth century. It is interesting to note that one of Jung's clients was instructed that psychoanalysis alone would not cure him of his chronic alcoholism. In a letter written to this client, Jung suggested that his best chance for cure was a "spiritual conversion." After Bill W.'s recovery, which he attributed to spiritual enlightenment, he and a friend started an organization for problem drinkers called Alcoholics Anonymous. Although this program is not tied to any religion, it has a very strong sense of spirituality about it.

Shortly before his death in 1961, Jung was interviewed by the British Broadcasting Corporation. When asked if he believed in God, he replied, "No." Then he paused for a moment and stated, "I know."

Rachel Naomi Remen: To Be of Service

A S A PHYSICIAN, RACHEL NAOMI REMEN is one of the earliest pioneers of holistic medicine. She is a professor of clinical medicine at the University of California at San Francisco School of Medicine. Although she began her medical career as a pediatrician, her focus over the past 20 years has changed to working with cancer patients. In 1985 she and her colleague Michael Lerner founded the Commonweal Cancer Help Program, a retreat program for terminal cancer patients. Remen herself is no stranger to disease. For over 47 years she has suffered from Crohn's disease. Her experience as a patient has given her a deep appreciation of the power of scientific medicine and a profound sense of its limitations.

Remen has dedicated her life to restoring the values of the Hippocratic Oath to the practice of scientific medicine and has answered a calling to reintroduce human spirituality back into the healthcare industry. More than just "doing no harm" as the Hippocratic Oath directs, her message is one of service.

In a speech given at the fifth annual Noetic Sciences Conference, "Open Heart, Open Mind," Remen summed up her philosophy of service as follows:

> **Service** is different from helping. Helping is based on inequality; it is not a relationship between equals. The wholeness in us serves the wholeness in others and the wholeness in life. The wholeness in you is the same wholeness in me. Service is a relationship between equals.

> Service rests on the basic premise that the nature of life is sacred, that life is a holy mystery which has an unknown purpose. When you serve, you see life as a whole. From the perspective of service, we are all connected.

Dr. Remen has received many honorary degrees in recognition of her pioneering work in unifying mind, body, and spirit and in the role of human spirituality in the healing process of disease and illness. The most requested reprint in the Institute of Noetic Sciences journal, *Noetic Sciences Review*, is Remen's essay written in 1988, titled "On Defining Spirit." The following is a passage from it:

> The most important thing in defining spirit is the recognition that spirit is an essential need of human nature. There is something in all of us that seeks the spiritual. This yearning varies in strength from person to person, but it is always there in everyone. And so, healing becomes possible. Yet there is a culture-wide tendency to deny the spiritual—to delegate it at best, to ignore it at worst.

Remen is an unconventional healer; a doctor to the soul. She heals through the power of stories. In her book *Kitchen Table Wisdom*, she recounts several stories of her cancer patients who have made the pilgrimage from illness to wholeness, with cancer being the common thread that weaves each human journey into a patchwork quilt of human spirituality. The theme in each story is similar—as we move from fear to love, healing occurs:

> It is not that we have soul. We are a soul. The soul is not an idea or a belief. It is an experience. It may awaken in us through illness or suffering, through dreams, music, or art, or work, or parenthood or sometimes for no reason at all. It overtakes us at times in the midst of daily life. Spiritual experience is not taught: it is found, uncovered, and recovered.

> There are many practices which can awaken us and deepen our sense of the soul, among them prayer, meditation, chanting, fasting and ritual. One of the

most surprising of these is the experience of loss. I have learned much about the power of the soul from people who have lost almost everything they once thought was important and found what has the most enduring meaning.

Abraham Maslow: To Be Self-Actualized

IT HAS OFTEN BEEN SAID that the role psychologists play today is that which was performed by the priests, rabbis, and ministers of the past. Keeping in mind that the word *psyche* actually means "soul," a few professionals in the field of psychology have taken what is called a *humanistic* (rather than mechanistic) approach to their field. Abraham Maslow is one such individual.

Greatly influenced by the atrocities of destruction in World War II, Maslow was convinced of the existence of a brighter side of human nature, and he became committed to the development of a theoretical construct to support this hypothesis. In the course of his career, Maslow chose to study the supreme examples of men and women who epitomized the height of human potential—individuals exhibiting a unique combination of creativity, love, self-reliance, confidence, and independence. Maslow called this **"self-actualization."** His faith in humankind led him to believe that by understanding individuals with positive personality characteristics and admirable traits, one would have a model framework to serve as an example for others in their pursuit for self-improvement.

Maslow's study of personality and behavior revealed a hierarchy of needs that must be met for a person to reach his or her highest human potential. This hierarchy of needs consists of five tiers, or levels. A metaphor to illustrate this concept is a series of steps up a mountain, as presented in **Figure 3.1**.

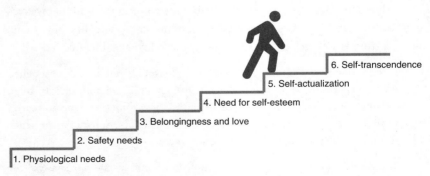

6. Self-transcendence
5. Self-actualization
4. Need for self-esteem
3. Belongingness and love
2. Safety needs
1. Physiological needs

FIGURE 3.1 Maslow's Hierarchy of Needs.

The first tier comprises the most basic physiological needs to ensure survival of the human organism. These include food, sleep, and sex. The second tier, safety needs, also contributes to one's survival and includes factors that provide security, order, and stability to one's life, such as clothing, money, and housing. Affection and strong bonding relationships comprise the third stage of belongingness and love. The fourth tier he called personal-esteem needs, a need and desire to seek or prove self-worth. Maslow called the final level the need for self-actualization, a stage of personal fulfillment in which ego boundaries and attachments are virtually eliminated, resulting in a feeling of oneness with the universe. This is the level at which one's human potential is maximized. Ideally, self-actualization is the fulfillment of one's highest human potential and capabilities. Maslow writes in *Religions, Values, and Peak Experiences,* "Self-actualization is the point where one is ultimately at peace with oneself."

Maslow noticed that until the basic needs at the bottom of the hierarchy are met, the needs at higher levels cannot be achieved. Notice that self-actualization is the top step. In essence, Maslow explained, the focus of attention here is directed toward the connection to the divine. However, if a person is struggling to pay bills, raise children as a single parent, keep a job, or take care of an elderly parent—needs that appear to be at ground level—all spiritual matters take a back seat, sometimes indefinitely. Moreover, even a person who has reached the level of self-actualization does not stay there forever. In a theoretical sense what makes the level of self-actualization so challenging to attain is the requirement that one must regularly lower the walls of the ego and explore the unknown with anticipation, not fear. In fact, Maslow states that the need to know (curiosity), taking risks, and the active pursuit of self-understanding are paramount to reaching self-actualization.

A quick browse through Maslow's work reveals that he observed and interviewed thousands of people, several of whom he considered both healthy and prime examples of quality human beings. From his research, cited in *Motivation and Personality,* Maslow noticed many characteristics that were common to people whom he identified as being self-actualized. It is this collection of characteristics that appear to contribute to the resilient nature of people who have achieved some degree of self-actualization. These include such attributes as a sense of humor, creativity, acceptance, spontaneity, curiosity, wonderment, compassion, independence, and integrity. Also in this list are what Maslow called mystical or peak sensations—those natural feelings of euphoria achieved through some wonderfully profound experience, akin to kissing the face of God.

What Maslow came to realize is that individuals are not born self-actualizers. Instead, they have evolved or journeyed through a multitude of human experiences, smoothed the rough edges, and polished the surface of their personal existence. In doing so, they have developed a remarkable human potential and, in the process, a healthy example for others to follow. Basically, self-actualizers are people with a strong positive outlook on themselves and on life in general. They hold a tremendous amount of faith in themselves and in their work. They live life with a passion, not a grudge. They know themselves inside and out; without a doubt, they are their own best friend.

The exciting aspect of Maslow's theory of self-actualization is that we are all capable of this potential. We all have the ability to access our inner resources, and we are all capable of being self-actualized.

M. Scott Peck: The Four Stages of Spiritual Growth

IN 1978, M. SCOTT PECK ushered in a new age of spiritual awareness to the American culture with a book entitled *The Road Less Traveled*. A psychiatrist who spent many years counseling clients with neurotic and psychotic disorders, Peck became aware of what he noted as a commonality in virtually all his patients: an absence or immaturity of spiritual development. He also noted that not all people were at the same level of spirituality, which made it a challenge to treat each person. Through an intense reflection of his own spiritual beliefs, coupled with what he observed in his clients, Peck developed a framework he called the "Road to Spiritual Development." This framework, closely associated with J. Fowler's "Stages of Faith," consists of four systematic, or hierarchical, stages of spiritual growth and development: chaotic antisocial, formal institutional, skeptical, and mystic communal. Peck states in his book *Different Drum* that not everyone falls neatly into one of these four categories. Some people hover between stages, and others migrate back and forth from one stage to another. Despite the shortcomings that Peck admitted to, this model (**Figure 3.2**) provides a basis from which we can begin to understand the maturation process of the human spirit.

Stage 1: The Chaotic Antisocial Individual

The first stage of Peck's road to spiritual development marks an underdeveloped spirituality and, in some cases, a spiritual absence or bankruptcy. Although many young children might appear to fall into this category, at an adult level the chaotic antisocial individual is a person whose life is in

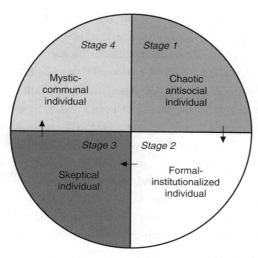

FIGURE 3.2 A symbolic representation of Peck's conception of human spirituality as a maturation process with four hierarchical stages.

utter chaos. This chaos may be represented by several attitudes and behaviors, including drug and alcohol addiction, codependency, or a helpless or hopeless attitude. Individuals at the **chaotic antisocial stage** can be very manipulative and unprincipled, and they often find that controlling others is easier than taking responsibility for their own lives. Individuals at this stage have a poor self-relationship; completely avoid the self-awareness process; maintain very poor relationships with family, friends, and co-workers; hold a weak value system with many unresolved conflicts; and have an absence of meaningful purpose in their lives. Some people remain at this stage their whole lives. A life-threatening situation, however, may be the catalyst to move to the next stage. In preparation to leave this stage, the chaotic antisocial individual will look for some kind of structure to help make order out of his or her personal chaos and to help slay some personal dragons that mask themselves as chronic stressors.

Stage 2: The Formal-Institutionalized Individual

Institutions such as prisons, the military, and, in many cases, the church provide structure or rules to live by. They offer rules, structured guidelines, and dogma to help individuals leave personal chaos behind and rebuild their lives. People who make the transition to this **institutional stage** from the chaotic antisocial stage desperately need rules, dogma, and guidance to survive.

Although many young people enter this stage through the influence of family (e.g., parents taking their children to church or temple), Peck finds that adults enter this stage by making an overnight conversion, almost a "born again" transformation. In essence, they adopt the dogma of the institution as a means of personal survival. Peck observed that when an individual advances to this stage, it may be very sudden and perhaps unconscious. A relationship with God parallels the parent–child relationship, where God is loving but punitive. In the words of Peck, "God becomes an 'Irish Cop' in the Sky." A Supreme Being is personified in human terms and, perhaps most important, God is purely an external figure. People who advance to this stage come looking for personal needs to be met and are looking for life's answers. Quite often they find what they came looking for. Comfortable with this stage, many people stay at this level for the rest of their lives. Some, however, may slip back into the first stage and continue an oscillation process between the two. Others eventually leave this stage because of unmet needs. They become skeptical of perhaps all institutions, yet remain spiritually stable enough to avoid slipping back to stage 1. At this point, such people begin a free-floating process, unanchored to anything.

Stage 3: The Skeptical Individual

When a person questions the dogma and rules necessary to maintain membership in a church organization or any organization that has provided some security and becomes skeptical of the answers or, more often than not, the lack of answers, he or she may eventually make a break, leaving the safety that the organization once provided. Peck said that this **skeptical stage** is crucial to spiritual development, when one begins to question the basis of understanding that the institution represents. This is also a very risky stage because there are no guaranteed answers. With tongue in cheek, Peck calls people in this stage "born-again atheists." People become skeptical when they find that the institution they joined doesn't fulfill or answer all their needs or expectations. Frustration turns into distrust, and they often leave the institution they once joined for refuge, becoming very cynical of the organization and perhaps even about life in general. The "skeptical individual" is looking for truth and, according to Peck, is more spiritually developed than many devoted churchgoers. Some college students, and even more college graduates, fall into this category after years of following their parents' religious lead, only to find that the beliefs on which they were raised do not seem to be adequate for the situations in which they currently find themselves. The skeptic individual finds him- or herself in a very tenuous position because one needs sure footing or an anchor to harbor oneself eventually. Two outcomes are likely. The first, like Goldilocks, is to sample other church institutions with a half-hearted compromise along the way; the second is to progress to the next and final stage of spiritual development.

Stage 4: The Mystic-Communal Individual

In the continual search for answers to life's questions, a person eventually comes to the realization that, like an unsolvable Zen *koan*, there are some questions that have no answers.

Unlike the skeptic who fights this premise, the mystic-communal individual takes delight in life's paradoxes. These people find comfort in the unanswerable, yet, like a sleuth, they seek out the continuing challenge, ever more hungry for possible clues and answers. People in this stage of spiritual development love a good mystery, and they love to explore. In this stage, mystic communals begin to depersonify God and come to the realization that God is equally an internal source (the power of love, faith, and will) and an external source (an unexplained energy or consciousness). Mystic communals begin to see an outline of the whole picture even when there are several pieces missing. These people see spirituality as a living process, not merely as an outcome or a heaven-oriented goal. Perhaps as important, these people see the need to build and maintain community within their environment by developing quality relationships built on acceptance, love, and respect. They see and feel the need to be connected. Individuals who reach this stage of spiritual development realize upon arrival that it is only the beginning of a very long but fruitful journey.

Like Jung, Peck hints that the inability to deal with psychological crises often manifests as a result of spiritual immaturity, from a lack of progression through these stages of spiritual growth. And as with Maslow's hierarchy of needs, Peck agrees that situations arise in which individuals "backslide" when stressful situations cause them to lose their footing on this road. For example, a person in the **mystic-communal stage** who experiences the death of a loved one may feel anger or guilt when the death is perceived as a form of punishment (Why me?). Many stressful situations cause individuals to focus on the external side of God or the lack thereof, often causing them to slip back into stage 2 or 3. While the road to spiritual development is an independent one, Peck suggests that we are not alone on this journey. Love and grace are the guides that lead the way when we choose to listen.

Black Elk: Mother Earth Spirituality

T HE AMERICAN INDIAN NATION and First Nation tribes of Canada include several hundred tribes. Although cultural differences abound,
from the Algonquins in the American Northeast to the Salish tribes on
Vancouver Island to the Navajo of the American Southwest, the spiritual
nature of the American Indian and First Nation people is fairly consistent
across the various Indian nations. One voice that ascended the heights of
consciousness in American Indian culture was that of Black Elk, a medicine
man of the Oglala Sioux (Lakota) tribe. His mystical vision, as recorded by
John G. Neihardt in the book *Black Elk Speaks,* has galvanized the understanding and appreciation of American Indian spirituality, which is also
referred to as **Mother Earth Spirituality**. In a culture that was nearly dev-
astated by European traditions and values, Black Elk's vision is quite profound and elaborate with respect to the essence and integrity of the human
spirit and the bonding relationship between the "two-legged" (human) and
the natural environment.

Perhaps the feature that most distinguishes American Indian spirituality
from that of other cultures is its incredible set of values, which demonstrate
a respect for Mother Earth and a connectedness to it seemingly unparalleled by other cultures. Black Elk is not alone in voicing this philosophy.
These same feelings have been expressed by a great many Indian people. In
the words of Shoshone shaman Rolling Thunder, who describes the Earth
as a living organism, "Too many people don't know that when they harm
the Earth they harm themselves." In his book, *Mother Earth Spirituality,* Ed
McGaa, Eagle Man, both expounds on Black Elk's vision and augments this
knowledge with additional insights into American Indian culture to provide
a more profound understanding of Black Elk's enlightenment. Following is a
brief synopsis of paths to American Indian healing.

Despite the initial assumption by Christian missionaries that Indians
were pagan, American Indians have a very profound relationship with the
divine essence. Unlike the Europeans, who appeared to personify this higher
power in human terms, American Indians accepted the divine power as the
Great Mystery, with no need to define or conceptualize God in a human
context. In the prophetic words of Chief Seattle, transcribed in a letter to
President Franklin Pierce in 1855 on land treaty negotiations: "One thing
we know, our God is the same God. You may think you own Him as you
wish to own land, but you cannot. He is the God of man; and his compassion is equal for the red man and the white. The Earth is precious to Him
and to harm the Earth is to heap contempt on its creator. Our God is the
same God. This Earth is precious to Him" (see **Box 3.1**). This preciousness

Box 3.1 A Letter from Chief Seattle (1855)*

The President in Washington sends word that he wishes to buy our land. But how can you buy or sell the sky, the land; the idea is strange to us. If we do not own the freshness of the air, and the sparkle of the water, how can you buy them? Every part of this Earth is sacred to my people. Every shining pine needle, every sandy shore, every mist in the dark woods. All are holy in the memory and experience of my people. We know the sap that courses through the trees as we know the blood that courses through our veins. We are part of the earth and it is part of us. Perfumed flowers are our sisters. The bear, the deer, the great eagle; these are our brothers. The body heat of the pony and man belong to the same family. The shining water that moves through the streams and rivers is not just water, but the blood of our ancestors. If we sell you our land, you must remember it is sacred.

Each ghostly reflection in the clear water of the lakes tells of the event and the memory in the life of my people. The water's murmur is the voice of my father's father. The rivers are my brothers. They quench our thirst, they carry our canoe and feed our children. So you must give to the river the kindness that you would give any brother. If we sell you our land, remember, that the air is precious to us. The air shares its spirit with all life which it supports. The wind that gave our grandfather his first breath also receives his last sigh. The wind also gives our children the spirit of life.

So if we sell you our land, you must keep it apart and sacred as a place where man can go to taste the wind that is sweetened by the meadow's flowers. Will you teach your children what we have taught our children? That the earth is our Mother? What befalls the earth, befalls all the sons of the earth. This we know, the earth does not belong to man, man belongs to the earth. All things connect, like the blood that unites us all. Man did not weave the web of life, he is merely a strand in it. Whatever he does to the web, he does to himself. One thing we know, our God is your God. The earth is precious to him and to harm the earth is to heap contempt on the creator.

Your destiny is a mystery to us. What will happen when the buffalo are all slaughtered, the wild horses tamed? What will happen when the secret corners of the forest are heavy with the scent of many men and the view of the ripe hills is blotted with talking wires? Where will the thicket be? Gone! Where will the eagle be? Gone! And what is it to say good-bye to the swift pony and the hunt—the end of living and the beginning of survival. When the last red man has vanished in his wilderness, and his memory is only the shadow of a cloud moving across the prairie, will these shores and forests still be here? Will there be any spirit of my people left? We love the earth as a newborn loves his mother's heart-beat. So if we sell you our land, love it as we love it. Care for it as we have cared for it. Hold in your mind the memory of the land as you received it. Preserve the land for all children, and love it as God loves us all. As we are part of the land, you too are part of the land. It is precious to us, it is also precious to you. One thing we know, there is only one God. No man, be he red man or white, can be apart. We are brothers after all.

*As interpreted by Ted Perry. Loosely based on Chief Seattle's 1854 oration, "The Great Ecology," as it appeared in the *Seattle Sunday Star*, October 29, 1887.

was and continues to be represented in the bonding relationship between each American Indian and the Earth's creatures, the wind, the rain, and the mountains.

North American Indians and First Nation people see Mother Earth as a symbol of wholeness, represented by their medicine wheel (**Figure 3.3**). Just as the seasons are divided into quarters, so, too, are many concepts within American Indian spirituality; for example, the four elements: earth, fire, water, and air; the four earth colors: red, yellow, black, and white; the four directions: East, West, North, and South; and the four cardinal principles or values of the Red Way: (1) to show respect for Wankan Tanka (the Great Mystery or Great Spirit), (2) to demonstrate respect for Mother Earth, (3) to

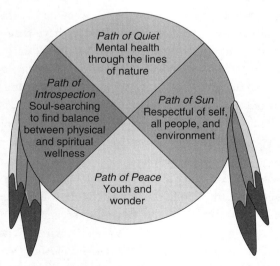

FIGURE 3.3 A symbolic representation of an American Indian medicine wheel described by Black Elk.

show respect for each fellow man and woman, and (4) to show respect for individual freedoms. The American Indian medicine wheel is a symbol of Mother Earth spirituality by which the lessons of nature are used to better understand oneself. Each quadrant of the wheel represents a specific aspect of spiritual growth, with various lessons to learn. The eastern quarter represents the Path of the Sun, where respect is shown for ourselves, others, and the environment. The southern quarter is the Path of Peace and is characterized by the traits of youth, innocence, and wonder. The western quarter is referred to as the Path of Introspection, where time is allocated for the soul-searching process and balance is strived for between one's physical and spiritual essences. The northern quarter represents the Path of Quiet. The Path of Quiet symbolizes the importance of mental health in which the intellect is stimulated by the lessons of nature.

Although several ceremonies celebrate American Indian spirituality—the most famous being a feast of Thanksgiving taught to the European settlers hundreds of years ago—one practice, the *vision quest*, exemplifies the strong bond with Mother Earth especially well. The vision quest is recognized as a time of self-reflection. Self-reflection helps one to understand one's purpose in life, to become grounded in the earth and centered with the Great Spirit, and to reach a clearer understanding of one's contribution to the community from which he or she came. During a vision quest, an individual isolates himself in the wilderness, such as on a hilltop, in a large meadow, or any area that provides privacy. The vision quest creates an opportunity for emptying the mind (meditation) and body (fasting). The emptying process allows the human spirit to be filled with an energy from the Great Spirit, leading the individual toward a path of self-enlightenment and self-improvement. Typically performed as a rite of passage from adolescence into adulthood, a vision quest can be taken any time there is a need for spiritual growth or guidance. Although many elements of American Indian spirituality were nearly extinguished by Christian missionaries a century ago, they are now beginning to be recognized and respected, particularly in light of environmental concerns about the poor health of planet Earth. Ironically, it is the white man who is now adopting this value from the American Indian.

Hildegard von Bingen: The Mystical Path

THE WORD *SPIRIT* OFTEN CONJURES up the term *mystic* for many, and in the case of Hildegard von Bingen this adjective is most accurate. However, the word **mystic** (someone who sees beyond the physical world) alone is not enough to describe this unique woman who lived in Germany at the turn of the twelfth century (1098–1179). The words *visionary, poet, composer, healer, artist,* and *saint* are also used to describe her, yet even these seem inadequate to capture the essence of Hildegard von Bingen. Born of a noble family near the town of Mainz, Hildegard was 8 years old when she first experienced a vision of light, which was followed by a period of intense illness. Because she was not at first familiar with the meaning of her experience, she did not realize that this vision was in some way a message from God. Not long after this first vision, she acquired a remarkable psychic ability that left her parents and family rather puzzled. As was the custom of her day, Hildegard, the tenth child in her family, was taken to a monastery to be looked after and raised in the hopes that her work and accomplishments would please the church.

The first vision was actually one of many throughout her life. Hildegard was encouraged by members of her order to write about these moments of divine insight and to tell what she saw in these visions. In her own words, she writes:

> What I write is what I see and hear in the vision. I compose no other words than those I hear, and I set them forth in unpolished Latin just as I hear them in the vision, for I am not taught in this vision to write as philosophers do. And the words of the vision are not like words uttered by the mouth of many but like a shimmering flame, or a cloud floating in a clear sky.

In what is considered to be her most impressive writing, *Scivias,* she describes a series of visions that illustrate the story of Creation, the dynamic tension between light and darkness, the work of the Holy Spirit, and words of encouragement to ponder and savor as we journey on our human path. Her writings did not go unnoticed. Word soon traveled to Pope Eugenius III, who then sent for copies of these writings. He was so impressed that not only did he give his blessings, but he also sent words of support to Hildegard to continue her writings, thus making her a celebrity.

In the time of the Dark Ages, the vision von Bingen saw was not just a ray of light in the shadows; it became a philosophy that breathed life into a people with a spiritual hunger. And in a time when women took a backseat to the dominance of male authority, Hildegard's presence and renown spoke to a higher order of humanity than was common in her day.

Her message was simple: that there is a holistic nature to the universe, just as there is a holistic nature to humanity. And just as man and woman are essential parts of the universe, so, too, is the universe an essential part to be found within each individual. In other words, this message is similar to the axiom, "As above, so below," or "As the microcosm, so the macrocosm." As if extending an invitation into nature, she encouraged the greening of the soul, a process whereby one engages with the natural world as a part of it, not shutting oneself off from the elements of nature. Hildegard also spoke to the principle of each soul. She routinely emphasized that our soul is not to be found in the body; rather it is our body that resides in our soul. The body, she said, is the instrument of the soul, a means by which our divine essence can function in the material world. The soul, a unique aspect of our divine nature, is boundless and contains our dreams, hopes, wishes, and desires. Can all things be spiritual? This, indeed, was the message of Hildegard von Bingen. From her visions she shared the wisdom that all things are sacred, "Every creature is a glittering, glistening mirror of divinity."

In times of spiritual hunger, people often look back to those in earlier times who were able to hold the light of divine essence and to share it. Perhaps this is why today, after nearly 1,000 years, the music composed by Hildegard von Bingen has been recorded and released. In fact, some of her music is on a popular-selling CD called *Vision.*

Joan Borysenko: The Feminine Path

NEW TO THE DISCIPLINE OF psychoneuroimmunology, Joan Borysenko hit the ground running as cofounder, therapist, and director of the Mind/ Body Clinic in Boston, Massachusetts, which is affiliated with the Harvard Medical School. Through the mentoring process provided by stress physiologist Dr. Herbert Benson, work with her patients, and her own personal journey of self-enlightenment, Borysenko began to synthesize an understanding of the connections between the body, mind, and soul. One aspect that inspired this journey was the observation of the personal faith of some of her clients— faith that seemed to be stronger than any clinical medicine; faith that caused cancerous tumors to go into spontaneous remission; faith that healed several illnesses; or faith that simply brought inner peace in the last moments of life.

But just as faith can heal, an absence of faith can quicken the pace of physical illness, even causing death. Borysenko is among a growing number of clinical specialists who believe that the mechanistic approach to medicine (i.e., the body is like a machine and fixing it requires one to repair or to replace parts) is very much outdated. As explained in her book *Guilt Is the Teacher, Love Is the Lesson,* the mind and spirit play a crucial role in the health and healing process of the body.

In her campaign of health promotion, including several books, interviews, and national presentations, Borysenko advocates healing the human spirit as an integral part of physical healing and the importance of the role of spirituality in the self-healing process. *Spirituality*, as defined by Bory-senko, is "a reconnection (remembrance) of our eternal connection with a life-force or power that we are a part of." Strongly influenced by the works of Carl Jung, Larry Dossey, and others, Borysenko advocates the importance of building a relationship with the inner self and of taking the time to get to know the real self. The distance that people keep from this self-center—distance created by shame, guilt, and the expectations of who we should be, rather than who we really are—becomes fertile ground upon which to sow the seeds of stress. She also believes that through the ability to know ourselves we strengthen the bonds with our higher consciousness as well as with the people within our community.

Borysenko left the Mind/Body Clinic in 1993 to devote her work to integrating the spiritual dimension of health back into health care. As a part of this mission, she has placed her primary focus on the issue of woman's spirituality. Raised in the Jewish faith, yet not quite comfortable there, she left to search out a more inclusive nature of God. She found out she was not alone with this quest. In her book *A Woman's Journey to God,* Borysenko notes that women comprise the greatest percentage of Americans she labels as "religious drop-outs"—those women who leave the institution of their religious upbringing to wander, drift, and possibly reconnect to another affiliation they find more accepting. One reason for this apathy can be found in the language of several religions in which male pronouns describing God exclude the female gender, which is a big issue to many women in an age of equal rights. She states that the white-male hierarchy has become a huge roadblock on the spiritual path to women of the baby-boomer generation, as well as to their children.

Borysenko describes each woman's quest for a relationship with the divine as a spiritual pilgrimage. While not outlining a systematic progression of steps on this pilgrimage, Borysenko shares her insights on how a woman might journey through various stages of the feminine quest. She suggests that each woman connect to the creative aspect of the divine and not see God entirely as a male entity. She cites menses and childbirth as examples of this creative process. Next, she conveys the importance of resolving anger issues that develop (some as early as childhood), which she sees as the first step to healing. Borysenko then speaks of rituals as a means to remember the divine connection. Rituals may include baby showers, candle ceremo-nies, retreats—anything to place one in the conscious recognition of God or Goddess. A final aspect of the feminine path that Borysenko talks about is the connection to other women through support groups, prayer circles, or other venues in which women can share their stories. For generations upon generations, stories have been the vehicle by which women have passed on spiritual truths to each other and to their children.

In *A Woman's Journey to God,* Borysenko writes:

> A quieting awakening is under way as women are coming together to worship, to tell stories, and find their place spiritually, if not always religiously, in the household of God. Women's spirituality groups are popping up everywhere. Women often report a deep sense of connection to God as part of friendship, or mothering. We see God in others.

It is this aspect of the feminine path that Borysenko shares in the hopes of inclusiveness and healing of the human spirit.

Ken Carey: Divine Messages

WHEN PEOPLE THINK OF MYSTICS, what usually comes to mind are elderly men with long white beards. Ken Carey is neither old nor gray. Raised in Chicago and educated at UC Berkeley, Ken opted to abandon the bright lights of the big city for a log cabin in the Ozarks. It was soon after graduation that he and his wife headed for Missouri and there carved out a lifestyle of simplicity and solitude.

One might think that those of a spiritual bent might be inclined to read volumes of books to seek a worldview of understanding, but wisdom can come from many sources, both conventional and nonconventional. Not long after Ken and his wife finished their cabin, he was awakened one night by a voice. He was led to a typewriter where he began to type what was to become his first book, *The Starseed Transmissions.* The voice he heard spoke of a spiritual path of loving kindness and a future bright with possibilities, but first the human race needed to wake up to its divine nature. The voice he knew intuitively was angelic in nature and promised to speak again. Twenty years later the voice awoke Ken once again in the night and for the next 11 days he sat in front of his typewriter, banging away at the keys, putting words to the thought forms delivered in his head. This collection was then edited to become the best-seller *Starseed: The Third Millennium.* A sampling of pages from this book includes the following:

> The God that lives within you lives also within all of humankind, though in some I am honored, and in some I am denied. My spirit manifests in all biological life, in all planetary life, in all stellar life, in all things from the greatest spiraling galaxy to the tiniest subatomic particle.

As gravity draws objects to fall, so too does it draw the thoughts of those who define themselves without reference to the Source. When you define yourselves in isolation, your senses deceive and blind. They lock you into a fractional perception of the universe in which you live.

In between Cary's two *Starseed* books, he wrote *Return of the Bird Tribes,* another book with messages from the spirit realm of angels. In the introduction to this book, he writes:

During the past decade, a growing number of people have had encounters with those beings of the spirit world that Western tradition rather simplistically refers to as angels. These creatures are worth getting to know. While these entities—who have been known on rare occasions to take human form—clearly have long-term purposes of a more general nature, their immediate goal is the freeing of our race from what they have termed "the spell of matter."

On first appearance, with a flannel shirt and blue jeans, one might take Ken for a country bumpkin, but this would be a gross error in judgment. Extremely articulate, well educated, and ever so humble, Ken now spends his time traveling to various parts of the world to share the series of divine messages he has received. When not on the road, he finds solitude back in the comfort of his home tucked away in the Ozarks, where he finds spirit in the healing power of nature.

The Dalai Lama: Compassion and Happiness

WHEN TENZIN GYATSO WAS BUT a young child, a knock sounded at the door to his parents' house. There on the doorstep was a group of Tibetan monks from Lhasa, guided through dreams, on a mission to identify their new leader, the Dalai Lama, spiritual leader and ruler of Tibet. When they left the house hours later, there was no doubt that indeed young Tenzin was the reincarnation of their former spiritual leader, soon to take his rightful place at the Potola in Lhasa, the capital of Tibet.

Anyone who has seen the movies *Kundun* or *Seven Years in Tibet* knows the story of how China invaded the secluded country of Tibet in 1959, killing thousands of people and driving hundreds of thousands of others, including the Dalai Lama, into exile in nearby India. Since that time he has served as goodwill ambassador for world peace. In 1989, he was awarded the Nobel Peace Prize for his nonviolent struggle for the liberation of Tibet and today is seen as an icon for world peace.

In his book *The Power of Compassion,* he writes:

Compassion is the most wonderful and precious thing. When we talk about compassion, it is encouraging to note that basic human nature is, I believe, compassionate and gentle. Love and kindness are the very basis of society. If we lose these feelings, society will face tremendous difficulties. The survival of humanity will be endangered. This is not a question of religious practice but a question of the future of humanity. There are various positive side effects of enhancing one's feelings of compassion. One of them is that the greater the force of your compassion, the greater your resilience in confronting hardships and your ability to transform them into more positive conditions.

Recognizing that there are roadblocks to an open heart, the Dalai Lama offered these words: "We cannot overcome anger and hatred simply by suppressing them. We need to actively cultivate the antidotes to hatred: patience and tolerance."

The Dalai Lama has become quite the public figure in the later years of his life, traveling to various countries to spread his message of peace as well as making appearances on selected television shows. You may wonder how someone who was forced to leave his own country could maintain an air of happiness, which he does quite easily with an undeniable giggle, but this, too, is his mission:

I believe that the very purpose of our life is to seek happiness. That is clear. Whether one believes in religion or not, whether one believes in this religion or that religion, we are all seeking something better in life. So, I think the very motion of our life is toward happiness. . . . I believe that happiness can be achieved through training the mind. When I say training the mind in this context, I'm not referring to mind merely as one's cognitive ability or intellect. Rather I'm using the term in the sense of the Tibetan word *Sem,* which has a much broader definition, closer to psyche or spirit.

There are those who call the Dalai Lama a living deity. He merely refers to himself as a kind soul. Never one to make a big deal of his role or legacy, His Holiness the Dalai Lama, thrust into public life, has taken his mission of service quite literally—to help raise the consciousness of the human race. His message is about our inherent ability to share compassion and happiness. He teaches by example.

Joseph Campbell: The Hero's Journey

THE WORD *MYTH* COMES FROM an ancient Sanskrit word meaning "the source" or "truth." Today, the word *myth* has become synonymous with the word *fallacy*, but it is fair to say that every myth is based on a source of truth, exaggerated perhaps to make a point, but truth nonetheless. Joseph Campbell is the most respected scholar in the study of mythology. For over 60 years, he studied myths, legends, and stories from all cultures: from the ancient Hindus to several American Indian tribes. Campbell left no stone unturned when it came to looking behind the message of each story. What he found was not only astonishing parallels (e.g., virgin births, resurrections, healings, etc.), but also remarkable patterns, regardless of the story's origin, that speak to the nature of the human spirit. His own quest brought him to the works of the psychologist Carl Jung, the mystic Jiddu Krishnamurti, the poet Robert Bly, and scores of luminaries around the world, all of whom added to his collective wisdom.

Campbell's work went largely unrecognized outside of academic circles during the twentieth century until PBS television host Bill Moyers aired a six-part special titled *The Power of Myth* with Joseph Campbell in the spring of 1987. Campbell died soon thereafter on October 30. Despite his death, his work continues to increase in popularity as people discover the links between mythology and spirituality, and he has left a legacy for all to share.

In the first episode with Bill Moyers, Campbell explained the connection between mythology and human spirituality like this: "Myths are clues to the spiritual potentialities of the human life. Our problem today is that we are not well acquainted with the literature of the spirit."

Having studied the myths and legends of every culture throughout the ages, from Zeus to *Star Wars* (George Lucas was a student of Campbell), Campbell noticed an interesting trend. In each myth there is a hero, and although the face of the hero may change through the ages, the storyline remains the same over time. In his book *The Hero with a Thousand Faces*, Campbell highlights the progression of the hero's journey, which, as it turns out, mirrors our own life's sojourn. The stages include departure, initiation, and return. Let's take a closer look at each stage.

Departure

The first step in any adventure is to leave your place of origin. Whether it's on a ship like Ulysses or on a spacecraft like Luke Skywalker, every hero must leave home to go find him- or herself. Campbell also referred to the departure stage as a "severance" or "separation," whereby the reluctant hero or heroine is forced into a situation unwillingly. Campbell cites Adam and Eve as examples of reluctant departure. Stepping outside of the classic mythical tale, departure may begin with the first year in college away from home, the death of a parent, or the end of a marriage. Departures can occur in a great many ways. With the first step out the door, across the threshold, the journey has begun.

Initiation

Traveling down the road far away from home, the hero is put to a test. Campbell calls this stage "the road of trials." For some it may be dragons (the symbol of fear), for others it may be a symbolic river to cross (the River Styx). For still others it may be an evil witch, a wicked stepmother, a rescue, or the betrayal of a close friend. In the legend of King Arthur, it was the apprenticeship with Merlin. In the life of a college student, initiation can manifest itself in thousands of ways, such as the roommate from hell or an abusive alcoholic parent. In every mythological story, the hero must demonstrate strength, courage, patience, and willpower. If the hero fails with the first test, another will appear until he or she is strong enough to conquer it and move on.

The initiation stage actually has two parts. Upon completion of passing the test (the first phase), the hero then receives a "boon" (the second part), a blessing of some kind, whereupon he or she ventures back home to share it with friends, family, or members of the community.

Return

At some point in the journey, usually upon success with the initiation process, the heroine must return home. Upon crossing the threshold of return, the heroine shares the wealth of riches acquired on the road. Symbolically, the return home is accompanied with a trophy of sorts: magical runes, the Holy Grail, the Golden Fleece, or Medusa's head. Campbell points out that there may be a reluctance to want to go home, either because of shame or the lust for additional conquests. But return we must to complete the story. The stage of return is also called "incorporation," whereby the returning hero is accepted by his family and peers as an equal, and everyone benefits from his wisdom. He is then a master of two worlds: the one he conquered and the one he has returned home to. The return phase offers a promise that all ends well.

There was a time when the sharing of myths was passed down from parent to child, not merely for entertainment purposes but as wisdom to guide the child on his or her own life journey. Stories from the Bible, the Bhagavad Gita, and other sacred scriptures as well as scores of legends, fairy tales, and folklore all serve the same purpose. However, for the most part, the tradition of finding wisdom from these stories has vanished from American culture. In a discussion about *The Power of Myth,* Campbell drew a connection between the rising state of spiritual hunger and the absence of our connection to mythological stories. As he explained, when a society forgoes the power of myth, instead replacing it with information, technology, or perhaps nothing, the society becomes less civilized, more destructive.

Knowing the power of myth himself, Campbell maintained an optimistic outlook on the journey of humanity itself, for he knew the end of the story. "We are at this moment participating in one of the very greatest leaps of the human spirit—to a knowledge not only outside nature but also our own deep inward mystery—the greatest leap ever!"

Barbara Marx Hubbard: Conscious Evolution

As the daughter of a toymaker tycoon, Barbara grew up in New York City during the Great Depression with a privileged life. Yet despite all the comforts that money can buy, she felt a need as a child to share everything she owned with her friends. Compassion was the foundation of her life as a child, and it has remained so throughout her life. Like most women of her generation, she married and raised several children. As her kids went off to college, she refocused her energies on world affairs and social activism. One of her greatest claims to fame was her nomination for vice president during the 1984 presidential election. Her platform: to create a new cabinet position, Secretary of Peace. Although these dreams never materialized, her efforts in social activism never ceased. As a citizen diplomat, she worked to build bridges between the United States and the Soviet Union in her efforts for world peace. She has been instrumental in the founding of many important organizations and initiatives, including the World Future Society, New Dimensions Radio, Global Family, Women of Vision and Action, the Foundation for the Future, and the Association for Global New Thought. Colleagues with Jonas Salk, Abraham Maslow and Buckminster Fuller, Barbara's vision of a new world was forged with the highest caliber of intellect and spirituality, all of which resides within us, she insists.

For the past 30 years, Barbara has written several books and addressed several hundreds of thousands of people about the evolution of consciousness taking shape over the human landscape. Her message, as wonderfully articulated in her best-selling book, *Conscious Evolution*, is simple: if we are going to make it as a species and avoid a social planetary collapse, we need to evolve our consciousness, and soon! The human spirit, she states, is eclipsed by the shadow of the ego, and this has to change.

Barbara is a firm believer in the concept of human potentials, that which helps us rise to meet our highest potential, through love, compassion, and integrity. As a midwife in the "birthing process" of this new consciousness, Barbara cites the need for all people to "wake up" to the power of the human spirit, rather than falling back asleep. She calls for a collective awakening of the human race as part of this **conscious evolution**. This new evolution is the realization of our divine nature, and the responsibility this holds with each of our thoughts and actions to make the world a better place for everyone. The shift in evolution is one from "me" to "we."

Barbara's platform for spiritual growth begins with a regular practice of meditation, what she calls entering the "inner sanctuary." When one can enter this quiet space and turn down the voice of the ego, then one can begin to hear a greater voice that leads to one's highest potential. In reaching our highest potential, Barbara explains that we become "Agents of Conscious Change."

Spiritual, but not religious, Barbara explains that spirit is at the center of everything we do, a divine invisible force that connects us in the web of life. Using the term *co-creator*, Barbara explains that we have an active role to play in the evolution of humanity; we are not passive victims in a cruel world. We are living in extraordinary times, she insists. Barbara's current work is a social media documentary video program called *Humanity Ascending* (www.humanityascending.com).

Deepak Chopra: Seven Spiritual Steps on the Divine Path

ONE MIGHT THINK THAT SPIRITUALITY and medicine would go hand in hand because both honor the essence of life, but that is not how Deepak Chopra, M.D., was introduced to the science of medicine, nor were any of his physician colleagues and peers. An endocrinologist by training, Chopra came from India to the United States where he landed a job in New Jersey in 1970. With his sights set on a bigger hospital, he soon ended up outside of Boston, working as chief of staff at New England Memorial Hospital. Frustrated at the limitations of Western medicine, Chopra returned to his Indian roots and began to explore Ayurvedic medicine, an ancient form of holistic health care and a word that, when translated, means the "science of life," where mind, body, and spirit connect as one. On a path that led him from allopathic to holistic medicine, Chopra soon discovered that mind–body medicine, or psychoneuroimmunology, as it is referred to clinically, is really mind–body–spirit medicine, in which the human spirit plays an integral role in the healing process. His search into psychoneuroimmunology and the essence of spirituality led him to study with the founder of Transcendental Meditation (TM), Maharishi Mahesh Yogi, with whom he began to understand the concepts of mind and consciousness. It was this exposure to consciousness that began to galvanize his understanding of the intricacies of the human condition in states of disease and health and matters of the soul.

But Chopra didn't rest there. An avid reader, he, like a child with a crayon, began to connect the dots of wisdom from all corners of the earth, including the writings of Einstein, Blake, Rumi, Lao Tzu, Tagore, and others, as well as sacred writings, such as the Bhagavad Gita, the Bible, and the Koran, to synthesize a comprehensive, if not universal, understanding of the nature of God and the laws that govern all creation.

The author of several books, including *Quantum Healing, Perfect Health,* and *Ageless Body, Timeless Mind,* Chopra has now focused his attention toward the matters of the soul. In his book *The Seven Spiritual Laws of Success,* Chopra presents a simple guideline of seven steps for embracing the spirit of life in everyday living.

The Law of Pure Potentiality

Understanding that at the core of our essence is pure consciousness, the law of pure potentiality reminds us to enter in silence the core of our being and to tap the universal wisdom in which to create and reach our potential. In Western culture, it is common to seek validation in external objects. The law of pure potentiality reminds us that we only need look inside to find our divine essence. Once this source is accessed, then we become co-creators and active participants rather than passive victims on the human journey.

The Law of Giving

According to this law, the universe is a dynamic cornucopia. Nothing is static. Energy flows freely. In support of the axiom, "as you give, so shall you receive," the law of giving reminds us to keep open the channels of our heart. For when the heart is closed, then the energy becomes blocked and the stagnation of universal energy leads to an atrophied spirit. Chopra points out that the derivation of the words *affluence* and *currency* do not mean money. Rather, they mean "to flow," a lesson the law of giving teaches. Nature abhors a vacuum; however, she is not fond of gluttony either. The law of giving reminds us to walk in balance.

The Law of Karma (or Cause and Effect)

As if taken from a law of physics in which every action has an equal and opposite reaction, the law of Karma invites us to become more responsible for our thoughts and actions. The law of Karma, similar to the Christian expression, "as you sow, so shall you reap," invites us to shed the habits that inhibit our growth, to break the bonds of conditioned thoughts, and to become responsible (the ability to respond) to our every action.

The Law of Least Effort

Nature teaches us that water finds its own level. The universe unfolds in its own time and place. If we try to rush it, we only tire ourselves. The law of least effort invites us to go with the flow and not resist that which we cannot change or influence. Chopra writes that nature's intelligence functions effortlessly. To be in harmony with nature means to go with the flow. One aspect of least effort requires us to accept those things we cannot change. A second aspect of least effort requires us to initiate self-responsibility rather than to cast blame on others. The law of least effort asks us to travel the human path lightly, discarding those opinions, beliefs, and attitudes that are defensive in nature, because when we carry these the human journey becomes a struggle rather than a delightful sojourn.

The Law of Intention and Desire

We attract that which we submit to the universal consciousness through intention. "Intention," writes Chopra, "grounded in the detached freedom of the present, serves as the catalyst for the right mix of matter, energy, and space–time events to create whatever it is that you desire." The Buddha once said that all suffering comes from desire. What is implied in the teachings of the Buddha is the partner of desire—detachment or letting go. Attachment to our desires will most likely create suffering when our intentions are not fully made realized. As you intend, so must you detach and let the universe take care of the details.

The Law of Detachment

The law of detachment is an invitation to let go of our desires, wishes, and dreams. It is not that we don't want the desired outcome, but detachment allows the desire to stand on its own two feet. This law serves as a reminder that we are co-creators in the universe of our lives, but not codependent on it. Detachment means to let go of the emotions that align with our desires— fear and anger—if our desires go unfulfilled. The law of detachment is one of the hardest laws to honor, because we often place our security in those things we keep near us. Implicit in the law of detachment is the concept of trust. When you let go of thoughts, wishes, and desires, implied is the trust that whatever the outcome, it is in our best interest. So if we apply for a job (intention) and we don't get it, we must realize that at a higher level of consciousness this was in our best interest. Those things in our best interest will come back to us as intended.

The Law of Dharma or Life Purpose

Each of us has a unique gift and talent in which we are here to share in the community of humanity. This law invites us to realize what our life purpose or mission is and to act on it so that we help raise consciousness for one and all. *Dharma* is the ancient Sanskrit word for "purpose" or "mission." The acceptance of life on Earth requires that we not only realize our purpose, but act to fulfill it so that all may benefit from it.

Chopra has become a bridge that unites not only spirituality and medicine but also many facets of humanity that have become divided through ego and fear. If asked, he, and others like him, will tell you that we, the human species, stand on the precipice of great change. For us to weather this change and become self-realized, we must work to evolve our soul, and this can be done by honoring and practicing the seven universal laws of spirituality.

Since the publication of the *Seven Spiritual Laws of Success*, Chopra has published several other books continuing his thesis on the role of the human spirit in health and wellness and the importance of higher consciousness in both one's own life and the world at large.

Larry Dossey: The Nonlocal Mind

As A WESTERN-TRAINED PHYSICIAN, Larry Dossey, M.D., is no stranger to the aspects of the divine. With a host of synchronistic events and mystical dreams too numerous to mention, Dossey has been gently guided to expand the perspective of the human condition to include and embrace the spiritual dimension in the healing arts. Although he is certainly not alone in this venture, nor the first, his collection of work in this area has sounded a clarion call throughout the healthcare industry, from medical education to the hospital setting, to abandon the reductionist method for a more holistic approach to life. To his credit, the concept of prayer as a healing agent is now taught in several medical schools around the country.

In the first few pages of his book *Recovering the Soul*, Dossey tells the story of a woman who is undergoing surgery. During the operation her vital signs dipped way below normal, but she was brought back to life quickly. In the time it took to revive her, the woman had what is commonly known as a near-death experience (NDE). In post-op, she explained her experience to the nurses. She described leaving her body and hovering over the operating room. She described it in exact detail, clear down to the color of the socks the surgeon was wearing. She also told the nurses that she found herself above the hospital, ascending. Before she was called back to her body, she noticed a green sneaker on a window ledge on the eighth floor.

What makes the story remarkable is that the patient was blind, yet the accuracy of her experience, rich in detail, was entirely correct. And indeed there was a green sneaker on a window's ledge, eight floors up. These and other experiences that Dossey has either experienced firsthand or has heard from others have led him to create a model of consciousness that he describes as "nonlocal."

Dossey borrowed the word *nonlocal* from the field of physics to describe the inability to confine consciousness entirely to the brain. One study about the healing power of prayer conducted by Randolph Byrd, M.D., in 1990 so intrigued him that he spent the next several years studying prayer as a function of the **nonlocal mind.** His findings can be read in his best-selling book *Healing Words: The Power of Prayer and the Practice of Medicine.* This collection of studies, perhaps more than anything else, has helped change the paradigm of Western medicine to recognize the role of spirituality as a function of conscious intent in healing.

In *Recovering the Soul,* he writes:

> The nonlocal view of man places mind and consciousness outside the person, the brain, and the body, and it leads to a theory of one mind, which is boundless in space and time . . . the next step in nonlocal thinking not only gets us outside the brain and body, and the individual person, it takes us beyond mankind altogether. It lands us squarely in the lap of God—or the One, Logos, Tao, Brahman, Buddha, Krishna, Allah, Mana, the Universal Spirit or Principle. To some degree, the borders of man and God overlap. This is a way of saying that there is an element of the divine within man which shows itself through man's nonlocal qualities.

Dossey contends that Western science is on the verge of a new era, what he calls Era-III medicine. Era I he describes as the mechanistic approach to health, where the body is viewed as a machine with fixable or replaceable pieces. The newly recognized Era II he defines as mind–body medicine. The next step in the evolution of Western consciousness is Era-III medicine (or nonlocal medicine) in which the role of the human spirit is not only acknowledged, but fully integrated into the healing paradigm. According to Dossey, Western medicine is on the vanguard of this new era, but the process of change is not a quick one.

To know Larry Dossey is to know a master of quotations (and a great appreciator for cartoons), for he is extremely well read in several disciplines. One of his favorite quotes, which speaks to the nature of the nonlocal mind and the acknowledgment of the divine force of the universe, is attributed to Hermes Trismegistus: "God is a sphere, whose center is everywhere and whose circumference is nowhere."

Albert Einstein: Light and Energy

IT MAY SEEM RATHER STRANGE to include a physicist among the people noted here who have speculated on the nature of human spirituality, yet at the same time it would be a gross oversight to omit this perspective. The fields of physics and theology, which were so bitterly divided over 300 years ago, are finding they have more commonalties than differences today. These commonalties were first brought to scientific light about a hundred years ago by a physicist named Albert Einstein, who took it upon himself to challenge the accepted principles of natural physics developed by Isaac Newton. Like an earthquake, his concepts of the physical laws of nature rocked the foundations of the scientific community. But as can be seen today, the ramifications of this challenge actually parallel, and may eventually validate, the concept of a higher power, albeit somewhat differently from the way that many people currently perceive it. In 1999, *Time* named Einstein "Man of the Century," not solely for his scientific theories or Nobel Prize, but rather for changing humanity's paradigm of thought in a nonthreatening way.

Curious about the nature of the universe and the laws that governed it, Einstein was convinced that all matter is energy and that time and space are not locked into a continuum, as previously thought. This thinking gave way to his famous theory of relativity ($e = mc^2$). Very simply put, this theory suggests that all matter that is not confined to the "local" concept involving space and time is energy. Although the complexities of this theory are beyond the scope of this book, the premise of Einstein's theory, once rejected by his peers, is now completely accepted by the scientific community. Moreover, the impact of Einstein's work has reached far beyond science to the fields of poetry, art, and even psychology (it was Einstein's theory of relativity that gave Jung the idea for the collective unconscious). With *energy* being the word that opened the door to understanding, theologians also gravitated toward Einstein's theories, giving the concept of light a solid foundation from which to explore the divine nature of the universe hand in hand with science.

Stepping out of the scientific box that Newton had created centuries earlier, Einstein paved the way for others to follow. Pioneers in the field of energy medicine credit Einstein with building a conceptual model from which to understand the human energy field and even human consciousness. Biophysicist Itzhak Bentov expounded on Einstein's concept that "energy equals matter" in his widely acclaimed book *Stalking the Wild Pendulum*. From his added insight we begin to see that consciousness is actually a form of energy that surrounds, permeates, and connects all living objects. Like the atom's electrons that vibrate to give off an energy field, so, too, does the human body produce an oscillation and energy field, which he refers to as "subtle energy." Bentov hypothesized that this subtle energy is composed of many layers, or "frequencies," which he suggests constitute various layers of human consciousness (and the soul itself).

With a greater understanding of the theory of relativity, several physicists have noted connections between the world of physics and the spiritual nature of the universe. In his book *The Tao of Physics*, Fritjof Capra outlined many similarities and parallels between the disciplines of physics and the Eastern mystical philosophies of Buddhism, Hinduism, and Taoism, suggesting that there is an incredible linkage between them. Whether it is called *energy*, the *Tao*, or the *Holy Spirit*, it all appears to be very much related. Capra writes, "Physicists and mystics deal with different aspects of reality. Physicists explore levels of matter, mystics levels of mind. What their explorations have in common is that these levels, in both cases, lie beyond ordinary sensory perception." Capra suggests that these two disciplines, in effect, are looking at the same mountain but from different vantage points and through different binoculars. To Capra, the paradigm shift that occurred in physics with Einstein's theory of relativity is currently rippling through other Western disciplines, including clinical medicine and psychology. In his autobiography *Memories, Dreams, Reflections*, Jung wrote, "There are indications that at least part of the psyche is not subject to the laws of space and time." The collective unconscious and subtle energy in which all things connect may, in fact, be the same component of human spirituality. As science continues to explore the realm of human energy and consciousness, the fields of physics and theology may not only connect, but someday become one and the same.

Those who knew him and studied his works say that Einstein was a spiritual but not a religious man. Yet these same people note that he appeared to be driven by a spiritual quest to understand the nature of the universe. One of Einstein's most famous quotes that speaks to this fact is: "I want to know the thoughts of God, the rest are just details." And although some people infer from his theory of relativity that his view of the cosmos is impersonal, at best (with the order of the universe simply calculated by mathematical equations), Einstein was noted to have said, "God does not play dice with the universe." From Einstein's writings, it is obvious that he was not only a scientific genius, but a world-class philosopher as well. A person who spent much time in deep personal reflection, he once wrote:

> A human being is part of the whole, called by us "universe," a part limited in time and space. He experiences his thoughts and feelings as something separate from the rest, a kind of optical delusion of his consciousness. This delusion is a kind of prison for us, restricting us to our personal decisions and to affection for a few persons nearest us. Our task must be to free our- selves from this prison by widening our circle of compassion to embrace all living creatures and the whole of nature in its beauty.

Einstein spent the better part of his later years conceiving his Unified Field theory (a thesis to explain the relationship between gravity and elec- tromagnetic energy) as well as in a more subtle role as pacifist for world peace—a moral position he took great pride in. Yet through it all, it was light, symbolically and literally, that fascinated Einstein. "For the rest of my life, I want to reflect on what light is," he said.

Matthew Fox: Creation Spirituality

MATTHEW FOX IS A FORMER Dominican priest and Catholic theolo- gian who was silenced by the Vatican for a year in 1988 for his "pro- gressive" views of human spirituality. He was excommunicated from the Catholic Church in 1995. The premise of Fox's theory, **creation spirituality**, states that the Judeo-Christian concept of spirituality, formulated when it was believed that the Earth was the center of the universe, has not kept pace with scientific discoveries substantiating that the Earth is but a piece of the whole universe and by no means its center. Fox has attempted to unite many concepts of theology with the laws and theories of physics in what he terms creation spirituality. His theory of creation spirituality (**Figure 3.4**) suggests that divinity can be found in any act of creation, from the atom to the far reaches of the cosmos and in every particle in between. The seed of creativity is energy, a binding element that unites all things together. And as stated in the First Law of Thermodynamics, energy is neither created nor destroyed.

Fox was inspired by the work of thirteenth-century German theologian Meister Eckhart, many American Indians, Einstein, and a divine presence he terms the "Cosmic Christ." Through these influences he has developed four

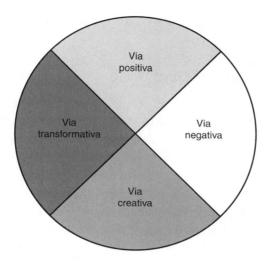

FIGURE 3.4 A symbolic representation of Fox's creation spirituality.

paths, or attitudes, of creation spirituality, which, in his opinion, raise individual consciousness and thus the spiritual level of humankind as a whole.

Path One: Via Positiva

Via positiva is a sense of awe and wonder at the design and creation of all aspects that surround us. Like the wonder of a young child, via positiva is a continual awareness and appreciation of all things, from the simplicity of a blade of grass to the mechanical complexity of the space shuttle. The creation of life should be celebrated, not feared or shamed.

Path Two: Via Negativa

Via negativa is a process of emptying or letting go of thoughts, feelings, values, and even possessions that weigh down, enclose, and even smother the soul, depriving it of nutrients for growth. Via negativa is a period of darkness, silence, even fasting of the soul, for only when emptiness occurs is there room for new growth. This process may be emotionally painful at times (also called the "dark night of the soul"), yet it is a necessary maturation process of the human spirit.

Path Three: Via Creativa

Via creativa is a breakthrough or explosion of enlightenment that fills the space vacated by the cleansing process of via negativa. This enlightenment may come in the form of divine inspiration, intuitive thoughts, or imagination. Via creativa is human creativity that increases the quantity and quality of awe in the universe.

Path Four: Via Transformativa

Via transformativa is the path of struggle, compassion, and celebration. With this path comes the responsibility to act on the enlightenment and inspiration from via creativa by channeling divine energy into personal acts of creation and using this positive creative energy for the betterment of humankind.

Fox suggests that all people see themselves as acts of creation, deserving of awe and wonder. In turn, the ability to use one's imagination and creativity will add to the awe of the universe. These four paths align themselves in what Fox calls a "sacred loop" or "circle" symbolizing wholeness, with each path nourishing the others to their full potential (see **Figure 3.4**). The connection between each element of this hoop is compassion. Compassion, as defined by Fox, is a continual celebration of life. This celebration includes the fulfillment of love, forgiveness, and a personal as well as public display of one's own spirituality.

Human spirituality involves the integration of all four paths, which unite to become one road, or what Fox refers to as a "personal cosmology," a relationship to the Divine Presence that dwells in us. When asked how to cultivate this divine relationship, Fox, in turn, asks these questions: what poets do you read? What music moves you? What acts of creation are you involved with? What social issues are your passion? What work do you most love doing? What pain is in your emptiness? And when do you feel a connection to the universe? From Fox's perspective, the fulfillment of these answers nurtures the growth of the human spirit.

Since the advent of his concept of creation spirituality, Fox has served tirelessly in the role as educator, motivational speaker, author of several books, and humanitarian in his efforts to promote world peace from the standpoint of inner peace.

Lao Tzu: Tao—The Balance of Life

AROUND 500 B.C. THE WRITINGS of China's most famous philosopher, Lao Tzu, entitled *Tao Te Ching*, were first published. Originally written primarily for the leaders of his country, this collection of 5,000 words soon became the doctrine of Chinese living, outlining the path to spiritual enlightenment through inner peace. Lao Tzu used the word *Tao* to describe the movement, path, or way of universal energy. The literal translation of Tzu's title means "the path that leads straight from the heart," and the Chinese character representing this title symbolizes "walking wisdom." Tzu's writings speak of building a peaceful world through inner peace. Only when peace is created within yourself can you move in tandem with the energies that circulate within and around you to establish world peace.

The Chinese concept of **Taoism** suggests that all things connect with a flow of energy called *chi*. Movement with the patterns of flow enables a peaceful coexistence with oneself and the environment. Movement against the flow causes internal as well as external disturbances, often with far-reaching consequences. This movement of life energy goes in cycles like the ebb and flow of the ocean tide. Among the many concepts the *Tao Te Ching* teaches is balance: the opposing forces of the *yin* and the *yang*, which, through equality, provide harmony, patience, and timing, to move with rather than against the flow, thus securing and maintaining inner peace. Tzu's Tao invites each individual to look inward, beyond the superficial facade of humanness, and to sense the inner rhythms that move in harmony with the universal rhythms. By doing this, not only is inner peace achieved, but harmony with nature and all relationships is also created and maintained. Tzu also spoke of the importance of self-reliance: "Wise people seek solutions, the ignorant only cast blame." Although initially Taoism may seem like a foreign concept, its core teachings can be found in many Western writings as well. Perhaps the best example of this is the Taoist mannerisms and character of Winnie the Pooh, as described by Benjamin Hoff in the renowned best-seller *The Tao of Pooh*. With a closer look, these same principles can be found virtually everywhere.

In her book, *The Tao of Inner Peace*, Diane Dreher explains that Tzu outlined four "great disciplines" to help achieve inner peace through the way of the Tao: the principles of oneness, dynamic balance, cyclical growth, and harmonious action (**Figure 3.5**).

The Principle of Oneness

The principle of oneness suggests that we are part of the whole, connected to a dynamic network of universal energy. Oneness means to be one with or a part of nature, not above or apart from it. When we see ourselves separate from the whole, we distance ourselves from other people and from the natural elements. This distance weakens our spiritual strength. Just as there is strength in numbers, there is also strength in oneness.

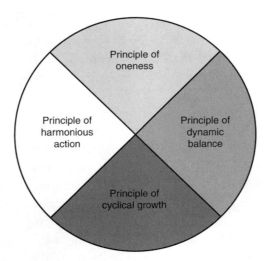

FIGURE 3.5 A symbolic representation of the four principles of Taoism created by Lao Tzu.

The Principle of Dynamic Balance

Tao philosophy speaks of the composition of life as two complementary opposites: the yin and the yang. In simple terms, yin is thought to be composed of the quiet, feminine, receptive elements of nature, whereas yang is seen as active, dynamic, and masculine. Alone, each side is overbearing. The union of yin and yang within the individual provides a perpetual movement striving for balance and harmony. For example, after rain comes sunshine, after disaster comes calm. To live in this dynamic balance, one must move with the flow, through the mountains and valleys of life. To stay static or dynamic goes against the laws of nature, of which both men and women are very much a part.

The Principle of Cyclical Growth

The natural world has many cycles: day and night, birth and death, winter and summer. Each human life is also filled with cycles, from the life cycle of a red blood cell to the highs and lows of our emotions. The wisdom of the Tao asks that these cycles be recognized and appreciated. Too often, impatience blinds human vision to the natural cycles of which we are a part. The universe is not still. The Tao encourages patience.

The Principle of Harmonious Action

As a part of nature, we must work in cooperation with it, not try to dominate, monopolize, or destroy it. The wisdom of the Tao invites each person to live in harmony with nature, respecting her many components, including the lives of others. To live in harmony means to live in moderation, not in excess; to live with simplicity, not in complexity; and to learn to slow down, to know oneself, and to make wiser choices in our lives. One concept of harmonious action is called the *wu wei*, which is knowing when to wait for the right moment and knowing when to be spontaneous—moving with the rhythms of life.

The attitude of the Tao philosophy can be reinforced in many ways. The most commonly known techniques include yoga, meditation, and t'ai chi. Tzu invited all individuals to be people of the Tao. The characteristics of a Tao person sound very similar to those characteristics of self-actualized individuals described by Abraham Maslow. These features include self-acceptance, humor, creativity, commitment, challenge, and self-control. In short, these traits serve as buffers to the possible perceptions of stress. Tao individuals have faith in themselves and in what they do. They carry no false pretenses of who they are. They embrace life joyously. This is what it means to be "One with the Tao."

> We look at it and we do not see it; Its name is The Invisible. We listen to it and we do not hear it; Its name is The Inaudible. We touch it and don't find it. Its name is The Subtle.
>
> —Lao-Tzu, *Tao Te Ching*, 14

Viktor Frankl: The Search for Life's Meaning

ON THE DAY THAT Viktor Frankl was walking to deliver a manuscript to his publisher (a book called *The Doctor and the Soul*), he was picked up by two Nazi SS officers and hauled off to the most notorious of all concentration camps: Auschwitz. It was there that he saw his theory of logotherapy—the search of life's meaning—no longer a theory but a fact. Ironically, this was the message he wrote about in his manuscript, yet with all his possessions stolen, including the manuscript, the book was never published. Instead, his experiences in Auschwitz and survival of the Holocaust led to a new book, now a classic, called *Man's Search for Meaning*.

From both his personal experience and his observations in the notorious death camp, Frankl augmented his understanding of the quest for the real meaning of human existence. Regarding the many prisoners who were fortunate enough to avoid the gas chambers and crematoriums, Dr. Frankl noted that it was largely the ability to choose one's attitude that ultimately decided the fate of those who lived and those who eventually perished from disease and illness in the concentration camps. Those who found and kept a reason to live were able to survive the hellacious conditions, whereas those who had no substantial meaning for living became physically and spiritually weak and succumbed to the shadows of death.

Many of Dr. Frankl's psychological theories center around the concept of human pain and the meaning of suffering. One does not have to experience firsthand the horrors of Auschwitz to feel the pain of suffering. Any experience that promotes feelings of emotional trauma, according to Frankl, contains the essence of a purposeful meaning. The death of a child, a terminal illness, retirement, the loss of a job—these are all candidates for personal suffering. Frankl was convinced that suffering is as much a part of life as happiness and love and, like love, suffering has a purpose in the large perspective of human nature. From his experiences, Frankl realized that suffering is indeed a universal experience. Therefore, he reasoned, it must have some significant value in the advancement of one's human potential or spiritual evolution.

Frankl writes in *Man's Search for Meaning* that "If there's meaning in life then there must be meaning in suffering. Suffering is an ineradicable part of life, and death. Without suffering and death, human life would not be complete." Frankl did not advocate avoiding suffering, but rather suggested that the cause of emotional pain be examined to try to make some rational sense out of it: to find a meaningful purpose in the suffering. This search for meaning is not a defense mechanism, a rationalization of pain, but the search for a truthful understanding. In fact, writes Frankl, meaning is not a fabrication of the mind but a truth uncovered by the soul.

A tool to augment the search for meaning, as defined by Dr. Frankl, is "tragic optimism." He defined it as the ability to turn suffering into a meaningful experience and to learn from this experience with a positive perspective on life's events. The history of humanity is filled with many inspiring examples of people who completed their grieving period by finding meaning in their stressful suffering. One such person was Candy Lightner who, after losing her young daughter to the recklessness of a drunk driver, assembled her creative energies and formed the national organization Mothers Against Drunk Driving (MADD). Another example is Jim Abbott, who overcame the mental anguish of a birth defect (no right forearm and hand) to earn a position as pitcher on the 1984 Olympic baseball team. In fact, many contemporary heroes and role models are individuals who overcame obstacles of biblical proportions and soon thereafter became examples of the epitome of human potential for others to emulate.

Moving from the state of suffering to finding meaning in a painful experience is not easy. Quite often, people tend to wallow in self-pity well beyond the time that it serves a beneficial purpose. How does one begin a quest for the meaning of one's own life? Dr. Frankl suggests that the best time for this to occur is when you feel mental anguish or emotional suffering of any kind. At the time that these conditions surface in your environment, you must journey into the garden of your soul and examine your conscious mind. A mental examination quite often leads to a questioning of your ideals, values, and a test of your will to fulfill or abandon these values.

Dr. Frankl notes that the purpose of meaning in most people is supported by something or someone, not merely by faith alone. Additionally, it is important to note that each person will find his or her own unique meaning, not a universal purpose, or a purpose that can be borrowed or adopted from others. In fact, there will be many different meanings to be searched for and recognized in one lifetime. Suffering awaits in between the periods of life's meanings.

Whereas Freud placed an emphasis on a person's childhood experiences as the root of personal problems, Frankl shifted the attention from the past to the present and future as if to say: "So, what happened, happened. What are you going to do with your life now? Where are you headed from here? What new contribution can you make to mankind?"

Frankl's theory of logotherapy advocates goal setting to help search for personal meaning in one's life. Goals and the accomplishment of them involve creativity—to visualize where you are going—and stamina—the energy to get you there. The fundamental purpose of personal goals, Frankl states, is to enhance one's human potential. Furthermore, pleasure should be a consequence of meaning, not a purpose in and of itself. Dr. Frankl also suggests that a true quest for meaning has a spiritual nature or quality to it (*logos* in Greek is defined not only as "meaning" but also as "spirit"). In this case, however, the term *spirituality* is not associated with a religious connotation, but rather refers to the human dimension of the inner balance between the faith of self-reliance and the individual's will.

Spiritual health is imperative to the search for one's own meaning in life and ultimately to dealing with the suffering of various life experiences, regardless of their cause. In his autobiographical story, Dr. Frankl spoke of those who, in the midst of a crisis, lost their belief in the future, themselves, and their spiritual hold. Consequently, they became subject to mental and physical decay and eventually premature death.

Although Dr. Frankl's existential theories may seem rather abstract, the fundamental messages are quite clear: (1) One must continually search from within for life's meaning to achieve inner peace. (2) In the absence of everything but one's body, mind, and soul, one has the ability to choose one's attitudes and in choosing we either perpetuate or resolve each circumstance. He writes, "We had to learn from ourselves and we had to teach despairing men that it did not matter what we expected from life, but rather what life expected from us."

Jean Houston: Our Human Potential

To those who know her or who have heard her speak, Jean Houston is a character—lively, animated, and enthralling. Those who know her also have no doubt that she is a genius. Her admirers call her a national treasure. All these things are true. Houston was born into a show business family (her father is credited with helping to draft the famous Abbott and Costello piece "Who's on first") who served as a catalyst for what was to become, in her words, "a mythic life." In her autobiography, *A Mythic Life,* Houston writes, "I grew up the daughter of a professional comedy writer who was, at the same time, a great innocent. I am afraid that I am also. I see comedy where others see neurosis. I am fascinated by the depths of the psyche, but I find story and allegory where others find madness and mayhem. I mythologize where others pathologize."

Jean's list of mentors ranges from Joseph Campbell and Margaret Mead to the famed theologian Teilhard de Chardin. The wisdom of Helen Keller, Albert Einstein, and Edgar Bergen have also left their trace on her soul. Perhaps Houston is best known for her work in the Human Potential Movement. She has taken her worldly experiences from her days of walking around the sound stages of Hollywood and the wisdom of Ancient Greece to formulate what she calls a sacred psychology: a passion for the possible.

In *A Mythic Life,* Houston writes: "The joining of local life to a great life is a central experience of what I call sacred psychology. It requires that we undertake the extraordinary task of dying to our current, local selves and of being reborn to our eternal selves. When we descend in the forgotten knowings of earlier or deeper phases of our existence, we often find hidden potentials, the unfilled and unfinished seedings of what we still contain, which myth often disguises as secret helpers or mighty talismans." From her explorations in the Human Potential Movement, Houston has observed that many people are not even close to meeting their inherent potential for creativity, passion, and love. She is convinced that we don't need to go far to uncover this potential. It's inside us. According to Houston:

> We humans endure that loss of many exquisite abilities, and many balanced
> and beautiful ways of functioning have become distorted, inhibited, or

blocked. . . . Almost everybody is much less than he or she has the capacity to be. I have come to the belief that life is allied with myth in order that we may advance along an evolutionary path carrying us nearer to the spiritual source that lures us into greater being.

Houston states that a psychology based on the premise of myth and sacredness demands that each person have the courage both to detach from the personal baggage accrued from woundful experiences and to begin to access the wealth of energy stored as inner resources or muscles of the soul:

> A psychology with a mythic or sacred base demands that we have the courage both to release the limitations brought about by old wounds and toxic bitterness and to gain access to the undiminished self, with its vast storehouse of capacities . . . then like the hero or heroine of myth, we may, regardless of our circumstance, become an inspiration for helping culture and consciousness move toward its next level of possibility.

Ever the eternal optimist, Houston states a simple truth that she knows from personal experience: "So many of the problems that we see outside ourselves can be solved only by answers we find within."

As part of her extensive research into human potential, Houston studied 55 of the most creative thinkers, scientists, and artists alive in the United States. What she found was that each person had the ability to delve below the waters of the conscious mind and to tap into a reservoir of archetypal energy—what Houston refers to as a cast of characters lending their experience for the asking. Houston also borrows upon the wisdom of the ages to invoke what she calls the spirit of I AM: "The I AM is the supreme fractal wave from which everything branches, out of which everything comes forth. This is the realm many know as God . . . a realm of which nothing and everything can be said."

Houston states that the role of the human journey involves the recognition of mystical events and divine experiences, yet the human mind is quick to deny that these ever happened. Jokingly she says that "It has been said unkindly that mysticism begins in a mist and ends in a schism. This is both unfair and untrue." Echoing the words of her mentor, Joseph Campbell, "The hero's journey is an allegory of the soul's journey toward enlightenment."

Jesus of Nazareth: Unconditional Love

OVER 2,000 YEARS AGO, a unique man appeared in the Middle East, and his presence has since left a profound and indelible mark on humankind. His teachings were profound, his healings miraculous, and his death a mystery. Some people called him a prophet, others called him the Messiah. Still others called him a heretic. These same names can be heard today. Little background is known about Jesus of Nazareth, other than he was born in a barn, raised as the son of a carpenter, shared many profound philosophies of a divine nature, and died a cruel death. As a teacher, he never wrote down on paper any of his philosophies. Rather, he passed his simple, yet profound wisdom on to those who yearned to understand his enlightenment and, in turn, they created a community from which Christianity was established. Years after his death, in an effort to remember those teachings, his followers recorded his wisdom, stories, and healing practices in a series of documents that have now come to be known as the New Testament of the Bible. Today scholars and theologians continue to study and interpret his words of wisdom as a harbinger in troubled times. It may be difficult, if not impossible, to separate the messenger from the message, but if for a moment we were to focus on the most fundamental principle taught by this unique individual, we would find that the basic premise of his teachings was the power of love. What follows is a small sampling of insights and reflections of this theme.

At the time that Jesus began his teaching in the Middle East, there was much civil conflict and strife. People in Jerusalem were oppressed by the Romans and, in essence, were second-class citizens in their own country. Many were searching for a political leader to save them and to return them to a life of undisturbed peace. In this time of ambivalence and hatred, Jesus preached and practiced the power of love. His words were charismatic, his style was uniquely humble, and he attracted many followers who in their own hearts believed he possessed the qualities of great political leadership. But Jesus of Nazareth regarded himself as a spiritual leader. By his examples and teaching, he showed men and women how to restore and maintain inner peace through a loving relationship with God. Beyond all else, it was his belief that love was the greatest of all emotions, for through love all things were possible.

From the inspirational words of Jesus and his followers, many people have attempted to illustrate the concept of love from the canvas of their own hearts. Scottish theologian Henry Drummond described love as a spectrum of several attributes, including patience, kindness, generosity, humility, unselfishness, and sincerity. Theologian Thomas Merton wrote in his book *The Ascent to Truth* that love is the source of one's merit and, as such, it is love where God resides. Psychiatrist Gerold Jampolsky defines love as an experience absent of fear with the recognition of complete union with all life. To Jesus, the expression of love is like a passageway. For love to be effective as a channel of communication or healing energy, there must be no obstructions and no conflicting thoughts that pollute the feeling of love. In other words, there must be no conditions or expectations placed on the expression of love. Like a child who acts spontaneously, the expression of love must be uninhibited, not filtered by conscious thought. As Jesus elaborated, people under oppression, whether it be by foreign rulers or the perceptions of their own minds, begin to close and harden their hearts. Their ability to feel and express love is overridden by critical, judgmental, and conditional thinking, thought processes often rooted in fear. As described by Ken Carey in the book *Starseed,* these two concepts are mutually exclusive, because one cannot experience love and fear at the same time. From the writings of Jesus' followers we see that it is fear, expressed in terms of hatred, greed, and guilt, that is the greatest obstacle to love.

Love has an inherent healing power all its own, and it was this power that Jesus demonstrated to perform his miracles, giving sight to the blind and health to the infirm. Inspired by the book, *A Course on Miracles,* Dr. Gerald Jampolsky cites love as a divine energy that knows no bounds. In his own book, *Teach Only Love,* Jampolsky explains that when love is undiluted it becomes the most powerful source of healing energy. When there is a conscious shift from the motivation of fear to the motivation of love, then nothing real is impossible.

Once, during his teachings, Jesus was asked what the greatest rule to live by was. His reply was to love unconditionally, specifically to love God and to extend love to each human being as you would to yourself. For as Jesus explained, God resides in each and every one of us, "the Kingdom of God is within you." These words, while not new, were novel in their meaning. Much hatred and fear existed in the hearts of people at this time, and it seemed quite incongruous to love your enemy as Jesus suggested. The implied message of the Golden Rule is that forgiveness is a crucial element of unconditional love (**Box 3.2**). To elaborate on this theme, Jesus shared the story of the Prodigal Son, a young man who wasted his inheritance on foolish pleasures and came crawling back home destitute. Yet his father welcomed him back with complete forgiveness. This is an example that expresses the depth of God's unconditional love for all people.

Just as Jesus spoke of love, he spoke equally about faith and its relationship to love. Faith, a confident belief and conviction in the power of God's love, is the intent or desire to express love. As Jesus explained, it does not take much. In his usual way, Jesus explained the concept of faith through metaphors and parables. In one such case he compared faith to a tiny mustard seed. In noting the size of this type of seed, it was implied that a small seed

Box 3.2   The Golden Rule

For millennia, spiritual luminaries the world over have cited the Golden Rule as the most important criterion to live one's life by: do unto others as you would have them do unto you. So important is the Golden Rule as a hallmark of the human condition that its message can be found as the cornerstone to nearly all the world's religions. Simply stated, the Golden Rule, as a measure of common respect, is the perennial philosophy.

Christianity: Treat others as you wish to be treated in all things. Don't criticize others, nor should they criticize you.

Buddhism: Do no harm to others. Treat all with respect as you wish to be treated.

Confucianism: What you do not wish to have done to you, refrain from doing to others. This action will allow no resentment against you or your family.

Hinduism: Your responsibility in life is to treat all others with the respect that you wish upon yourself: this is the sum of the duty.

Islam: You should only desire for yourself that which you desire for your brother.

Judaism: What is hateful to you, do not do to your fellow man. This is the entire law: all the rest is commentary.

Taoism: Delight in your neighbor's gain, and grieve in his loss, for his gain and loss are yours. To those who are good to you, return kindness; to those who are not good, return kindness. Be sincere in all kindness.

of faith could expand to phenomenal proportions to overcome the trials of human experience. To paraphrase the words of theologian C. S. Lewis, faith is a necessary virtue to complete the will of God. And in the words of President John F. Kennedy, "God's work must truly be our own."

As the strongest of all emotions, love was described this way by one of Jesus' earliest followers, Paul, in a letter to his friends in the city of Corinth. It has since been recited at many weddings:

Love is patient and kind, never jealous or envious, never boastful or proud, never haughty or selfish or rude. Love does not demand its own way. It is not irritable or touchy. It does not hold grudges and will hardly ever notice when others do it wrong. It is never glad about injustice, but rejoices whenever truth wins out. Above all there are three things that remain, faith, hope, and love. The greatest of these is love. Let love be your greatest aim.

Paramahansa Yogananda: To Be Self-Realized

YOGANANDA IS CONSIDERED TO BE one of the greatest spiritual teachers of all time. The story of his life, as recounted in his classic book, *Autobiography of a Yogi*, introduced him to the world as an authentic and gifted master of divine thought. Raised and educated in India and tutored by the saintly Sri Yukteswar, Yogananda first came to the United States in 1920 for a world conference of religions, only to make this country his permanent residence.

Though Hindu by birth, Yogananda taught of the universal truths that form the foundations of all world religions: love, forgiveness, patience, and humbleness. "Truth is timeless and impossible to trademark," he often said. His mission was to teach a process of heart-centered awareness that he called "**self-realization**," a name that describes the conscious realization of our divine nature. Yogananda spoke of "being fully conscious," rather than falling asleep to the hypnotic suggestion of materialistic pleasures. He often spoke of consciousness as energy and would on many occasions speak to the nature of human form as energy, chakra, and the kundalini energy, each holding a level of consciousness to be explored and cultivated.

Throughout his adventurous life, he not only described his meetings with remarkable luminaries such as Mahatma Gandhi, St. Theresa Neuman, and Rabindranath Tagore, but he was also able to bring the mystical side of his teachings and miracles into a scientific language that is only now, more than 50 years later, fully being understood.

Yogananda taught lessons in Kriya Yoga, a meditation practice that seeks to consciously unite the soul of the person with the soul of God. Yogananda writes:

> Introspection or sitting in the silence is an unscientific way of trying to force apart the mind and senses tied together by the life force. The contemplative mind, attempting its return to divinity, is constantly dragged back toward the senses by the life currents. Kryra, controlling the mind directly through life force, is the easiest, most effective, and most scientific avenue of approach to the infinite.

Throughout his writings and speeches, Yogananda always came back to the topic of love. When he spoke of love, he joined the terms *joy* and *bliss* with it to signify that the actual experience of love always accompanies joy: "Just as oil is present in every part of the olive, so love permeates every part of creation. But to define love is very difficult, for the same reason that words cannot fully describe the flavor of an orange. You have to taste the fruit to know its flavor. So it is with love. A spark of this divine love exists in most hearts in the beginning of life, but is usually lost, because man does not know how to cultivate it. " It was Yogananda's mission to teach people how to recapture that spark and to cultivate it at the start of each waking day.

Yogananda wrote several books, and several more were published as a collection of his speeches and seminars over his 20 years spent in the United States. The following are a handful of some of his quotes:

- "Reality is light. Change your consciousness: Open your eyes. In every atom of space you will see the twinkle of God's light and laughter."
- "Whenever you want to produce something, do not depend on the outside source. Go deep and seek the Infinite Source."
- "Unite the heart's feeling and the mind's reason in a perfect balance."
- "If you open the door to the magnetic power of friendship, souls of like vibrations will be attracted to you."
- "When one has realized God, he no longer feels that others are different from himself."
- "To develop pure and unconditional love between husband and wife, parent and child, friend and friend, self and all is the lesson we have come on earth to learn."

His remarkable life was no less remarkable than his death. On March 7, 1952, he finished a speech in honor of the ambassador of India at a gathering in Encinitas, California. He then retired to a supine pose and took his last breath. In a letter written by the funeral director, it was stated that the body showed no signs of decay for 20 days, at which time his body was buried.

Ken Wilber: The Spectrum of Consciousness

IN 1977, KEN WILBER, a young man in his late twenties, published his first book, *The Spectrum of Consciousness,* a comprehensive examination of the mind and various thought processes. In what was soon to become a classic study into the depths of consciousness, Wilber is credited with jump-starting the transpersonal psychology movement via his idea of the **spectrum of consciousness.** Greatly influenced by the works of Freud, Jung, and Maslow, as well as Krishnamurti and several leaders in the Buddhist community, Wilber's vast synthesis of information is profound, particularly when you realize that he is self-taught (the story is that he ordered hundreds of books from Shambhala Press and devoured them). Among his peers and fans alike, Wilber is unequivocally recognized as a tour de force in the understanding of human spirituality.

The premise of his thesis in *The Spectrum of Consciousness* rests on a continuum of consciousness, a playful dichotomy between the extension and retraction, the exhalation and inhalation of spirit. Wilber refers to these as "evolution" and "involution." *Evolution* is a term he uses to suggest a movement away from the source, an exploration or unfolding, to which at some point each person must return. *Involution* is a word that Wilber uses to describe returning to the source. In a sense, evolution is getting lost, he writes, whereas involution is getting found. Like the two halves of the Taoist yin/yang symbol, both evolution and involution make up the whole.

Just as Campbell, Peck, and Maslow outlined a linear progression of the spiritual path, Wilber takes a very analytical approach to the connection of our Divine Source. Noting the complexities of consciousness and the language to explain it, Wilber admits that human spirituality is a paradox of sorts. Using a ladder as a metaphor, Wilber states that spirit is both the highest rung of the ladder and the wood of which the entire ladder is constructed. Human spirituality, he states, is both the ground and the sky. Divine Spirit neither evolves nor involves; it merely is. The human experience is that the Divine Spirit lives through us; it travels in a progression similar to that of Maslow's hierarchy of needs.

Wilber's spectrum of consciousness is his take on what he calls the great "chain of being," the evolution of consciousness, which includes seven stages:

1. The external world: the awareness of external objects being separate from oneself.

2. Five senses: an awareness produced by the retrieval of stimuli via the five senses.

3. Shadow level: various unwanted and undesirable character traits that we would rather ignore than admit to having.

4. Ego level: the avoidance of death by living in the past or the future, but denying the present moment.

5. Biosocial bands: a state of dualism, where things are seen as either good or bad, positive or negative.

6. Existential level and transpersonal bands: an awareness where you move beyond the ego, beyond the self to join consciousness with the higher self.

7. Spirit (or the universal mind): being in conscious recognition with the divine presence in the present moment without slipping back into the past or moving ahead into the future.

Each layer is a complex matrix of highly organized patterns. What makes the progression of human spirituality so interesting, if not challenging, is that everyone seems to be at various levels, moving up and down the spectrum as different experiences come into our lives. Ideally, the goal is to evolve consciously to achieve a state of spirit consciousness.

However, Wilber makes very clear that the roadblock to spirit evolution is ego. In his landmark book, *Sex, Ecology, Spirituality,* Wilber describes in fine detail a model of human spirituality that is all encompassing. Enthralled with the issues of God, Goddess, realization, and self-destruction, Wilber has formulated an elaborate and complex matrix of interconnecting paths, what he calls "holons." Holons occur where Eastern philosophy meets Western materialism, and the future of humanity lies somewhere in the balance between despair and hope, between the individual and the social culture of which the individual is so tightly integrated. Creating a template of quadrants (Interior Individual, Exterior Individual, Interior Collective, and Exterior Collective) to explain consciousness and the growth of the human spirit, Wilber cites an imbalance, nicknamed "flatland," where too much attention is placed on the external and not enough on the internal aspects of self (in simple terms, soul-searching and meditation).

As thorough as Wilber's template of human spirituality appears to be, one aspect that continually gets neglected is the aspect of love and compassion.

In the past decade, Wilber has focused his energies on the concept of the Integral theory (similar in nature to Einstein's Unified Field theory that tries to unite all aspects of consciousness and broaden the appeal of Aldous Huxley's "perennial philosophy" to a much wider audience). Moving beyond theory to application, Wilber has also focused his energy on building the foundation of an "integral society" through his Integral Institute (www.integralinstitute.org). Fully aware of the problems facing humanity,

Wilber sees the awakening of the human spirit through consciousness as the essential step in human evolution.

With many books to his credit, Wilber is a prolific source of knowledge regarding matters of the mind and soul. Some argue that Wilber's approach to human spirituality is extremely cerebral and, indeed, even his biggest fans will agree that his books are not easy reading. But for as much as Wilber reads and writes, it is no secret that, as a practicing Buddhist, he spends the early morning hours in contemplative meditation seeking the counsel of his higher self as well.

⚜ SUMMARY

AMONG THE PAGES OF THIS chapter are 20 philosophies and theories of human spirituality shared by both men and women from various global cultures spanning a time period of more than two millennia. The purpose of this chapter was to present a brief overview of various theories and philosophies that, in turn, will lay the groundwork of information for the remainder of the text. A review of these selected theories finds that some individuals, including Jesus of Nazareth, the Dalai Lama, Rachel Naomi Remen, and Yogananda, focus on one particular aspect of spirituality, such as love, compassion, joy, or optimism, whereas others, including Joseph Campbell, M. Scott Peck, Matthew Fox, Abraham Maslow, Barbara Marx Hubbard, and Deepak Chopra, present a systematic approach toward higher consciousness—achieving a higher point on the mountain. All philosophies highlighted in this chapter recognize and honor the divine mystery.

⚜ TERMS AND CONCEPTS

chaotic antisocial stage
conscious evolution
creation spirituality
divine consciousness
institutional stage
Mother Earth Spirituality
mystic
mystic-communal stage
nonlocal mind

self-actualization
self-realization
service
the shadow
skeptical stage
spectrum of consciousness
synchronicity
Taoism

EXERCISE 3.1
HIGH ON A MOUNTAINTOP

Spirituality is an individual matter, based on one's own personal experience. As the saying goes, there is no substitute for personal experience. As we begin to explore our own human spirituality, we often look toward others who are farther along the path or higher up on the mountain for guidance or validation that we are headed in the right direction. The following questions are meant to serve as a rest stop and refueling station as you work your way up toward the top of this mountain, to gain a better perspective of the big picture.

1. Of the theories or individuals you have read about in this chapter, is there one with whom you can most identify or relate? Why? Please explain.

2. Two of the most powerful questions we can ever ask ourselves are (1) Who am I? and (2) Why am I here? How does Viktor Frankl's concept of human spirituality relate to your own? What is your purpose in life?

3. Human spirituality certainly includes an acknowledgment of the divine, particularly with regard to the mystical aspects of life that cannot be explained logically, rationally, or scientifically. How do the perspectives of Hildegard von Bingen, Ken Carey, and Albert Einstein compare? Have you had a mystical experience that you felt it was best not to share for fear of being ridiculed?

4. Barbara Marx Hubbard speaks of the concept of conscious evolution, but she is not alone. Jean Huston, Ken Wilber, and Abraham Maslow also speak to the concept of our highest potential. Each hints at the tension between ego and soul. Please explain your perspective on

this "tension." How does consciousness relate to human spirituality? Why is the Golden Rule so hard to follow?

_____

_____

_____

_____

5. The philosophies of M. Scott Peck, Matthew Fox, Lao Tzu, Ken Wilber, and Black Elk each have four aspects. In your opinion, why might the number four be so significant?

_____

_____

_____

6. The philosophies of the theorists in this chapter share many common themes. Can you identify a common theme among Einstein, Jung, and Black Elk? Please explain.

_____

_____

_____

7. From the divine perspective there is no difference between male and female spirituality (all is one), yet for so long the feminine voice has been silenced by the patriarchal social structure, not allowing a full picture from this vantage point. Joan Borysenko, Barbara Marx Hubbard, Jean Houston, Rachel Remen, and Hildegard von Bingen anchor the voice of the feminine aspect of human spirituality in this chapter. How do their voices, experiences, and perspectives add to your own?

_____

_____

_____

_____

_____

Please feel free to add any additional comments here:

_____

_____

_____

_____

EXERCISE 3.2
THE ROAD LESS TRAVELED: STAGES OF SPIRITUAL GROWTH

Human spirituality is so complex that it seems to defy an adequate definition or description. It is often compared to love, self-esteem, faith, and other human characteristics that seem to be related to it. This we do know: human spirituality involves a strong self-relationship, strong relationships with others, a strong personal value system, and a meaningful purpose in life. Unlike religions that have integrated these components, human spirituality has no rules, no dogma, and no set agenda. These concepts are related but separate entities. Psychologist Carl Jung once said, "Every crisis over the age of 30 is spiritual in nature." There is a definite relationship between stress and spirituality.

Over the years, M. Scott Peck, author of *The Road Less Traveled*, has studied the concepts of human spirituality and has developed a four-stage model to understand spiritual development. Each stage has many layers, and although some people seem to hover, these categories can help us to focus on our spiritual path. The stages are detailed below:

1. **Chaotic/antisocial stage.** At this stage, a person is manipulative, unprincipled, and governed by selfish pleasure under spiritual bankruptcy. His or her lifestyle is unorganized, in chaos or crisis, and headed for the rocks, which, in turn, causes much pain. All blame is externalized and projected onto others.

2. **Formal/institutional stage.** At this stage, a sudden conversion occurs where a person finds shelter in an institution (prison, military, or church) for security, structure, rules, and guidance. People in this stage see God as a loving but punitive figure, an "Irish cop in the sky." God is personified with human characteristics (a human face, a masculine pronoun, *He, His,* etc.). Institutions do, however, make some order out of the chaos.

3. **Skeptical/individual stage.** At this stage, the person, while searching for answers, rejects the institution that claims to have them. He or she becomes a "born-again atheist," a person who no longer buys into the system of rules and dogma but still believes there is something out there and wants to find it. According to Peck, this is a crucial stage of development.

4. **Mystical/communal stage.** The most mature stage is reached when someone actively searches for new answers to life's age-old questions but feels comfortable knowing that he or she may never find the answers. A person's vision of God at this stage is as internal as it is external. Additionally, such an individual sees the need for community, or bonding, and tries to foster this. Finally, those who reach this stage realize that it is only the beginning.

As described by Peck, spiritual well-being is an unfolding, an evolution of higher consciousness. Spirituality is also very personal; we each travel on our path at our own pace.

1. How would you define *spirituality*?

    _____

    _____

    _____

2. What state of well-being is your human spirit currently in?

    _____

    _____

    _____

3. In what stage of development in Peck's model do you see yourself?

    _____

4. Is your perception of God personified? Please explain.

    _____

    _____

    _____

5. Do you have a relationship with God? If so, how strong or weak is it? What steps could you
    take to improve this relationship?

    _____

    _____

    _____

EXERCISE 3.3
THE HERO'S JOURNEY

Exploring the Wisdom of Joseph Campbell

An ancient proverb states, "It takes a brave soul to walk the planet earth." In the eyes of God, we are all heroes. The role of a hero is not an easy one. To depart from home can promote feelings of insecurity and even abandonment. Initiations, and there are many in one lifetime, are demanding and arduous; the phrase "baptism by fire" comes to mind. Yet through it all we are assured a warm reception upon our return, no matter the outcome of our journey.

The hero's journey is a mythical quest. Myths are clues to the spiritual potential of human life. They offer meaning and significance as well as values. A myth is a source of truth, which often becomes exaggerated, but still holds its own essence. According to Joseph Campbell, a myth does four things to assist us on this remarkable journey:

1. A myth brings us into communion with the transcendent realms and eternal forms.

2. A myth provides a revelation to waking consciousness of the power of its sustaining source.

3. A myth tells us that no matter the culture, the rituals of living and dying have spiritual and moral roots.

4. A myth fosters the centering and unfolding of the individual in integrity with the ultimate creative mystery that is both beyond and within oneself and all things.

Campbell was of the opinion that the greatest danger of the hero's journey is to fail to use the power of myth as a guide on the spiritual path. He was keenly aware that contemporary American culture had abandoned its association with myths, a clear and present danger to any society.

The Spiritual Quest: Your Mythical Journey

The plot of every myth includes a beginning, a middle, and an end. In this case, the beginning is a departure from the known and familiar, the middle is a set of trials (called *initiations*), and the end is the return back home. In truth, we engage in this process of the hero's journey many times during the course of our lives.

1. **The departure.** Are you in the process of moving out of the familiar into the unknown? What are you departing from? Some people refuse the call. This is often based on a fear of the unknown. Are you ignoring a call to move on?

   _____

   _____

   _____

2. **The initiation.** The initiation is the threshold of adventure. Mythically speaking, the initiation is to slay the dragon or monster. In real life, initiations come in many forms, from rites of passage to issues, problems, and stressors. What is the single major life issue, concern, or problem that you are facing at the present moment?

   _____

   _____

   _____

3. **The return home.** The return is symbolized by coming home; home to the old life but with a fresh perspective. The return home bears a responsibility of sharing what you have learned on the journey. What have you learned from your most recent journey?

   _____

   _____

   _____

4. **A working myth.** What myth (source of truth) do you hold as a compass on your spiritual quest? Where did you learn this myth, and how has it helped you in your life?

❖ REFERENCES AND RESOURCES

A note to the reader: because the work in this chapter is a synthesis of each person's work, this chapter is referenced differently. References are listed alphabetically.

Bobko, J., *Vision: The Life and Music of Hildegard von Bingen.* Penguin Books: New York, 1995.

Borysenko, J., *A Woman's Journey to God: Finding the Feminine Path.* Riverhead Books: New York, 1999.

Borysenko, J., *The Ways of the Mystic: Seven Paths to God.* HayHouse Books: Carlsbad, CA, 1997.

Borysenko, J., *Fire in the Soul: A New Psychology of Spiritual Optimism.* Warner Books: New York, 1993.

Borysenko, J., *Guilt Is the Teacher, Love Is the Lesson.* Warner Books: New York, 1990.

Boyd, D., *Rolling Thunder.* Delta Books: New York, 1974.

Campbell, J., *The Power of Myth* (with Bill Moyers). Doubleday Books: New York, 1988.

Campbell, J., *The Hero with a Thousand Faces* (2nd Edition). Princeton Bollinger: Princeton, NJ, 1968.

Capra, F., *The Tao of Physics* (3rd Edition). Shambhala Publications: Berkeley, CA, 1991.

Carey, K., *The Starseed Transmissions* (reissued). HarperSanFrancisco: San Francisco, 1991.

Carey, K., *Return of the Bird Tribes.* HarperSanFrancisco: San Francisco, 1988.

Carey, K., *Starseed: The Third Millennium.* HarperCollins: New York, 1991.

Chopra, D., *Ageless Body, Timeless Mind.* Harmony Books: New York, 1993.

Chopra, D., *How to Know God.* Harmony Books: New York, 2000.

Chopra, D., *The Seven Spiritual Laws of Success.* New World Library: San Rafael, CA, 1994.

Chopra, D., *The Path to Love.* Harmony Books: New York, 1996.

A Course in Miracles. Foundation for Inner Peace: Mill Valley, CA, 1975.

Cousineau, P. (Ed.), *The Hero's Journey.* Element: Shaftsbury, England, 1999.

Dalai Lama, H. H., *The Art of Happiness: A Handbook for Living.* Riverhead Books: New York, 1999.

Dalai Lama, H. H., *Ethics for a New Millennium.* Riverhead Books: New York, 1999.

Dalai Lama, H. H., *The Power of Compassion.* Thorsons: San Francisco, 1995.

Dalai Lama, H. H., *Beyond Dogma.* North Atlantic Books: Berkeley, CA, 1989.

Dossey, L., All Tangled Up: Life in a Quantum World, *Explore* 7(6):335–344, 2011.

Dossey, L., *The Power of Premonitions.* Dutton Books: New York, 2009.

Dossey, L., *Reinventing Medicine: Beyond Mind-Body to a New Era of Healing.* HarperSanFancisco: San Francisco, 1999.

Dossey, L., *Healing Words: The Power of Prayer and the Practice of Medicine.* HarperSanFrancisco: San Francisco, 1993.

Dossey, L., *The Meaning of Medicine.* Bantam Books: New York, 1991.

Dossey, L., *Recovering the Soul.* Bantam New Age Books: New York, 1989.

Dossey, L., *Space, Time, and Medicine.* Bantam New Age Books: New York, 1982.

Dreher, D., *The Tao of Inner Peace.* HarperPerennial: New York, 1991.

Einstein, A., *Ideas and Opinions.* Crown Publishing: New York, 1954.

Fox. M., *One River, Many Wells.* Tarcher Books: New York, 2004.

Fox, M., *Creation Spirituality.* Harper Books: San Francisco, CA, 1991.

Fox, M., *Original Blessing.* Tarcher Books: New York, 2000.

Fox, M., *A Spirituality Named Compassion.* Winston Press: Minneapolis, MN, 1979.

Frankl, V., *Man's Search for Meaning.* Pocket Books: New York, 1984.

Frankl, V., "Logo-Therapy." A seminar presented at Johns Hopkins University, April 17, 1984.

Hoff, B., *The Tao of Pooh.* Penguin Books: New York, 1982.

Houston, J., *Jump Time: Shaping Your Future in a World of Radical Change.* Tarcher/Putnam: New York, 2000.

Houston, J., *A Passion for the Possible: A Guide to Realizing Your True Potential.* HarperSanFrancisco: San Francisco, 1997.

Houston, J., *A Mythic Life.* HarperCollins: New York, 1996.

Houston, J., *The Search for the Beloved.* G. P. Putnams's Sons: New York, 1987.

Hubbard, B. M., Available: http://www.barbaramarxhubbard.com.

Hubbard, B. M. *Conscious Evolution.* New World Library: Novato, CA, 1998.

Hubbard, B. M., *Emergence: The Shift from Ego to Essence.* Hampton Roads Publishing: Hampton, VA, 2001.

Jampolsky, G., *Teach Only Love.* Bantam Books: New York, 1983.

Jung, C. G., *Man and His Symbols.* Anchor Books: New York, 1964.

Jung, C. G., *Memories, Dreams, Reflections.* Vantage Press: New York, 1964.

Jung, C. G., *The Undiscovered Self.* Mentor Books: New York, 1958.

Jung, C. G., *Modern Man in Search of a Soul.* Harvest/HBJ Books: San Diego, CA, 1933.

Maslow, A. H., *Motivation and Personality* (3rd Edition). Harper and Row: New York, 1987.

Maslow, A. H., *The Farther Reaches of Human Nature.* Penguin Books: New York, 1976.

Maslow, A. H., *Toward a Psychology of Being* (2nd Edition). Van Nostrand Reinhold: New York, 1968.

Maslow, A. H., Self-actualization and Beyond. In J. F. T. Bugental (Ed.). *Challenges of Humanistic Psychology.* McGraw-Hill: New York, 1967.

Maslow, A. H., *Religion, Values, and Peak Experiences.* Penguin Books: New York, 1964.

McGaa, E. and Eagle Man, *Mother Earth Spirituality: Native American Paths to Healing Ourselves and the World.* HarperCollins: San Francisco, 1990.

Neihardt, J. G., *Black Elk Speaks.* University of Nebraska Press: Lincoln, NE, 1972.

Pearson, C., *The Hero Within: Six Archetypes We Live By* (expanded edition). Harper: San Francisco, 1989.

Peck, M. S., *The Different Drum: Community Making and Peace.* Touchtone Books: New York, 1987.

Peck, M. S., *The Road Less Traveled.* Touchtone Books: New York, 1978.

Remen, R. N., *My Grandfather's Blessing: Stories of Strength, Refuge and Belonging.* Riverhead Books: New York, 2000.

Remen, R. N., Foreword to *Stand Like Mountain, Flow Like Water.* Health Comm. Inc.: Deerfield Beach, FL, 1997.

Remen, R. N., *Kitchen Table Wisdom.* Riverhead Books: New York, 1997.

Remen, R. N., "In the Service of Life." *Noetic Science Review,* No. 37, pp. 24–25, 1996.

Remen, R. N., "On Defining Spirit." *Noetic Sciences Collection,* p. 63, 1988.

Remen, R. N., "Spirit: Resource for Healing." *Noetic Science Collection,* pp. 61–65, 1988.

Yogananda, P., *Mystical Meditations.* Self-Realization Fellowship: Los Angeles, 1986.

Yogananda, P., *The Divine Romance.* Self-Realization Fellowship: Los Angeles, 1986.

Yogananda, P., *Autobiography of a Yogi.* Crystal Clarity Publishers: Nevada City, NV, 1946.

Wilber, K., *Integral Psychology: Consciousness, Spirituality, Psychology and Therapy.* Shambhala: Boston, 2000.

Wilber, K., *The Marriage of Science and Religion.* Random House: New York, 1998.

Wilber, K., *A Brief History of Everything.* Shambhala: Boston, 1996.

Wilber, K., *Sex, Ecology, Spirituality.* Shambhala Press: Boston, 1995.

Wilber, K., *The Spectrum of Consciousness.* Quest Books: Wheaton, IL, 1993.

Wilber, K., *Grit and Grace.* Shambhala Press: Boston, 1993.

⦿ ADDITIONAL REFERENCES

Bolen, J. S., *The Tao of Psychology.* Harper & Row: New York, 1979.

Bopp, I., Bopp, M., Brown, A., and Lane, P., *The Sacred Tree: Reflections on Native American Spirituality.* Four Worlds Development Press: Madison, WI, 1985.

Byrd, R. C., "Positive Therapeutic Effects of Intercessory Prayer in a Coronary Care Unit Population." *Southern Medical Journal,* No. 81(7): 826–829, 1988.

Byrd, R. C., "Cardiologist Studies Effect of Prayer on Patients." *Brain/Mind Bulletin.* March 7, 1986.

Clark, R. W., *Einstein: The Life and Times.* Avon Books: New York, 1971.

Crow-Dog, M., and Erdoes, R., *Lakota Woman.* Harper Perennial Books: New York, 1990.

Foster, S., with Little, M., *Vision Quest: Personal Transformations in the Wilderness.* Prentice Hall: New York, 1988.

Hoyman, H., "The Spiritual Dimension of Man's Health in Today's World." *Journal of School Health.* February 1966.

Klivington, K., Sloan, D., Smith, R., Cunningham, A., "Does Spirit Matter?" Four Commentaries. *Advances,* No. 8(1): 31–48, 1992.

Leichtman, R., *Einstein Returns.* Ariel Press: Columbus, OH, 1982.

McFadden, S., *Profiles in Wisdom: Native Elders Speak about the Earth.* Bear and Co: Sante Fe, NM, 1991.

McTaggart, L., *The Bond; Connecting Through the Space Between Us.* Free Press: New York, 2011.

Pilch, J., "Wellness Spirituality." *Health Values,* No. 12(3): 28–31, 1988.

CHAPTER 4

The Nature of Human Spirituality

Be humble, for you are made of earth. Be noble for you are made of stars.

—Serbian proverb

PERHAPS SINCE THE VERY FIRST person looked up in the sky and began to realize that she was a small but crucial part of the universe at which she gazed, humans have been courting a special relationship with an intangible, indescribable, unique, yet essential, aspect of life. This relationship is one that the heart knows intuitively at a very profound level, yet it is a connection on which the mind is troubled when asked to explain rationally.

Definitions of Human Spirituality

HOW DO YOU DESCRIBE the indescribable? By all accounts the topic of **human spirituality** is difficult to articulate, either in general or specific terms. Perhaps it is safe to say that we as the human species—no matter what language is spoken, whether English, Arabic, Chinese, or Swahili—just do not possess the vocabulary to give the concept of spirituality an adequate definition or description. So how does one describe the indescribable?

It should come as no surprise that human spirituality has been the topic of countless conversations since the dawn of humanity. Yet, despite the millions of phrases used and philosophies articulated to illustrate this concept, it is fair to say that human spirituality is a phenomenon for which no one definition seems adequate. In truth, the words of the human language are insufficient in even coming close to defining this concept, because the moment we entrap the essence of spirit in the confines of words, all we are left with is an empty cage.[1]

By its very nature, a definition teases and separates from everything else that which it attempts to define long enough to gain a sense of clarity of the concept. Yet spirituality is inclusive in nature, not exclusive. In fact, human spirituality encompasses so many factors—possibly everything—that to separate anything out denies a full understanding of its true meaning. To eliminate or delete any aspect would serve as gross injustice to the concept. Spirituality has an ageless quality to it that knows no bounds and holds no allegiance to one group, continent, or religion. For this reason, the rational/judgmental mind has a hard time with this elusive and inclusive concept.

For millennia, the topic of human spirituality was held tightly by theologians, those individuals who spent their whole lives studying the nature of the divine and the mysteries of the universe. Peasants, bankers, fishermen, tailors, and all other mere mortals were not encouraged to ponder such a heavy topic. In fact, they were often discouraged from doing so. Until the sixteenth century, the average person could not even read, leaving the Bible and other sacred scriptures in the hands of those who could. With knowledge came power, and, in some cases, the abuse of power. But if there is one thing we know about human spirituality, it is that it is not just intellectual, it's experiential. As such, everyone has a direct connection with a personal knowing of the nature of our divine connection. Today, perhaps for the first time, poets, CEOs, playwrights, actors, athletes, soccer moms, and (some) politicians all speak of human spirituality, and, because of its inclusive nature, they are all right in their description of it.

Renowned Harvard philosopher Aldous Huxley dedicated the better part of his career to the study of human spirituality. Although most noted for his book *Brave New World*, Huxley is equally noted for his idea of **perennial philosophy,** a phrase he uses to describe human spirituality. Synthesizing years of study, he came to the conclusion that the human spirit is a uniquely divine gift bestowed on each individual. The perennial philosophy he describes transcends three things: religions, egos, and politics. True to the nature of inclusiveness, spirituality is all-encompassing, despite the best efforts to describe it otherwise.[2]

Spirit: The Breath of Life

IF YOU WERE TO EXPLORE its derivation, you would find that in many cultures the world over the word *spirit* means "breath," not just the inhalation of air, but also the continual exchange of air. In and out through the lungs, it is the flow of energy that gives us life. It is that which enters our physical being with the first inhalation at birth and continues throughout life. To inspire—that is, to breathe life-giving oxygen—is to be inspired by the breath of God. In Western culture, we make passing reference to this with the words *inspire* (inhale) and *expire* (exhale). In a clinical sense, these words refer to the physiological dynamics of breathing; however, they also take on a symbolic sense. To be inspired suggests a divine source of guidance, whereas expiration typically means a point of termination.

In the Jewish tradition, the Hebrew word for breath is *ruah*, in acknowledgment of the divine connection, and even as you speak this word, you can hear the rush of wind pass through your lips. In Hindu culture, *pranayama*, or diaphragmatic breathing, is believed to have a spiritual essence that enhances physical tranquility by uniting the mind, body, and spirit. This occurs by breathing with the flow of universal energy. In fact, in many Eastern cultures, the word *spirit* conveys a sense of energy, a free-flowing source of divine energy called the life force, represented by the words *chi, ki,* or *qi.*

Similarly, the ancient Greeks used the words *pneuma* to connote spirit and *psyche* to describe the human soul. The word *psyche* is now associated primarily with psychology, the study of human behavior. Although psychologists such as Carl Jung and Viktor Frankl recognized and honored the spiritual essence of humanity, it is fair to say that with the exception of offshoots of humanistic and transpersonal psychology, the general field of psychology, vying for credibility in Western science, has done little to acknowledge the existence of the soul growth process. Rather, brain chemistry has become the preferred paradigm to explain a host of mental and emotional conditions. As a result, the human soul or psyche has been left entirely out of the picture.

Assuredly, the human spirit includes the facets of higher consciousness, a hybrid of self-reliance, self-efficacy, self-actualization, enlightenment, creativity, self-assertiveness, community, love, faith, compassion, forgiveness, and transcendence, as well as a multitude of other components. Yet, each characteristic alone is not sufficient to describe the essence of human spirituality. Because the concept of spirituality is so ineffable, we are simply left with the option to describe it through analogy, simile, metaphor, and allegory.

Take a moment to reflect on a time when you found yourself in conscious recognition of your divine connection. Perhaps it was standing on top of a mountain or at the edge of the ocean and looking upon the vastness of nature. Perhaps it was riding a horse with snow lightly falling. Or maybe it was celebrating a joyous event with several lifelong friends. This type of experience can and does leave one speechless. In our best attempts to express in words our thoughts and feelings, we search the memory banks of our vernacular to explain how we feel, only to come up short. So we reach for a comparison. We say, "It was as if . . . ," "It was similar to . . . ," "It was like . . . ." Such is the nature of human spirituality.

However, just because spirituality is ineffable doesn't mean that we should abandon efforts to acknowledge this essential aspect of the human condition. The consequences would be horrendous, as is so often depicted in our current healthcare system in which patients at odds with their HMOs insist they are being treated in less than humane terms. In recognition of the Western mind–body separation consciousness, the World Health Organization (WHO) made an attempt to place the spiritual dimension prominently on the healthcare map. Although the definition may appear inadequate, the significance of the statement cannot be denied. The WHO defines *human spirituality* as "That which is in total harmony with the perceptual and nonperceptual environment." But the WHO didn't stop there. It went so far as to say this as well: "The existing definition of health should include the spiritual aspect and that health care should be in the hands of those individuals who are fully aware of and sympathetic to the spiritual dimension."[3]

One Source, Many Names

REGARDLESS OF ONE'S BACKGROUND OR perspective, it is assumed that when people speak of human spirituality that there is an implicit understanding of a higher power that goes by a great many names. In the words of primatologist Jane Goodall: "I believed in a spiritual power I called God. But as I grew older and learned about different faiths, I came to believe that there was after all but One God with different names: Allah, Tao, the Creator."[4] The list of names is rather long and includes Brahman, The Great Mystery, the Absolute, the Source, the Universe, and the Big Kahuna, to name a few. As is the case with Jane Goodall, who finds human spirituality a rather personal topic yet is open to share, various people, including Muhammad Ali, Nelson Mandela, Richard Gere, Vaclev Havel, Phil Jackson (coach of the Los Angeles Lakers), Adam Yauch (singer with the Beastie Boys), and scores of other less famous, but equally important, people are sharing their faith and their experiences publicly.[5] Spirituality is something that each of us just has to experience, and experiences will certainly vary on the human path, as will the interpretation of those experiences.

Although spirituality and religion are separate but related concepts that often overlap, it is inconceivable to separate the concept of spirituality from the divine aspect of the universe. Regardless of what perspective we come from, there is an implicit understanding that when we speak of human spirituality we are speaking of our connection to the divine source, however we choose to call it.

Definitions of Religion

SOMETIMES DEFINING WHAT a concept *is not* becomes a type of definition in itself. For instance, human spirituality is neither a religion nor the practice of a religion. The word *religion* comes from a French word that means "to regulate" or "to tie back." Religion involves a commitment to a specific observance of faith, as outlined by the leaders of its institution. The purpose of religion is to foster a sense of spirituality and nurture a person toward the divine. Unlike spirituality, which is rather freeflowing, religions are based on rules, regulations, and dogma, with the sole purpose of directing one toward a heavenly aim or reward. In addition to an initiation (e.g., baptism, bar mitzvah, etc.), most religions offer various rules of obedience to maintain membership, such as attendance, holy days of obligation, penance, tithing, and rituals. By not obeying the rules as stated, the fear of expulsion, or excommunication, exists.[6] Each religion is based on a specific dogma, a living application of a specific set of organized rules based on the ideology of the human spirit. Most people generally agree that being actively involved in a particular religion is considered a means to enhance one's spirituality—to bring one closer to God. This is the primary objective of all religions, and, on the whole, they are very effective in doing so. But recently, several experts in the field of humanistic psychology have noticed that, like too much of anything at one time, religion can stifle the growth of the human spirit. In other words, religions may serve as a path, but they can also form a roadblock as well. This fact has led some behavioral psychologists to observe that people can form an addiction to a religion as a means to continually validate their existence.[7,8] This is not to say that religions are bad. However, the power they yield can certainly be abused.

Ego also comes into play when people begin to identify themselves solely with a particular religion. With labels soon come comparisons and judgments over which religion is better. In some cases, division turns to violence, the antithesis of spirituality.

For those who wash their hands of religion, and a divine spirit as well, by calling themselves agnostics or atheists, take heart! This rebellious nature is considered by many to be an essential but very challenging part of the spiritual process, as noted by M. Scott Peck in his concept of human spirituality.

The Perennial Philosophy

L ET THERE BE NO DOUBT that religion, as a whole, can certainly promote spiritual evolution; the two are very compatible. Yet, you can be very spiritual and not "religious" (e.g., attend temple, church, or mosque), just as you can be very religious but have a poor awareness of your own spirituality. Spirituality and religion are like two independent circles that integrate with a common ground, yet each maintains its own uniqueness (**Figure 4.1**). Once, while talking to a colleague of mine who spent several years in the seminary, the topics of spirituality and religion came up. Father Bill said, "Of course they are not the same thing. We're taught this in our first year. In fact, there is a phrase which I'll share with you; it goes like this: 'God has many the Church has not, and the Church has many God has not.'"

In a day of synchronistic events, the same afternoon Father Bill and I talked I drove home from work to hear a conversation on National Public Radio's "All Things Considered." A musical conductor from a European symphony orchestra was being interviewed by the radio show host regarding

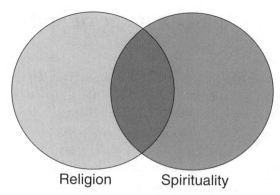

Religion   Spirituality

FIGURE 4.1 Like two circles that overlap with common ground yet are also separate, so, too, are religion and spirituality: two separate concepts that share a common theme.

his profession and his deep love of music. "Music," he said, "is a universal language." Then he added, "Music is a very spiritual language. When you listen to music, you eavesdrop on the thoughts of God." After taking a pause, he continued, "Do you know what the difference is between spirituality and religion?" Without taking a breath, he answered his own question. "Spirituality unites, where religions divide and separate."

Once, while giving a speech at the National Wellness Conference in Stevens Point, Wisconsin, I addressed the topic of stress and human spirituality and shared that particular story. A woman in the front row raised her hand and, with her tongue partially in her cheek, added this bit of wisdom, which I'm sure came from her personal experience: "Religion is for those who are trying to avoid hell, and spirituality is for those who have already been there."

Today, as pieces of the cosmic puzzle are being assembled from all cultures, religions, and societies—specifically those pieces that highlight various aspects of ageless wisdom—we are beginning to see that despite subtle nuances and a few obvious differences, there are several common denominators that thread and weave the integrity of the human spirit, a universality of all humanity. It is true that spirituality unites, whereas religions divide and separate. Bearing this in mind, it becomes imperative that as we honor our uniqueness we learn to set aside our cultural, religious, and political differences and work together as one people. Today, the world itself is experiencing many wake-up calls in an effort to raise consciousness regarding our interconnectedness. As such, the answers to global problems will not come from division or separateness but from the recognition of unity expressed as one people.

Metaphor: The Language of Spirit

THE CONSENSUS AMONG THOSE WHO study the topic of human spirituality is that, at best, the topic is ineffable, meaning that it is beyond the limitations (and confines) of mere words. Yet, if there is a language of human spirituality, most likely it is the language of metaphor, simile, and stories such as fairy tales. Here is one example from a host of metaphors that only begins to hint at the mystery: spirituality is like water—it flows freely everywhere. Water, like spirit, may take on different shapes (e.g., rivers, mist, fog, thunder clouds, or ice), but its properties are consistently found everywhere and always. Religions, again using metaphor, are like containers that hold water, and they come in all shapes, sizes, and materials. Water doesn't need a container to exist, and should a container crack the water is still there. Simply stated, spirituality, like water, and religions, like the various containers that attempt to hold it, are related yet separate concepts.

Perhaps because of the personal nature of the divine, there is no end of the use of metaphors to describe the concepts involved with human spirituality. However, one of the most common metaphors known the world over is that of the spiritual path often described as a journey, a quest, or a sojourn—a lifetime voyage that brings one to a greater understanding of one's place in the universe. It is typically described as a mountain trek. With the metaphor of the path comes a description of the destination. In no uncertain terms the mountain is *the* spiritual metaphor, a majestic mountain, one with the most incredible views. The spiritual path is the way to the top of the mountain. The journey is the collection of experiences garnered along the way.

The Path and the Journey

SEVERAL YEARS AGO I TOOK a trip to Switzerland with the intention of climbing the Matterhorn, one of the world's most dynamic mountains, a rugged peak that stands alone, majestic and proud. The town of Zermatt is itself a picturesque storybook town with narrow cobblestone streets and Tudor architecture—the quintessential Swiss Alpine village. Upon arrival, I learned that the Matterhorn goes by several names, for it sits on the border of both Switzerland and Italy. The Italians call it *Mounte Cervino.* The French refer to it as *Mont Cervin.* For several years, the British called it the *Citadel.*

Although not considered a difficult technical climb, the Matterhorn is renowned for becoming enshrouded in clouds, which, in turn, makes climbing extremely dangerous. The north face of the Matterhorn, which looks down on the village of Zermatt, has four distinct routes to the top and perhaps just as many on the Italian side. The morning I set out to reach the summit, the sky was a deep blue with clouds nowhere in sight. I made it three-quarters of the way up before I was forced back down by bad weather. As I made my descent, I pondered the symbolism of the mountain's many names and the numerous paths to the top. Like the metaphor it represented, the message was equally profound. (As a side note, the Matterhorn is now designated as an international peace park!)

Ask any alpine hiker his or her destination and the answer is nearly the same: the summit of some mountain—not merely because of the challenge of the climb, inasmuch as the height of a summit offers a breathtaking and unparalleled vista of the vast surroundings. Likewise, the drive that inspires the human journey is the desire to have such a view of life—an understanding of life's mystery and our role in it.

If life can be compared to an expedition, then the realization of our divine connection is analogous to reaching the mountain summit. To stand on a mountain peak with arms stretched overhead in the familiar "Rocky pose" epitomizes the expression, "I have touched the face of God." Initially, a mountain peak may offer itself as a metaphor for the completion of the journey, but as any alpine hiker will remind you, the hike doesn't end on the mountaintop. One stays there only long enough to enjoy the view and become inspired again before beginning the descent back down.

Converse with any hiker on the best route up a mountain and he or she will tell you there is no one best path. Rather, several paths are available to reach the peak's summit, each offering a different experience. Ask any sage, master, mystic, or healer, one who truly speaks from the heart, which is the best path to the divine source, and he or she will smile. Like the hiker, you will be told there is no one path, only the path that is best for you. As Carlos Castaneda writes in *The Teachings of Don Juan*, "Look at every path closely and deliberately. Try it as many times as you feel is necessary. Then ask yourself and yourself alone, one question. Does this path have a heart? If it does, it is good; if it doesn't, then it is of no use."[9]

As you focus your attention on the matters of the heart and issues of the soul, you will find that the path you are on will frequently intersect, align, and parallel with other trails over the course of your life. Although these words may seem to contradict religious dogma, it matters not which path you take—Christianity, Judaism, Islam, Mother Earth Spirituality, or another, but only that you keep moving forward (growing) on the path you have chosen. Choosing to rest on the sidelines indefinitely is perhaps the greatest sin known to humanity (the word *sin* is derived from the word *inertia*) and serves no one. Additionally, for a path to enhance the maturation or evolution of your spiritual well-being, there are some recommended caveats. First, the spiritual path must be creative, not destructive. It must be a progressive, not regressive, path. It must stimulate and enhance, not stifle, spiritual well-being. Second, true to the nature of any expedition, it is important to pack light. As author Glen Clark reminds us, "If you wish to travel far and fast, travel light. Take off all your envies, jealousies, unforgiveness, selfishness and fears."[10] Remember, unlike a trip to Everest, there are no Sherpas or porters on the spiritual path. We each have to carry our own baggage. Traveling light is great advice, but too often we are burdened by the weight of our thoughts and emotions, many of which no longer serve us.

Spirits on a Human Path

OUR LIVES ARE A SERIES of events strung together through the spirit of each breath and heartbeat. Some circumstances may appear more meaningful than others because they mark significant changes in the growth and development of our existence, such as marriage, childbirth, divorce, or the death of a spouse. These are known worldwide as "rites of passage," the milestones of each human journey. Theologian and mystic Teilhard de Chardin once said, "We are not humans having a spiritual experience. Instead, we are spirits having a human experience." Jungian analyst and author Jean Shinoda Bolen, quoting him, put it in these words: "We are not humans on a spiritual path. Rather we are spirits on a human path."[11] If we see ourselves as the former and something goes wrong, we tend to feel we have been punished by some divine force. However, if we recognize that indeed we are spirits on a human path, then every situation we encounter is provided to be a learning experience, and that is how we grow. Learning from experience is a choice not everyone is willing to make because of the responsibility that goes with the lesson.

Believe it or not, every aspect of life has meaning, even if we cannot see it as it unfolds in front of us. Human spirituality does not merely reflect the dynamic peak experiences throughout life's expedition. For sure, these constitute the more memorable moments, but human spirituality is as equally subtle as it is dynamic. Moments of strife, conflict, boredom, and tension offer their spiritual perspectives as well. However, in the midst of stress, the lessons offered may seem muddled by fear. But when viewed from the perspective of hindsight, the focus of the soul's consciousness is remarkably clear as we say to ourselves, "Oh, that's why that happened." More often than not, each stressor that appears like a thick cloud overhead turns out to have a magnificent silver lining. And although it's been said that the road to happiness is always under construction, I prefer this clever adage: "Stressed is desserts spelled backward!"

The path of human experience would be mighty crowded if everyone were to embark at the same point in time during the soul growth process. Therefore, it would stand to reason that not only are there numerous paths, but that we each move at a pace conducive for our own soul growth process. Take a moment to glance around the spiritual landscape and you will notice that it appears anything but congested. In fact, the stressors we face often make us feel isolated, forgotten, and lost. But it is nearly impossible to get lost on the spiritual path. In truth, we can only become immobilized by our own fears.

The destination of our life process cannot be measured in miles, nor can our success be measured in material wealth. The evolution of the soul is gauged entirely by our capacity to love. Those who have shared the moments of a near-death experience remind us that the most important lesson in life, perhaps the only lesson, is to expand our capacity to love—both giving and receiving unconditionally.

Of Spirit and Soul

ALL LIFE IS TEEMING WITH spirit, a divine life force that permeates every inch of the universe. It is spirit that animates the densest matter, and it is spirit that inspires the thoughts and dreams of humanity. Gifted healers and sages claim to actually see spirit as energy, yet it would be naive to think of spirit merely as tiny particles of mystical light floating randomly throughout the cosmos. Despite thoughts to the contrary, there is a divine order to all life, even if it may look like chaos at times from the human perspective. Spirit encompasses all aspects of existence, even those undefined by the laws of science or yet to be described through the lyrics of poets and songwriters. Spirit exists despite the disbelief of some and the skepticism of others. It delights in appreciation, yet never wavers in those who doubt.

Imagine, if you will, that the source of all Creation, pregnant with a curiosity to know itself from all sides, aspects, and perspectives, fragmented (or birthed) itself into a multitude of pieces for the sole purpose of self-exploration. Each piece is equal in divinity yet unique in its experience, accrued over time. There is a part of our human entity, our divinity, which is both identical and universal in essence. There is equally a part of our essence that is unique to each individual, that aspect we call the soul.

In the dualistic nature of Western philosophy and science, where things are separated and categorized, we tend to see ourselves as a body—placing emphasis and attention on all that is physical. At times we are convinced that all we are is a physical body. From the vantage point of divine consciousness, we are not a body, but a soul. The body is merely a means of transportation in this three-dimensional world. Metaphorically speaking, the body is a costume. As a soul, we are a single entity and, at the same time, a part of the collective whole, much like a cell in an organism is a single entity but part of the organism.

Ancient myths and legends suggest that the source or Prime Creator scattered itself to the four directions in an adventure called human existence, with the promise that each scattered piece would collectively return at some point and share all the life experiences and the meaning each one holds. Like a personal journal that documents the memories and experiences of a journey, our life experiences are stitched into the fabric of our souls to remind us of what we intend to share when we return to the Source in celebration. It is the spirit of universal life that binds us to the source of God at all times, and this connection can never be broken, despite any illusions to the contrary. The wisdom of spirit and soul is as old as time itself. The relationship between the soul and the spirit can be described as a symbiotic one. Spirit nourishes soul. Soul invigorates spirit.

Simply put, in our effort to explore the human landscape, we channel our experience back to a collective source far greater than the human mind can conceive so that God can know God-self in every conceivable way possible. An ancient proverb reminds us that only brave souls walk the human path, for the earthly existence is enshrouded in a veil of illusion. It is a brave soul on a noble adventure who attempts to lift this veil. In doing so, courageous souls are no strangers to stress.

If the spiritual path were an easy coast downhill, it would prove to be less than challenging. The spiritual path is anything but easy. Every journey will have its moments, and the spiritual path is no different. In fact, you can be sure to encounter what can best be defined as stressful moments. In fact, stress and human spirituality are partners in the dance of life.

What Is Stress?

FROM THIS PERSPECTIVE, EXACTLY what is stress? Here are some insights I have collected on my travels on the human path:

- Stress is the tension between divine will and free will.
- Stress is the tension between ego and soul.

- Stress is coming to terms with the responsibility to venture into uncharted territories.

- Stress is resistance to living in the present moment.

- Stress is learning to employ the power of spirit through love at times when it seems there is none left to give.

Day to day, stress provides the greatest opportunity for the soul growth process, providing the chance to uncover the facets of the human diamond that lie hidden beneath hardened cakes of dirt (made up of unresolved fears and angers).

Any time we encounter stress, it serves as an invitation to explore and develop one or more of the following parts of the human landscape: the relationship we hold with ourselves (including our relationship with God, however we conceive God to be) and others; our personal value system; and fulfilling a meaningful purpose in life, all under the auspices of unconditional love.

Regardless of how events are selected or encountered, the task is still the same: to shed light where there is darkness, to overcome fear with love. Kahlil Gibran, the author of *The Prophet,* once said, "I have learned silence from the talkative; tolerance from the intolerant and kindness from the unkind. I should not be ungrateful to those teachers."[12] We must remind ourselves regularly not to confuse the costume for the actor inside, nor must we forget that every life experience is a lesson, a reminder, and an opportunity to practice the art of unconditional love.

What Is the Soul?

THE CONSCIOUS, ANALYTICAL, RATIONAL MIND begs to know what the soul looks like, even what it's made of, but these questions are irrelevant to the soul. Unlike the ego, which is well versed in the language of the five senses, the soul comes from a realm familiar with, but invisible to, sensory perception: an ethereal realm rich in energy beyond the comprehension of conscious thought. The soul—curious, eager, and enthusiastic—incarnates in physical form with a body as its vehicle (and a specific personality) to explore the human landscape and to gain wisdom through experience that can only be obtained via the dynamics of this setting.

The eternal soul comes from a place of divine origin and at some point will return to that very place with its wealth of experience to share with

All-That-Is. It may seem a quagmire to the conscious mind, but each soul, identical in its divinity, is unique in its personality and mission. Furthermore, all souls gifted in various talents are diverse in their dreams but united in the noble effort to raise consciousness through love, though the "earth plane," being dense in fear, often causes souls to forget their mission (and in many cases their connection to the source).

On occasion, the soul has been compared to a diamond caked with earthen soil, whereby the collection of human experiences makes certain facets not only visible but noteworthy as well. Various references to the soul describe a ledger where our earthly experiences are continually recorded. Stories have been told about selling the soul as if it is a possession, but the soul is not a piece of real estate that can be bought, sold, or negotiated. The soul is none other than "a gift from God," and as the expression goes, "how we nurture it, how we live our life, is our gift in return." This we do know: the body is the vehicle of the soul, but the soul does not die with the body. It returns to that from which it came, more polished, more refined, more educated, and more divine.

Compassion, intuition, imagination, faith, courage, free will, humor, and humbleness are just several of the aspects that constitute the backbone and muscles of the soul, for it is the use of these inner resources that comprises the currency of motion on the human journey. The soul seeks opportunities to exercise these muscles and gravitates toward people, situations, and circumstances that allow for optimal soul growth. If you are in doubt as to the direction of your soul journey, or curious about what lessons are offered to you in your present setting, take a careful look at the people in your life. The planet Earth is often said to be a school where lessons are continually offered. Furthermore, we are surrounded by teachers everywhere.

What is soul work? Perhaps it can best be described in terms of our capacity to love—a capacity exercised through each of our inner resources. The soul is called to work when it encounters intolerance, blame, greed, anger, fear, and intolerance. In his acclaimed book *The Seat of the Soul,* author Gary Zukav states:

> The soul is. It has no beginning and no end but flows toward wholeness. The soul is not physical, yet it is the force field of your being. The body is the instrument of the soul. Every soul that agrees consciously to bring to a level of human interaction the love and compassion and wisdom that it has acquired is trying through his or her own energy to challenge the fear patterns of that collective.[13]

The Three Pillars of Human Spirituality

I F YOU WERE TO TALK to the shamans, healers, sages, mystics, and wisdom keepers of all times, of all ages, and all languages, and ask them what constitutes the core of human spirituality, you would hear them say the same three things time and time again—relationships, values, and purpose in life—all leading one to a higher consciousness of the divine (**Figure 4.2**). Even with the understanding that human spirituality is extremely difficult to articulate, relationships, values, and purpose in life are understood to be the heart of what it's all about.

To repeat the wisdom of Carl Jung, "Every crisis over the age of 30 is a spiritual crisis."[14] People often thought he was talking about the midlife crisis, but Jung insisted that there was more to a spiritual crisis than age. I am convinced that if he were alive today he might drop the age limit down to 18 and, quite possibly, get rid of the age limit altogether.

It was 1983 when I taught my first undergraduate stress management course. Intrigued as to why college students were taking such a course, I would often ask the first day of class their reasons and expectations of the course. Among their peers, a few would jokingly say that they needed three credits to graduate. But after each class was over, students would corner me as I left the room and confide in me why they were taking the class. For eighteen years the answers were almost always the same. They would say things

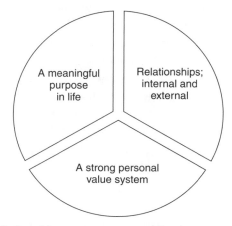

FIGURE 4.2 Relationships, a strong personal value system, and a meaningful purpose in life constitute the cornerstones of the foundation of spiritual well-being.

like, "I need help in dealing with my girlfriend or boyfriend," or "I need help coping with my roommate." Some would talk about the guy down the hall playing his stereo too loud. Almost every college student talked about the stress in dealing with parents. It occurred to me early on that what they were talking about was relationships.

Students would also talk about values and value conflicts, although they didn't quite use these words. Instead they would say things like, "I really like the freedom of college—I can eat pizza every night of the week and no one cares. But I'm not too crazy about this thing called responsibility."

At some point during the semester, every student would say something like, "I have to declare a major in two weeks, and I have no idea what I want to do with the rest of my life," or worse, they would say, "I am going to graduate in about a month, and I don't want to get a job in this field. I studied this major for my parents." At the core of their anxiety was the issue of a meaningful purpose in their lives.

What I realized upon hearing this was that students were wrestling with issues of spiritual importance: relationships, values, and purpose in life. I also realized just how connected stress was to the aspect of human spirituality and that spiritual crises do not just happen after age 30. They can happen at any time in one's life, at any age.

Let's take a closer look at these three pillars.

Pillar 1: Relationships

One common theme among the various spiritual philosophies is that they each speak to the nature of **relationships**—those that we hold with ourselves and those that we create with each other. Through the wisdom of the Dalai Lama, Carl Jung, Rachel Naomi Remen, and Jesus of Nazareth, we see how essential the concept of relationships is to our spiritual growth. In my research on the topic of relationships, it became evident that this component of human spirituality has two aspects, which I call *internal* (personal) and *external* (interpersonal) relationships.

The **internal relationship** is how you relate to yourself, how you govern yourself, and how well you know yourself. The internal relationship involves a fair amount of habitual soul-searching through reflection, meditation, or prayer. The internal relationship also involves keeping the ego in check. Most important, the internal relationship involves a relationship with your higher self (e.g., God, Jesus, or a Higher Power), whatever you conceive this to be. Some would even say the internal relationship is the integration of the self in conscious recognition with the higher self. At the heart of the internal relationship is the idea that we are whole, yet, at the same time, we are a part of a much bigger whole. And although we may seem infinitesimally small in the scope of the universe, we are unequivocally essential to it.

External relationships comprise how we relate to everyone and everything outside ourselves. Friends and family come to mind as people involved in our external relationships, but they also include acquaintances and strangers. To go one step further, external relationships include how you relate to everything. In American Indian culture, it is said that "all life is relationship," not just our relationships with people, but also those with the trees, the water, the plants and animals, and Mother Earth herself. Similar to this idea was Einstein's idea that everything is interconnecting energy.

External relationships are often a reflection of how we see and treat ourselves. Having lived in Washington, D.C., I learned it was important to speak in a vernacular that people could understand. In the land of politics, I used a political metaphor. If your internal relationship is like your domestic policy, then external relationships are like your foreign policy. And as the expression in Washington, D.C., goes, "If your domestic policy is bad, your foreign policy is worse." Relationships are the core of the Golden Rule, to treat others as you would treat yourself. Simply stated, if we do not treat ourselves with respect, honesty, integrity, and love, how can we possibly do the same for others?

Pillar 2: A Strong Personal Value System

Ever stop to ask yourself what your values are? Not many people do! Perhaps, as the expression goes, "If you really want to see someone's values, look at his checkbook register." Some people may say they value wealth; others might prefer leisure; still others value privacy. Ask anybody over the age of 60 and most likely they will say their health. Love is at the top of many peoples' lists as well.

Values are abstract ideas that we give importance to. Though intangible by nature, values are often symbolized in material form. For example, money is a symbol of wealth, a diploma is a symbol of education, and caller ID is a symbol of privacy. Though many people may not be able to list their values off the top of their head, they can certainly tell you what's important to them. Values have a very subtle yet powerful way of directing our lives, for we tend to gravitate toward those things we consider important. Likewise, our world seems to fall apart when values conflict or shift in importance. Each theory of human spirituality speaks to the nature of values—love, compassion, honesty, respect, or faith—because values constitute how we conduct our relationships.

It is said by those who study values that each person has a value system.[15,16] This value system is composed of about six core values, such as love, honesty, freedom, or leisure, and another ten to twelve supporting values, which support the core values, such as creativity, wealth, education, or friendship. From month to month, year to year, our value system changes. Our hierarchy of values shifts, much like the Earth's tectonic plates, with various values coming in and out of positions of importance. Think back to a period of about ten years ago. Ask yourself what was important to you back then. Compare that with what you find to be important in your life today. If you are like most people, you will see that, indeed, there has been a shift in your hierarchy of values. Sometimes this shift brings about a sense of conflict as two values jockey for position in the value system. For example, freedom and responsibility are two values that are often at odds in a value system. The result may be a level of stress or tension until resolution occurs within the value hierarchy.

Although it may seem that values and morals are synonymous, this is not necessarily the case. Greed is a value, yet it is fair to say that not many people would cite greed as a moral. Some values may hold great spiritual significance; others may not. Values and relationships often go hand in hand. Typically, people tend to associate with others who share similar values, giving them common ground to walk on. One's value system is also tightly integrated with a meaningful purpose in life.

Pillar 3: A Meaningful Purpose in Life

Perhaps the two most important questions you can ever ask yourself are: "Who am I?" and "Why am I here?" These two questions are the catalysts for profound thought when one goes on a retreat or modern-day vision quest. The question "Why am I here?" speaks to the heart of finding a **meaningful purpose in life,** and although it may appear that the answer changes over time, there is an underlying purpose to everything we do as well. As a teenager, it may seem like the purpose in life is to have fun. Later on, it may be to raise a family or care for family members. Although all of these are valid reasons for living, philosophers speak of greater meaning in life, such as learning to love.

In his book *How Then Shall We Live?* author Wayne Muller proposes four questions that collectively act as a compass in the soul-searching quest for life's meaning. They are "Who am I?" "What do I love?" "How shall I live, knowing that I will die?" and "What is my gift to the family of the Earth?" Muller explains that the answer to the last question is an expression of love, yet the way that this is expressed is unique to each individual.[17]

Viktor Frankl, in his classic book *Man's Search for Meaning*, speaks of a purposeful meaning as being the most important aspect on the spiritual journey.[18] It was Frankl's observation from his time spent in a Nazi concentration camp that people who had found meaning in their lives found a reason to live through the horrors of the Holocaust, whereas those who lost their meaning succumbed to death. It was Frankl's opinion that suffering arises when meaning seems to evaporate, yet we can always find a new meaning in life. In the words of Carl Jung, "As far as we can discern, the sole purpose of human existence is to kindle a light in the darkness of mere being."[19]

Here is a definition of human spirituality that brings these three aspects together: *human spirituality* is the maturation of higher consciousness as developed through the dynamic integration of three facets: an insightful and nurturing relationship with oneself and others, the development of a strong personal value system, and the cultivation and fulfillment of a meaningful purpose in one's life.

Desire + Commitment = Discipline

DID YOU EVER HEAR THE joke about the man who paused on the street corner in New York City? When the first person walked by him, he asked, "Excuse me, sir, how does one get to Carnegie Hall?"

The man replied, "Practice, my dear man, practice."

If the question were posed, "How does one progress on the spiritual path?" the answer would undoubtedly be the same: practice.

The word *discipline* derives from the word *disciple* or *follower*. Quite simply, it means that to follow guidance requires both desire and commitment. In a country and culture in which freedom reigns supreme, discipline has become a lost art of sorts. Responsibility goes hand in hand with discipline. Americans certainly don't lack desire, yet discipline seems to be in short supply. Perhaps because of the Puritan ethic (worth equals work), which still holds an amazingly strong influence on today's culture, commitment to work often eclipses commitment to other aspects of one's life, particularly one's inner life.

If you were to think of the spiritual path as an endurance athletic event, much like a marathon, you would soon realize that it takes considerable training to complete the event with any degree of success. Training would include long endurance runs, perhaps some sprints, definitely some stretching and perhaps even a weight-training routine, as well as a sound nutrition program and quality sleep. All of these are necessary to promote the health of the cardiovascular system for this event. The health of the human spirit is no different in its need for a structured program. The foundation of this program, like that of any other, is discipline.

With regard to human spirituality, discipline is required to domesticate the ego so that it does not sabotage the soul's growth. Meditation, service, and humbleness are just some of the ways in which discipline cultivates human spirituality. From these aspects alone, it is easy to see why people would rather sit and watch television than nurture the health of the human spirit. There is no denying that discipline requires work, but ask people who have applied themselves and they will tell you that the result is always worth it.

There is one more pillar of human spirituality. It is often referred to as the *Pillar of Mystery*, that which addresses all the things that cannot be explained rationally, even scientifically. Examples might include spontaneous healings, remarkable synchronicities, and even angelic events.

✤ SUMMARY

THE CONCEPT OF HUMAN SPIRITUALITY cannot be adequately expressed in words. The words *spirit* and *breath* are often used synonymously in various cultures to convey a sense of life force and energy. **Religion**, from the French word that means "to regulate," comprises regulations, rules, and dogma to nurture one's sense of spirituality. Spirituality is inclusive, but religions tend to be exclusive (e.g., one cannot be Baptist and Jewish at the same time). Although the topics of spirituality and religion overlap, they are not the same. If there is a language of human spirituality, it is the language of metaphor, a symbolic expression of intangible concepts. Every description of human spirituality describes some connection to a Greater Power. There is agreement among mystics, sages, and wisdom keepers that human spirituality involves the maturation of higher consciousness through relationships, values, and a meaningful purpose in life. These three components are considered the pillars of spiritual well-being.

✤ TERMS AND CONCEPTS

human spirituality	perennial philosophy
external relationships	relationships
internal relationship	religion
meaningful purpose in life	values

EXERCISE 4.1
THE THREE PILLARS OF HUMAN SPIRITUALITY

Every crisis over the age of 30 is a spiritual crisis. Spiritual crises require spiritual cures.

—Carl Gustav Jung

The shamans, healers, sages, and wisdom keepers of all times, all continents, and all peoples in their ageless wisdom say that human spirituality has three components: relationships, values, and purpose in life. These three components are so tightly integrated it may be hard to separate them from each other. But if this were possible, take a moment to reflect on each one of these aspects of human spirituality to determine the status of your spiritual well-being.

I. Relationships

All life is relationships! In simple terms, there are two categories of relationships: internal and external. The internal relationship (i.e., domestic policy) encompasses how you deal with yourself and how you nurture the relationship with yourself and your higher self. External relationships (i.e., foreign policy) address how you relate, support, and interact with the people, and all living entities, in your environment. How would you evaluate your internal relationship, and what steps could you take to cultivate it? Moving from a perspective of domestic policy to foreign policy, how would you evaluate your external relationships?

_____

_____

_____

_____

II. Your Personal Value System

We each have a value system consisting of both core and supporting values. Your four to six core values are those that form the foundation of your personal belief system. Supporting values support the core values. Intangible core values (e.g., love, honesty, freedom, and compassion) and supporting values (e.g., education, creativity, leisure, and integrity) are often symbolized by our material possessions. Quite regularly, our personal value system tends to go through a reorganization process, particularly when our values conflict. Think about your core and supporting values, and list them below.

Core Values

1. _____
2. _____
3. _____
4. _____
5. _____
6. _____

Supporting Values

1. _____
2. _____
3. _____
4. _____
5. _____
6. _____

7. _____
8. _____
9. _____
10._____
11. _____
12. _____

III. A Meaningful Purpose in Life

A meaningful purpose in life is that which gives our life meaning, purpose, and value. Some might call it a life mission. Although it is true that we may have an overall life mission, it is also true that our lives are a collection of many meaningful purposes. Suffering awaits those times in between each purpose. What would you say is your life mission, and what purpose are you now supporting to accomplish this mission?

_____

_____

_____

_____

EXERCISE 4.2
PERSONAL AND INTERPERSONAL RELATIONSHIPS

It is often said that all life is relationships—how we deal with ourselves and how we relate to everything else in our lives. It's no secret that relationships can cause stress. For this reason alone, all relationships need nurturing to some degree. Reflect for a moment on all the many relationships that you hold in your life, including the most important relationship—that which you hold with yourself. Relationships also constitute the foundation of your support system. Relationships go further than friends and family. This core pillar of human spirituality also includes our relationship with the air we breathe, the water we drink, and the ground we walk on. How is your relationship with your environment? Write your name in the center circle and then begin to fill in the circles with the names of those people, places, and things that constitute your relationship with life. Finally, place a * next to those relationships that need special nurturing and then make a strategy by which to start this process.

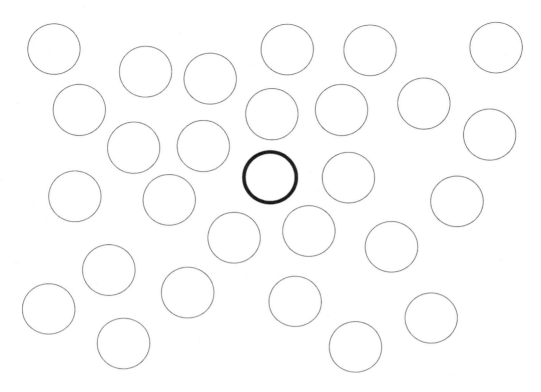

EXERCISE 4.3
YOUR PERSONAL VALUE SYSTEM

We all have a personal value system, a core pillar of the human spirit that is constantly undergoing renovation. What does your value system currently look like? Perhaps the following diagram
can give you some insights and, in turn, help resolve some issues that might be causing stress.
The circle in the center represents your core values: abstract or intangible constructs of importance that can be symbolized by a host of material possessions. It is believed that we hold about
four to six core values that constitute our personal belief system, which, like a compass, guide the
spirit on our human journey. Give this concept some thought and then write in this circle what
you consider to be your current core values (e.g., love, happiness, health, etc.). The many circles
that surround the main circle represent your supporting values, those values that lend support to
your core values (these typically number from five to twelve). Take a moment to reflect on what

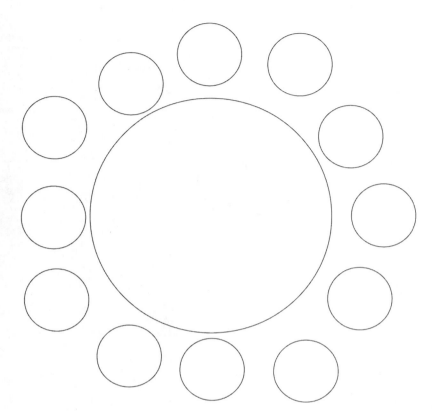

these might be and then assign one value per small circle. Also inside each small circle include what typically symbolizes that value for you (e.g., wealth can be symbolized by money, a car, a house, etc.). Finally, consider whether any stress you feel in your life is the result of a conflict between your supporting and core values.

EXERCISE 4.4
YOUR MEANINGFUL PURPOSE IN LIFE

Considering that your purpose in life may change many times in the course of your life, for this exercise first write down what you consider to be your life purpose now, at this point in time. Then take a moment to briefly describe what you considered to be your purpose in life at the start of each decade of your life (e.g., at age 20 it might be or have been to graduate with a college degree, at age 30 it might be or have been to raise a family or start a business etc.).

NOW: _____

Age 60: _____

Age 50: _____

Age 40: _____

Age 30: _____

Age 20: _____

EXERCISE 4.5
MANDALA OF THE HUMAN SPIRIT

The wellness paradigm is universally depicted as a circle, the symbol of wholeness. In every culture, the circle represents a yearning for and a coming to wholeness—a sense of peace through mind, body, spirit, and emotions. A mandala is a circular-shaped object symbolizing unity with four separate quarters that represent seasons of the year, directions of the universe, or four specific points of reference. The origin of the mandala can be traced back to the dawn of humanity. Mandalas can vary in their size, design, colors, and symbolism. They are often used in meditation practice as a focal point of concentration. In addition, they are also hung as decorations in many cultures. Examples include the American Indian medicine wheel and Tibetan artwork.

The mandala of the human spirit is a symbol of wholeness. This exercise is a tool of self-awareness that allows you the opportunity to reflect on some of the components of the human spirit: a meaningful purpose in your life, personal values, and the implicit chance to learn more about yourself in the precious moments of solitude. Each quadrant represents a direction of your life with a symbol of orientation. The East is the initial point of origin. It represents the rising sun, the point of origin for each day. The South symbolizes that which nurtures you. The West represents the future, and the North symbolizes that which inspires you and that for which you give gratitude.

The focus of the mandala begins with the East. It then moves South and then to the West and finally to the North. Each focal point of the mandala of the human spirit provides questions for reflection. Notice that each of the four directions deals with the components of human spirituality: relationships, values, and purpose in life. They could also represent the four quadrants of emotions, body, mind, and spirit in the life cycle. The parts of the whole will represent different aspects for different people.

Each quadrant or direction has a list of several soul-searching questions. Using the first mandala as a guide, read through the questions of each quadrant, one at a time, answering the questions of that quadrant before moving on to the next. Using the blank circle template on the next page, begin by writing your name in the small center circle. Then take a few moments to reflect on the directions of the mandala to get a better perspective on the well-being of your

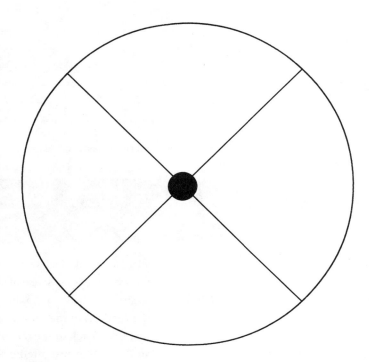

human spirit. For an added exercise, make a mandala collage incorporating photos, images, and words for the four areas. Then display the mandala in a place where you can see it regularly. Let it serve to remind you of the health of your human spirit.

❖ ENDNOTES

1. Krishnamurti, J., *On God.* HarperSanFrancisco: San Francisco, 1992.
2. Huxley, A., *The Perennial Philosophy.* Perennial Library: New York, 1944.
3. The World Health Organization (WHO). *Health Promotion and Chronic Illness.* Ed. A. Kaplun. WHO: Geneva, 1992.
4. Goodall, J., *Reason for Hope: A Spiritual Journey.* Warner Books: New York, 1999.
5. Van Biema, D., "Buddhism in America." *Time,* pp. 72–81, October 13, 1997.
6. Houston Smith is the foremost authority on the study of religions. He is the author of the acclaimed book *The Religions of Man.* These comments are from a presentation made at the International Conference on Science and Consciousness, Albuquerque, New Mexico, April 20, 1999.
7. Booth, L., *When God Becomes a Drug.* Tarcher Books: Los Angeles, 1991.
8. Schaef, A. W., *When Society Becomes an Addict.* Harper & Row: New York, 1987.
9. Castaneda, C., *The Teachings of Don Juan: A Yaqui Way of Knowledge.* Washington Square Press: New York, 1968.

10. Clark, G., as quoted in *The Promise of a New Day.* Casey, K., and Vanceburg, M. (editors). Hazelton Books: New York, 1984.

11. Bolen, J. S., Keynote Address, Common Boundary Conference, Washington, DC, April 1991.

12. Gibran, K., *The Prophet.* Knopf Books: New York, 1945.

13. Zukav, G., *The Seat of the Soul.* Fireside Books: New York, 1989.

14. Jung, C. G., as interviewed by John Freiman on the BBC, 1961.

15. Rokeach, M., *Beliefs, Attitudes and Values.* Jossey-Bass: San Francisco, CA, 1972.

16. Lewis, H., *A Question of Values.* Harper & Row: New York, 1990.

17. Muller, W., *How Then Shall We Live?* Bantam Books: New York, 1996.

18. Frankl, V., *Man's Search for Meaning.* Pocket Books: New York, 1984.

19. Jung, C. G., *Memories, Dreams, Reflections.* Vintage Books: New York, 1963.

◈ ADDITIONAL REFERENCES

Burch, J. *The New Trinity.* Devorss Publications, Camarillo, CA, 2011

Covey, S., *The Seven Habits of Highly Effective People.* Fireside Books: New York, 1990.

Ó Murchú, D., *Reclaiming Spirituality.* Crossroad: New York, 1998.

Ó Murchú, D., *Religion in Exile.* Crossroad: New York, 2000.

Rinpoche, S., *The Tibetan Book of Living and Dying.* HarperCollins: New York, 1992.

Trungpa, C., *Shambhala: The Sacred Path of the Warrior.* Shambhala Press: Boston, 1984.

CHAPTER **5**

Mountains, Molehills,
and Muscles of the Soul

Giving up is the final solution to a temporary problem.

—Gerta Weissman Klein, Nazi concentration camp survivor

I F YOU WERE TO READ through any collection of mythical lore, fairy tales, or Celtic legends, before long you would begin to discover a distinct pattern to the storyline. One or more characters sets off on an adventure, trouble ensues, lessons are learned, and finally he or she makes it back home—safe and sound. Whether it is Pinocchio, Hansel and Gretel, Dorothy and Toto, Luke Skywalker, or Snow White, the structure is a familiar one, familiar perhaps because in one way or another it mirrors our own human journey. Yet at the same time, the framework of the story guides us as well. We embark on this journey leaving the comfort of home, we encounter countless roadblocks and obstructions along the way, we are easily distracted, and we learn some lessons (hopefully). And, if we are lucky, we return home once again in one piece. Keeping in mind that the best language of human spirituality is metaphor, simile, and allegory, this chapter is framed in the context of many metaphors to bring several spiritual concepts to light. The mountain serves as a popular metaphor for reaching the pinnacle of spiritual well-being.

The Metaphorical Mountain

K 2, A BROADWAY PLAY, TELLS the story of two men's attempt to climb the second highest mountain in the world, K2. In the first act, one climber is injured, and the other must save him or they will both die in the frigid cold. One of the most memorable lines in the play is: "The mountain is the metaphor." It is how one of the characters describes his quest to meet God through the mountain expedition.[1] The movie *The Sound of Music* has a song, "Climb Every Mountain," that conveys a similar message. Indeed, the mountain is a universal metaphor for all of us, no matter where our paths may take us— either with breathtaking views from the valleys or peaks, or both.

Abraham Maslow used the metaphor of a mountain when he described the "peak experience" of self-actualization. Eastern cultures often describe consciousness as a mountain, with the goal being to rise above the clouds (symbolizing the ego) to gain a clear perspective of one's true life mission or purpose. Jung reframed the mountain metaphor as an iceberg to describe both the conscious (above water) and unconscious (below water) minds. Reaching the peak of a mountain is akin to reaching enlightenment or wisdom (which is why so many cartoons show aged yogis sitting on mountaintops). Just like studying for exams, wisdom takes time and energy. For those of you who have actually climbed a mountain, you know the challenges involved and the reward of hard work. Of course, some people exaggerate and see mountains when there are really only molehills. Then there are others who see the mountain as an obstacle itself. Perceptions will certainly vary. All things considered though, no one ever said the spiritual journey was easy. Eventually, one way or another, just like in the fairy tales, everyone makes it home.

Molehills: Roadblocks on the Spiritual Path

To REITERATE A VERY IMPORTANT point, no one ever said that the human journey would be an easy one. Even those who were born into what appears to be the lap of luxury with silver spoons and bottomless trust funds typically find themselves at odds with uncovering their true purpose in life. Whether the path you are on is a dirt road or a six-lane superhighway, of this you can be sure: the path you take will undoubtedly have ruts, potholes, and major obstructions—**roadblocks on the spiritual path**. Of course, everyone has heard the expression "Don't make a mountain out of a molehill," which people tend to do when the ego overrides the soul in times of stress. The ego distorts the soul's perspective of a given problem and tries to overwhelm and confuse it. But why is it that one person's molehill is another person's mountain? Most likely it is the perception or interpretation of the vantage point from where he or she stands. Recognition of a problem is the first step toward resolving it.

Roadblocks can take many forms. A dead-end job. A chronic illness. An alcoholic parent. The roommate from hell. What does your list of stressors, problems, and issues look like? Take a moment to search your mind and ask yourself what problems you are dealing with in your life right now. Some of the obstacles might seem like mountains. Spiritually speaking, they are referred to as "roadblocks" and they can appear quite formidable. In truth, roadblocks are part of the journey toward the summit. Undeniably, our first reaction is to do an about-face when encountering events, situations, and people we would rather not deal with. However, avoidance only perpetuates the stress and ultimately leads to stagnation on the spiritual path.

Avoidance might be the most popular coping technique for stress, but it is also the least effective one. With age and a whole lot of experience, you find out that roadblocks are as much a part of the spiritual path as the beautiful vistas. Ask anyone who is honest enough to tell you about his or her adventures on the human journey and soon you will learn that every person who has turned his or her back on a stressful situation and headed in the opposite direction will ultimately meet the same roadblock (with a different name or face) 5, 10, or 15 miles down the road—patiently waiting. Whether we like it or not, roadblocks are actually part of the human journey! And they must be addressed.

Now take a closer look at your list of stressors. Are these problems a symbolic representation of some deeper issues? Quite likely these problems are a reflection of your perceptions, attitudes, and beliefs (e.g., fears and frustrations) that at one time might have been helpful, but at the present moment inhibit the flow of spirit. At best they are a nuisance; at worst they keep us immobilized.

Every roadblock represents an issue begging for resolution, and with it an emotion begging to be reconciled—fear, anger, greed, laziness, guilt, and worry, to name a few. These unresolved issues of anger, fear, greed, jealousy, and guilt not only immobilize the human spirit, they can cause permanent paralysis as well. Stated simply, these unresolved issues drain our energy and eventually seem to stop us dead in our tracks. Perhaps it is no surprise that the two biggest roadblocks on the path of human experience are the primary stress emotions: anger (the fight response) and fear (the flight response). It doesn't take a saint to realize that these two emotions, when left unresolved, violate the moral codes of society: acts of lying, cheating, stealing, and killing are all based on insecurities rooted in unresolved anger or fear.

While avoiding life's problems (e.g., the semester from hell, the traffic from hell, the ex-spouse from hell, etc.) is not the answer, neither is sitting at the foot of the obstruction doing nothing. Laziness quickly weakens the human spirit. Once again, using the metaphor of water as spirit, water that flows along a path tends to filter itself along the rocks and gravel, keeping itself clean and fresh. Flowing water that pools becomes stagnant and eventually toxic. Our spirit becomes toxic when it becomes stagnant.

In addition to the terms *spiritual hunger* and *spiritual dormancy*, we can add the expression *spiritual constipation*. This describes someone who, enveloped by fear or laziness, sits at the foot of a roadblock and does absolutely nothing. This scenario is referred to as "getting stuck," and it is quite a common problem these days. Like its physical counterpart, spiritual constipation is definitely not healthy. No fairy tale ever ended at the foot of a roadblock. However, it is sad to say that thousands of people have concluded their earthly journey unsuccessfully this way.

Roadblocks may not seem like they are a necessary step on the spiritual path, but in truth they are an essential, if not critical, component of the soul's growth process. As discussed by several people, from M. Scott Peck to Ken Wilber, the progression of spiritual well-being is punctuated with roadblocks. To underscore this point, roadblocks on the human path are meant to be dismantled, circumnavigated, or transcended so we can move on. The issues they represent should not be avoided, ignored, or obsessed about indefinitely.

Distractions on the Spiritual Path

YOU ARE PROBABLY FAMILIAR WITH the expression, "Don't forget to stop and smell the roses." There is a side of human nature that gets so focused, mistaking the destination for the journey, that the best parts of the sojourn, those metaphorical roses, are often missed. They are simply passed over in the rush to cross the finish line. The people who remind us to smell the roses are often the same ones who remind us that the destination *is* the journey itself. Smelling the roses along the way is surely advocated, but with this sage advice: don't pause so long you stop and forget where you are going. As is the case with most warnings, this one sadly falls on deaf ears until it's usually too late.

Within the pages of each fable or tale, whether it's a witch with an apple (Snow White), a seductress (the femme fatale), or candy (Hansel and Gretel), some attraction presents itself to pull the character off the path; these are **distractions of the human spirit.** Distractions are every bit as dangerous on the human journey as they are in fairy tales and fables. Television, the Internet, drugs, alcohol, food, even codependence are common distractions today. In Judeo-Christian culture, distractions are called "temptations." Although not all temptations are bad (chocolate comes to mind), the human condition has a tendency to overindulge in simple pleasures (if some is good, more must be better), which then sets the stage for conflict and turmoil. No matter what path you take on the human journey, life is full of wonderful sights and attractions. However, attractions can easily become distractions that can lure you off the path. Unlike those in fairy tales, today's distractions can lead one off the path indefinitely. The results can be devastating for everyone involved.

So remember that distractions begin as attractions. A beer is an attraction. Alcoholism is a distraction. Making love is an attraction. Sexual addiction is a distraction. Perhaps today the most common distractions fall under the heading of addictions, for what starts as an attraction quickly becomes a distraction, drawing one onto the sidelines, sometimes for a very long time or, in some cases, a lifetime. Alcohol, drugs, excessive television watching, and Internet surfing top this list, and they have become some of our biggest health concerns today as well as contributors to spiritual dormancy.

Addictions come in many forms but they typically fall in one of two categories: (1) substance abuse (e.g., alcohol or drugs) or (2) process addictions that involve a repetitive behavior (e.g., gambling, sex, shopping, or eating). Like quicksand, addictions are slow but extremely powerful, and one almost always requires assistance from others or divine intervention to prevent a total demise. Pulling off the side of life's highway indefinitely serves no beneficial purpose. In terms of the health of the human spirit, prolonged distractions can be downright hazardous. Distractions dull the senses and drain the spirit. Moreover, distractions have a hypnotic effect, which, over time, can zap the strength of our spiritual muscle and rob us of our true destiny. In fairy tales, the characters always seem to find their way home, but not without learning their lessons. In real life, people are not always as lucky, often getting sidetracked long enough that they never reach their full potential. In the language of fairy tales, their voyage home is extremely arduous, painful, and prolonged.

Muscles of the Soul

I HAVE BEEN VERY FORTUNATE TO meet several special people on my life journey who are nothing less than remarkable heroes. I call them remarkable because they have quite literally made a trip to hell and back and done so quite gracefully. These are people who have encountered horrific stressful circumstances (e.g., a kidnapped child, three years in the Auschwitz concentration camp, or terminal cancer) and come out the victors. There are two ways you can emerge from a stressful situation, no matter how hellacious it is. The first is to play the victim, complaining, criticizing, and blaming others for the rest of one's life to generate sympathy. Simply stated, these people feel sorry for themselves and carry around tons and tons of emotional baggage for what seems to be an eternity. The second way to emerge from this type of circumstance is to do so with grace, with neither a sense of resentment nor an air of animosity toward others.

When I meet people who have returned victorious from their trip to hell, I ask them how they did it without any sense of remorse or indignation. Their responses are almost always the same, as if they all got together one day and pooled their answers (which I know they didn't). This is what they say: "It was my sense of humor, my sense of patience, a sense of forgiveness, a sense of optimism." The list goes on and on. As I listen to these attributes, what some call inner resources but what I have come to term *muscles of the soul*, I realize that these are not the gifts for a chosen few—they are every person's birthright. Whether stated directly or indirectly, every philosophy of human spirituality speaks of these inherent qualities to survive: Jesus of Nazareth spoke of faith and love, Jean Houston refers to these attributes as our "entelechy," Joan Borysenko speaks of "spiritual optimism," and Abraham Maslow grouped them together as "self-actualization."

I call these muscles of the soul because, like the muscles of our arms and legs, they will never disappear. However, like our physical muscles, they can certainly atrophy with disuse, making them weak and potentially vulnerable in times of need. Without a doubt, the time of need is when we encounter roadblocks and obstructions on the human journey. It is these spiritual muscles of the soul that enable us to dismantle, deflate, circumnavigate, or transcend the roadblocks, and, quite literally, "get on with our lives."

Whether we believe that we have arrived on planet Earth as a random act or if at some higher level we have actually chosen to come to this earthly existence (and I believe we do), we did not appear on the scene spiritually naked. The operating instructions were clearly written in a language that the heart understands and strives to articulate through our inner resources, the muscles of the soul. What are these spiritual muscles that reside in the heart of each person? A short list might include humor, creativity, optimism, courage, willpower, patience, acceptance, forgiveness, intuition, compassion, curiosity, humility, faith, and love, to name a few.

Muscles of the soul are those intangible assets that we use to help us cope with stress, from the everyday problems we encounter to the trips to hell and back. In times of stress, no matter how intense, it is these remarkable qualities that either individually or collectively help us to dismantle, remove, circumscribe, or transcend the barriers that befall our steps on the path of life. These inner resources comprise the sinews of our spiritual muscles, and they are within each of us.

We don't need to meet catastrophe head-on to utilize our muscles of the soul. They can and should be employed every day. Standing in line at the post office or driving in traffic may require unyielding patience. Dealing with an abusive alcoholic parent demands a strong degree of acceptance. Resolving a conflict with a fellow co-worker or roommate may require one to swallow some pride and have a sense of humbleness. Each inner resource is represented by a color in the heart's rainbow. There are no stressors, big or small, that will not give way to the strength of our inner resources. Furthermore, we are never asked to carry a burden that we alone cannot bear.

It has been said that faith can move mountains, but can it melt cancerous tumors? Like most people getting ready to retire, wondering what to do with the next phase of their lives, John's faith ebbed and flowed over the years. At age 64, he was diagnosed with four cancerous tumors in his brain. Surgery wasn't an option and, at his age, neither was radiation. That left chemo-therapy as his last medical option. Partially paralyzed and unable to speak, John looked at his options and decided to take matters into his own hands. Recognizing that the odds of using chemotherapy were awful at best, he called up all his friends in the Denver area and asked them to pray for him. He was specific with his prayer request. He did not want to live forever, just long enough to celebrate his 45th wedding anniversary in August of 1998. He was told by his team of physicians he would not be alive by June. So heal-ing intentions were sent on the wings of prayers—repeatedly. John prayed, too. To the spiritually naive eye, his chances did not look good, but John had faith that could move mountains. And in this case, his faith melted away the tumors, too. A full year later, John is the picture of health.[2]

Considering the magnitude of our inner resources, our spiritual potential is awesome. Yet the degree to which we utilize our inner resources determines the true health of the human spirit. It is this aspect of spiritual health that author Marianne Williamson describes in the following passage, which was later used by South African President Nelson Mandela in his inauguration speech in 1994:

> Our deepest fear is not that we are inadequate. Our deepest fear is that we are powerful beyond measure. It is our light, not our darkness, that most frightens us. We ask ourselves, who am I to be brilliant, gorgeous, talented, and fabulous? Actually who are you not to be? You are a child of God. Your playing small doesn't serve the world. There is nothing enlightened about shrinking so that other people won't feel insecure around you.
>
> We were born to make manifest the glory of God that is within us. It is not just in some of us. It's in everyone. And as we let our own light shine, we unconsciously give others permission to do the same. As we are liberated from our own fear, our presence automatically liberates others.[3]

The following briefly highlights the more common muscles of the soul:

Humor: A mental perception that makes us giggle and laugh. Humor isn't a mood, but it can promote a positive mood of happiness. Between parody and irony, between double entrendres and slapstick humor, there are literally hundreds of things to make our lips curl and faces laugh. Mark Twain once said that humor is mankind's greatest blessing. There are many people who insist that a sense of humor is what truly saved their lives in times of stress.

Forgiveness: The capacity to pardon those who we feel have violated us as well as the capacity to forgive ourselves for our mistakes and foibles. Forgiveness is not letting someone off the hook when we feel violated or victimized. Forgiveness is a gift of compassion we give ourselves so that we can move on. If someone else benefits, great, but forgiveness is not done for that someone else. It is done for ourselves.

Curiosity: In the effort to learn, the soul has a wide streak of curiosity. Some may call this an "inquiring mind," whereas others call it "information seeking." Either way, seeking options, answers, and ideas to learn makes life's journey more interesting.

Persistence: A persistent person is someone who doesn't take "no" for an answer until he or she has exhausted every conceivable option. There are variations on this theme. Some people stretch the meaning of persistence to encompass aggressive, in-your-face tactics. The spiritual approach is one of being pleasantly persistent (not aggressive), like flowing water that ever so slowly softens the hardest rock.

Courage: The word *courage* comes to the English language via two French words meaning "big heart." Courage often brings to mind the idea of bravery, and this is certainly a hallmark of courage. Perhaps courage can be thought of as the opposite of fear. It is courage that allows one to go forward, whereas fear holds one back. Courage is a brave heart.

Patience: Patience is the ability to wait and wait and wait till some sign is acknowledged that it is time to move on. Just as there is strength in motion, there is power in stillness. The Western culture is big on immediate gratification, the antithesis of patience. Impatience often leads to intolerance and anger. Patience quells an angry heart.

Optimism: Optimism is an inherent quality of being positive. This is not to say that every stressor is meant to be a Pollyanna moment. Rather, it is seeing the best in a bad situation. A great definition of an optimist is someone who looks at a pessimist and sees hope.

Faith: Faith is one part optimism, one part love, and two parts mystery. Faith is more than a belief that things will work out okay; it is an innate certainty that all will end well. Faith is an inherent knowing that we are part of a much bigger whole and that the whole has a loving, divine nature to it.

Intuition: This muscle of the soul may not help you win lottery tickets, but it is useful in sensing good from bad, right from wrong, and up from down. Research delving into the lateralization of the left- and right-brain hemispheres suggests that intuition is a right-brain function. Intuition is an inherent knowing about something before the ego jumps in to confuse things. Premonitions, sudden insights, intuitive thoughts, inspiration, and pure enlightenment are examples of how this level of consciousness surfaces in everyday use.

Compassion: To love without reciprocation, to care for someone or something without recognition or reward, this is compassion. Compassion is the ability to feel and express love when fear is an easier choice. Mother Teresa was compassion personified. You don't have to be a saint to feel compassion. Love is the fabric of our souls.

Integrity: When you meet someone of integrity, the first thought that comes to mind is honesty. Although this is certainly the cornerstone of integrity, there is more to it. Integrity is honesty over time. It is a code of conduct with a pledge to the highest ideals in the lowest of times. Integrity literally means the integration of many muscles of the soul.

Humbleness: The ego begs to go first. The soul is content going last. Humbleness is a trait that is called upon when we are reminded to serve others. Humbleness is manifested in acts of politeness, yet it never undermines self-esteem. Humbleness is based on the Golden Rule, by which you treat others as you would have them treat you. In a fast-paced world where rudeness prevails, acts of humbleness are greatly appreciated.

Creativity: Creativity is two parts imagination, one part organization, one part inspiration, and one part perspiration. Creativity is not a right-brain function; it is an inner resource that requires both hemispheres of the brain. Creativity starts with imagination and then makes the ideas happen. Creativity is the synthesis of imagination and ingenuity.

Unconditional Love: To extend love and compassion from your heart without conditions or expectations is the hallmark of this muscle of the soul. Some say that humans are not capable of unconditional love, but just ask any mother of a newborn baby and you will learn quite quickly that indeed we possess this attribute. Unconditional love is egoless.

I have noticed repeatedly in talking to these everyday heroes that rarely do they tend to use just one "muscle" in the face of stress. More often than not, they combine several attributes in an allied force to deal with whatever challenge they find in front of them.

Spiritual Potential and Spiritual Health

I T IS A GIVEN THAT we all have what it takes to get through any situation— if we apply ourselves. Interviews with prisoners of war and survivors of devastating earthquakes, terminal diseases, category-five tornadoes, as well as several manmade disasters attest to this fact, giving credence to the saying that "legends are comprised of ordinary people performing extraordinary tasks."

Assuming that we have each come to planet Earth equipped with a set of these spiritual tools, these muscles of the soul, one can also assume that we each hold the potential not only to survive but also to thrive in any situation and come through any hellacious circumstance gracefully. I call this promise *spiritual potential*, and it's a potential we all possess. Everyone has the inherent qualities. The overriding question is, do we make regular use of them?

Spiritual health is a phrase I use to describe the cultivation and utilization of these spiritual attributes, these divine birthrights within each of us: calling on the power of faith when every conceivable option is exhausted; employing a sense of humor when feelings of anger persist longer than a few moments; using a sense of intuition when a decision is needed with less than adequate information; or drawing upon courage of the heart to diplomatically confront fear head on. We are called upon regularly to exercise our spiritual muscles. Each time we do, they increase in strength. So how is your spiritual health?

As more and more people come forward and share their life experiences, new light is being shed on the connection between spiritual well-being and physical well-being (**Figure 5.1**). For example, Joanne is a physician with severe back pain. She connects this to unresolved anger from an event years ago. A gracious act of forgiveness absolved the pain, allowing her to cancel her back surgery. Likewise, Anne can positively link her breast cancer to an unresolved relationship. Phil's migraine headaches were unbearable, and he knew the medications were merely masking the symptoms. Some profound soul-searching revealed a deep-seated anger with his father. As he worked to resolve this relationship, the migraines disappeared. Once again, Descartes was wrong—the human spirit is undoubtedly linked to physical health.

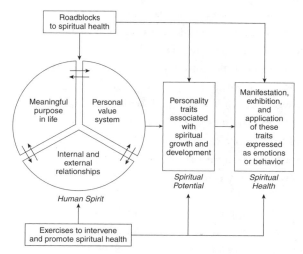

FIGURE 5.1 An integrative model of spiritual well-being that depicts spiritual potential and spiritual health as parts of spiritual well-being. © 1997, Inspiration Unlimited. Reprinted with permission.

Rainbows and the Yellow Brick Road

RAINBOWS REPRESENT AN ARCHETYPAL symbol of faith. L. Frank Baum, the author of *The Wizard of Oz*, no doubt knew this when he penned this story nearly a century ago. Since the release of the movie in 1939, the story of *The Wizard of Oz*, like so many other fables, has captured the hearts of millions of people throughout the years because it speaks to the essence of the spiritual journey and the human heart. It has been said that Baum's work had political overtones; however, I would like to share a far different perspective. My understanding became even clearer when I learned of Baum's interest in human spirituality and his association with mystic Helena Blavatsky, founder of the theosophy movement.[4] Here are some of my reflections on the ageless wisdom of this story as a spiritual metaphor of life, which nicely parallels the contents of this chapter.

Dorothy is not a happy camper! Frustrated with some of life's problems, she decides to run away from home (avoidance) with Toto (her soul). In a strange sequence of events, she winds up in a bizarre, yet wonderful land. Once she's there, however, all she wants to do is go home (home to the source, the Garden of Eden). From a black-and-white world (the conscious mind) to one filled with color (the unconscious mind), she is told, "follow the yellow brick road" (follow the spiritual path!). On her way, she meets three companions who represent very weak muscles of the soul: the Scarecrow represents intuition, which has become more like buffoonery; the Tin Man represents compassion, which is almost dried up; and the Lion represents courage, which has become more like cowardice. Weak as they are, they learn to stand strong to help Dorothy against the Wicked Witch of the West (fear, a roadblock personified). Dorothy overcomes fear through an act of compassion, wanting to save the Scarecrow from becoming toast—Dorothy throws water on the witch's burning cape, and the Wicked Witch (an illusion of sorts) melts and disappears. To her credit, actress Margaret Hamilton refused to revive the role of the Wicked Witch, forfeiting what she estimated to be millions of dollars in salary, because she wanted every child who saw the movie to know the Wicked Witch was *never* coming back. With the Emerald City practically in sight, the crew soon encounters fields and fields of poppies (a distraction with overtones of addiction) and falls asleep on the spiritual path. With some intervention from Glinda, the good witch (a divine presence), they are back on the path and off to see the Wizard—to get Dorothy home. When she misses the Kansas-bound hot air balloon ride, Glinda reminds Dorothy that with the possession of the ruby red slippers, she had the means to return home the whole time anyway (the Kingdom of God is within you). And with the click of her heels, she does, but not without learning and sharing a lesson or two about love upon her return.

Seasons of the Soul

IF YOU WERE TO EXPLORE the spiritual traditions and converse with the sages, masters, and mystics—the wisdom keepers of all cultures and countries over the millennia of human existence—you would come to learn there is no one curriculum for spiritual growth. Nor is there a designated series of sacred rituals for spiritual evolution. In fact, the paths of human spirituality are as varied as the people on them. In searching the wisdom of the ages you will find four unique processes, like the seasons of the earth, that continually nurture the health of the human spirit.

These life passages go by many names, but I refer to them as the *seasons of the soul*. They include (1) *centering*—a time of solitude to quiet the mind, be still, lower the ego walls, and tune into the voice of the higher self; (2) *emptying*—the process immediately following the centering process to cleanse, detach, and let go of old thoughts, perceptions, attitudes, and beliefs that occupy or obstruct one's attention, thus becoming a roadblock to one's highest human potential; (3) *grounding*—a time following the emptying process in which to access and cultivate one's powers of intuition, imagination, and intellect; and, finally, (4) *connecting*—a period dedicated to responsibly sharing the insights, creative expressions, and compassion gained in the grounding process with all members of our collective community so that we may enrich all lives and raise consciousness for all of humanity.

In this way, the seasons of the soul offer us the unique opportunity to examine the landscape of the human journey, the terrain we commonly call the spiritual path. In turn, these seasons offer insight into two of the most important questions we will ever ask and seek answers to: "Who am I?" and "Why am I here?"

Although the timing of these passages varies, it appears that the cycle of the seasons—from centering, to emptying, to grounding, to connecting—follows a rhythmical order. It is a natural flow in the evolutionary process of soul growth. For just as we would not see the full moon reverse to first quarter, nor midnight precede sunset, likewise it is impossible to become grounded in intuitive wisdom before there is receptivity to this wisdom—made available by the emptying process of the soul. But the comparison between the soul's growth process and the phases of the moon stops there. The human agenda varies so greatly, from day to day and from person to person, that the length of time spent in each phase will certainly contrast, as will the rate differ, when we repeat the cycle from day to day and week to month. Moreover, it is not uncommon to see the soul growth process in concurrent seasons, emptying with one experience while in the connecting phase of another. Admittedly, the intensity and duration of each soul season clearly depend on the experiences we encounter, our level of soul maturation, and how much we desire to make progress.

Sages from all corners of the globe share an ageless wisdom that describes four aspects of the human condition, four components that collectively comprise the whole: mind, body, spirit, and emotions. Elisabeth Kübler-Ross explained that of these four components, the spiritual dimension, or, more specifically, where the soul evolves, is the most challenging one of human existence. From a physical perspective, health challenges are very tangible and, whether we like it or not, we can see obvious changes in our body as we age. Likewise, we can appreciate the repeated challenge of intellectual stimulation and the maturation of our mental processes over the life span, particularly from the years in high school through college and beyond. Our emotional maturity—that is, our ability to feel and express the entire range of human emotions—may occasionally be stifled throughout the life cycle, but it is seldom compromised. Nevertheless, it is the soul's growth process (our evolution of higher consciousness—the realization of the divine nature of our inner self) in the midst of the journey that is the least understood and the most challenging. Yet, ask anyone who has been through this cycle of seasons a few times, and they will tell you that the spiritual domain is by far the most rewarding. If you have read the book *Eat, Pray, Love* by Elizabeth Gilbert (or seen the movie starring Julia Roberts), you may recognize that her journey, like so many personal sojourns that Joseph Campbell describes as the Hero's Journey, follows this seasonal template (*eat*, centering; *pray*, emptying; *love*, grounding; and the entire book was the sharing of her story, connecting).[5]

These four processes, like the planetary seasons they represent—centering (autumn), emptying (winter), grounding (spring), and connecting (summer)—are equally subtle and dynamic, challenging and uplifting (**Figure 5.2**). All provide a sense of balance to the soul's growth process. If you take a moment to revisit the three pillars of spiritual well-being—relationships, values, and a meaningful purpose in life—you will see that these aspects are interwoven through the passage of each season. Let's take a closer look at each one.

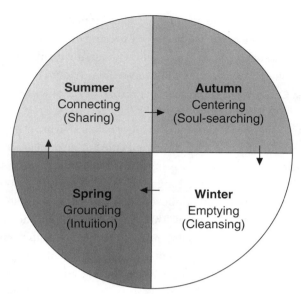

FIGURE 5.2 There are four seasons of the soul, which nicely correspond to the earth's seasons. The seasons of the soul also progress in a cyclical pattern.

The Centering Process

The **centering process** is a time where we sit still and quiet the mind. The word *center* means "to enter the heart." In doing so, we explore the vast landscape of the soul. During the centering process, one sits still and initiates what is known the world over as the soul-searching process. It begins by simply sitting calmly in quiet contemplation. Like the shorter days of autumn that gently usher us indoors at an earlier hour, the centering process invites us to tune into our inner self by unplugging from the external world. For just as there is a world to discover through our five senses, there is a world, if not a whole universe, to explore within the realms of the human mind.

You might have noticed that in the Western culture, people are not encouraged to be still and to initiate the soul-searching process. Rather, all senses are directed outward to gather information—continually. Now, more than ever, we live in a world where we are constantly bombarded with sensory stimulation. The end result is sensory overload and burnout, an all-too-common product of American culture. In truth, centering is as natural and necessary as eating and sleeping. To seek balance in life—balance of mind, body, spirit, and emotions—one must dedicate time to shut off external stimulation to focus on internal wisdom. Simply stated, it's clear that we need to strike a balance between exposing ourselves to the richness of external stimuli and the absence of it by habitually turning our attention inward. Only then can we access the deep-seated wisdom of the higher self. Psychologist Carl Jung believed that this vast resource of wisdom extends to the depths of our unconscious mind.

To center ourselves is a means to achieve balance, to bring equity back to the soul. We do this by making a concerted effort to reconnect with that part of our consciousness we know as the higher self, universal consciousness, the Divine Essence, or God (the Kingdom within). Chinese philosopher Lao Tzu wrote these words in his philosophical teachings of Taoism: "Be still and discover your center of peace. Through nature, the ten thousand things move along, but each returns to its source. Returning to center is peace. Find Tao by returning to source."[5] Spiritual teacher Paramahansa Yogananda gave the same message in these words: "Calm the mind, that without distortion, it may mirror Omnipresence."[6] From Psalms (46:10) comes the wisdom: "Be still, and know that I am God."[7]

When comparing the seasons of the soul, the centering process may appear to be short in duration. Although this step is small, it is mighty, because the real work of the soul cannot begin until this season starts.

The Emptying Process

Once the mind is quiet, it is time to start cleaning your house of nonessentials, and that is what the **emptying process** is all about. This process goes by many names (e.g., cleansing, emptying, detaching, letting go, and releasing), all of which mean the same thing. These nonessentials (sometimes referred to as "baggage") may be recognized as thoughts, perceptions, beliefs, attitudes, memories, and feelings that, once useful, no longer serve the soul's growth process. In fact, they hold it back. In theory, the emptying process occurs as a way to make room for new insights, ideas, intuitive thoughts, or enlightenment, yet these can only come when there is room for them—space we are typically reluctant to make. Metaphorically speaking, the emptying process is a time to plow the fields so that new crops can be planted and harvested. To use another metaphor, the emptying process is a time to weed the "garden of the soul." The wisdom of the Tao also suggests to empty oneself. To quote Lao Tzu: "Close your mouth, shut your doors and live close to the Tao. Open your mouth, be busy all day and live in confusion."[8]

By and large, humans are still hunters and gatherers. But today, most of what we hunt and gather is information. As a result, the mind gets overloaded. And every bit of information has an emotion attached to it. When you combine external sensations with the thoughts generated in the mind itself, coupled with more emotions, sensory overload becomes a major issue to be reckoned with. This is not a new phenomenon, and the solution is not new either. Ancient Chinese, Greeks, Mayans, and Essenes all adopted the emptying process in their cultures.

The sensation of emptiness is neither appealing nor desired in the American culture. In fact, in our consumer society we are constantly barraged with media messages to buy, consume, and fill up rather than to empty, cleanse, and eliminate those polluting aspects of our lives. Thus, the emptying process understandably brings up feelings of fear, trepidation, and avoidance (notice the word *avoidance* contains the word *void*). Very soon, fear can eclipse faith, resulting in what can best be described as spiritual stagnation.

The body empties several times a day, the mind empties hourly, if not more often, with thoughts slipping below the radar of the conscious mind. Catharsis (e.g., laughing, crying, etc.) is how emotional emptying takes place. The spirit needs to cleanse as well. The way it does this is by letting go of thoughts, attitudes, and perceptions that at one time might have been useful but now no longer serve a purpose. These also include frustrations, fears, grudges, and so on that actually hold us back—choking the spirit, so to speak. As a rule, people do not like to disengage from these thoughts and feelings because there is a sense of security with them—the ego's illusion of power. However, when we hang on too long, the end result is a lethal buildup of toxins or, as Max Erhmann wrote in his now famous essay *Desiderata*, "a vexation of the spirit."[9]

Perhaps the emptying process can best be compared to a dark hole or void. When we come to the edge of the void, we stop in our tracks, fearful of what might happen when we enter. Many people teeter on the edge, biting their fingernails. But go we must into the void to cleanse, detach, and let go of those things that hold us back. On first appearance, the void may appear to be a dark hole, but a more apt description is the womb of creation or the realm of possibilities.

Sometimes people refuse to take that first step for fear of falling into a black hole and never being seen again. They hesitate and freeze on the precipice. Eventually, they get a nudge, sometimes a kick in the butt, to continue moving. This nudge may come from a number of sources, such as the end of a relationship, the loss of a job, the death of a close friend. Through each experience of loss we are asked to release and let go. Ageless wisdom reminds us of the same message with the adage, "Be in this world, but not of it."

Of the four seasons of the soul, it is the emptying process that is the most painful and difficult to go through. The emptying process, which parallels the winter season, goes by several names, most notably the dark night of the soul and the winter of discontent. It is the one season that people tend to get stuck in. But just like the Earth's seasons, winter never lasts forever, and with night comes the promise of a new day. The emptying process holds the promise that whatever is released will always, without exception, be replaced by something of equal or greater importance. Yet no matter how many times we rotate through the emptying process, we always seem to forget this part the next time around. And we find ourselves again perched at the precipice of the void—timid, stubborn, and reluctant to take that next step. At these times, we must remember that nature, of which we are a part, provides us with many wonderful examples of our growth and balance on the human path: winter is always followed by spring, the new moon is always followed by a full moon, and darkness is always followed by light.

The following story illustrates this concept of emptiness:

> An American professor on sabbatical took a trip to the Himalayas to research a new book. Inquiries he made regarding mystical consciousness in the town of Katmandu led him to venture up a mountain path in search of a wise old yogi. After days of travel, he happened upon a hut where a man resided matching the description given to him. Once invited in for tea, the professor graciously sat down, patiently held a tea cup, and awaited the chance to converse with the yogi. As the tea was poured, the professor noted the cup was soon full, only to see the yogi keep pouring, next filling the saucer, and then spilling tea on to the floor. In as polite a way as possible, the professor insisted the yogi stop. The yogi replied: "Your mind is like this tea cup. You came to me searching for insights, yet your mind, like this tea cup, is quite full. It is so full of concepts and beliefs that there is no room for new wisdom."[10]

Lessons in detachment don't come easy. The first day Jennifer met Sam she knew she was going to marry him. Within the year they were making wedding plans. Later, with two kids, a big house, and vacations on the Cape every summer, Jennifer said that their first ten years together were heaven. But things began to crumble when Sam was downsized out of his job. Perhaps it was a midlife crisis, but Sam did not seem as interested in Jennifer or the kids for the next few months. Then came the shocking news that Sam wanted out of the marriage. There wasn't another woman, he insisted. He just needed to find out who he was. As it turns out, there was another woman in the wings. Jennifer was heartbroken. This was not how it was supposed to be. Sam moved out. Months later, Jennifer ended up selling the house and getting an apartment with the kids. The transition was rough. She thought it was the worst thing to ever happen in her life. But after a year of grieving, she realized it had become the best thing to have ever happened to her.

You don't have to quit school, divorce your spouse, or crash your car to initiate the emptying process. It can be initiated quite simply through your will and desire to meditate, keep a journal, exercise, fast, take in moments of silence, or partake of any quality time dedicated to clearing the mind. In fact, there are many ways to engage in the emptying process, each one offering the promise to cleanse the mind. For sure, the emptying process may seem like a dark void, but true to the cliché of the tunnel, there is light at the end, not a train light either, but a glorious light.

The Grounding Process

If the emptying process is like plowing the field, then the grounding process is like planting and harvesting a new crop. In this case, it's reaping new ideas, insights, and intuitive thoughts to help you get from point A to point B on the next leg of your human journey. The **grounding process** is a time of revelation and resolution with regard to relationships, values (and value conflicts), and, perhaps most important, the discovery of a meaningful purpose in your life. Every culture since the dawn of humanity has had an accepted occasion to seek the counsel of one's higher self, whether it be moments of solitude, periods of seclusion, or an organized retreat. In a literal sense, being grounded means to be connected to the Earth and to feel that you are indeed a part of nature. In a figurative sense, grounding is the ability to feel comfortable in your surroundings, in your own environment.

Years ago, a student shared with me a Chinese proverb that speaks to the nature of finding balance in one's life: "Stand like mountain, flow like water." In the Taoist philosophy, when two opposites are joined together in thought, they form a whole. To "stand like mountain" is a profound, yet simple, reminder to be grounded—to be deeply rooted in our own being. Mountains serve as a symbol of strength, stability, and resilience. We, too, become strong, stable, and resilient to the winds of change that stressors bring to our lives when we listen to the deep-seated wisdom of the soul. The image of mountains towering above the clouds conveys to many the mirror image of their own divine consciousness. For just as the mountain rises above the clouds, so, too, it connects to the very core of the Earth. To be grounded is an expression of security. To hear the voice of God, to receive a sign, a vision, a long-awaited insight, an epiphany, or a revelation reconnects us to that part of our divine essence that provides a sense of security, a sense of stability on the path of the human journey. But the connection doesn't stop there! Just as the vision quest is not complete until one has returned to the village to share the insights and wonders gleaned from that experience, so, too, is the grounding process just one more step in the quest to become whole.

Another Chinese proverb also speaks to the nature of grounding: "When the pupil is ready, the teacher will come." The implicit understanding is that we are both the pupil and the teacher. Only when the walls of the ego are lowered are we the most receptive to the divine whispers, insights, creative ideas, intuitive thoughts, and ageless wisdom that at some level we solicit and require for all situations we encounter.

Perhaps nowhere is the idea of the grounding process more evident than in the ritual of the American Indian culture known as the *vision quest*. In this rite of passage, a person departs from his or her community and spends a number of days in the wilderness—alone. The vision quest begins with an intense period of centering, a turning within to address the soul. Next comes the emptying process during which no food is eaten and little clothing is worn in order to reinforce detachment. The vision quest is an intense period of searching the corridors of the mind to connect with the divine source and to come to an understanding of the meaning of life, asking two basic questions: "Who am I?" and "Why am I here?" During this time, answers to these questions come, perhaps not always immediately, but in time a keen inner ear, an insight, or an intuitive thought process leads the way out of metaphorical darkness into the light of life. Listening at this level requires a unique receptivity to hear, to learn, to open up. But most important, we should not be afraid of the wisdom we might encounter through our thoughts, visions, or sensations.

You don't have to strip naked and wander through the desert for days to receive a vision. The entrance to universal consciousness can be accessed just about anywhere, including in the privacy of your own home. The grounding process can occur in meditation, through dreams, or in moments of synchronicity—those wonderful coincidences that leave you scratching your head in amazement. To quote Bernie Siegel, M.D., author of *Love, Medicine and Miracles*, "Coincidences are merely God's way of remaining anonymous."[11] You can seek insights on the spiritual path, but not order them on demand. We must be ready with an open heart and mind. Remember, just as you cannot push water uphill, you cannot demand enlightenment. Discipline and patience are essential requirements for the grounding process.

Artists, poets, authors, and songwriters will be the first to tell you that when the walls of the ego are lowered the most amazing thoughts will surface. And they happen during the most unpredictable times—while washing dishes, taking a shower, walking the dog, or lying awake late at night. One must constantly be receptive. Receptivity to divine insight is groomed not just through stillness of your mind, but also through the cultivation and refinement of your thoughts, perceptions, and attitudes. And although the flow of consciousness cannot be forced, it can be enticed. Relaxation is the key!

We climb the metaphorical mountain to gain a better view of the world. To glean an insight, to peek into the heavens and to see the light, is akin to kissing the face of God. But the journey never ends on the top of a mountain. Eventually we must descend from the peak, all the while savoring the taste of exhilaration.

The Connecting Process

When we come down off the mountain, when we emerge from the solitude of the soul, glowing with inspiration, we have an obligation to share that which we have learned, encountered, or experienced with friends, family, colleagues, and peers. Balance is derived from both receiving and giving. This is the expectation of the universe. Greed is not a spiritual value.

Call to mind those activities you do in the summer: barbecues, picnics, family reunions. The summer is a time of gathering and celebration. This is what the connecting process is all about: sharing and caring. And this is what most people think about when they speak of human spirituality—the "Disney World" effect—sharing exhilarating moments of euphoric joy and happiness with those you love.

The **connecting process** is all about relationships: cultivating, nurturing, and sustaining them. American Indian culture uses the expression "All life is relationship." Our interactions with family, friends, colleagues, acquaintances, and even strangers are a small fraction of the elaborate network of universal life. We are continually in relationship with everything and everybody, even when we are unaware of this profound association (not just people, but the earth, water, air, trees, and animals as well). Just as our interdependence on all humanity cannot be denied, neither can our inherent relationship to the natural world be ignored. The spirit of life flows freely through all things. Consider the poignant words of Chief Seattle: "All things connect. Man did not weave the web of life, he is merely a strand in it. Whatever he does to the web, he does to himself." All things are connected. To the inexperienced eye, there may appear to be separation and distance, but at the most profound level of understanding the wisdom of the soul knows differently—all is one. To quote the famous words of John Donne: "No man is an island entire of itself. Each is a piece of the continent of the main."[12] We must do our best to continually nurture the bonds of connectivity, rather than let them atrophy with fear, apathy, or indifference. Connectedness through our divinity holds the promise of our human potential.

The interrelatedness of life is just one of a handful of simple truths known among all the world's indigenous cultures. The African proverb, "It takes a whole village to raise a child," speaks to the heart of the connection process. Even the radical Apostle Paul recognized this and wrote that we are cells in the body of Christ. The wisdom of Taoism also emphasizes the interconnectedness of life. Nothing is separate.

Based on the ancient writings of Chinese philosopher Lao Tzu, the idea of connectedness is often referred to as the *principle of oneness:* "The Taoist embraces the One and lives in peace by its pattern."[13] The principle of oneness reveals that we are an integral part of the holographic whole, connected through a dynamic network of universal energy. Connectedness means to be one with or a part of nature, not above or apart from it. This Taoist perspective encourages us to transcend our thoughts and perceptions, which are so strongly based on the foundation of dualism and polarized thinking (e.g., mind vs. body, science vs. spirituality) and become one with God's universe. From a Taoist perspective, when we see ourselves as separate from the whole, we not only distance ourselves from nature, we isolate ourselves from other people as well. In turn, this distance weakens our spiritual health and suffocates our very essence. The nature of the Tao reminds us that just as there is strength in numbers, there is also strength in oneness. What does Taoism have to do with the field of physics? Some might say not much, yet others, such as Fritjof Capra, author of the classic bestsellers *The Tao of Physics* and *The Turning Point*, disagree.[14,15] Another who disagrees is Lynne McTaggart. In her highly acclaimed book, *The Bond*, McTaggart reveals the essence of the connection process, centered on the nexus of spirituality, nature, and science as part of our inherent nature. In her book, McTaggart pools data from renowned researchers to argue that science now supports the idea that everything is actually connected. More important, she argues that we (the human race) need to honor and nurture this connection.[16]

In various cultures around the world, children are raised to believe that they come to this world bearing a special gift. Given the right guidance from family, this gift is nurtured so that when shared, everyone benefits from it. The same idea is woven into the connecting process where our gifts are shared.

As we revolve through the seasons of the soul, the connecting process invites us to reemerge from solitude, isolation, or retreat and return to the fold of humanity. Like Moses who came down the mountain (the second time), we, too, must be willing to share the message, insight, wisdom, and fruits of creativity with all who wish to take part in community. In the spirit of the connecting process, our mission is to build bridges, not walls; to offer our hands in guidance, rather than turn our backs with indifference. In the true sense of connection, what we do for each other helps to uplift the spirits of all people. In reality, the connection between all people already exists, and the only request we are given as we complete the grounding process and move in is to acknowledge, sustain, and honor this connection. Someday we may even discover with great clarity that the web of life reaches well beyond the planet Earth, far into the galactic universe, and, with it, the true importance of connectedness.

⫸ SUMMARY

THE MOUNTAIN IS A UNIVERSAL metaphor of the spiritual journey. However, as on any journey, obstacles and roadblocks must be overcome. With this metaphor in mind, roadblocks (stressors) are thoughts and attitudes often grounded in unresolved fear or anger that impede our journey. As if obstacles are not enough, we can also become distracted and move off the path. Distractions begin as attractions. Ageless wisdom tells us that to get back on the path and keep moving toward the proverbial summit we need to exercise our spiritual muscles: faith, love, humor, optimism, and compassion, among others. Having these muscles of the soul is our spiritual potential; using these spiritual muscles ensures our spiritual health. Finally, as we progress on the spiritual path, we move through various seasons of the soul: the centering, emptying, grounding, and connecting processes, each with its own challenges and rewards.

⫸ TERMS AND CONCEPTS

centering process	muscles of the soul
connecting process	roadblocks on the spiritual path
emptying process	seasons of the soul
grounding process	spiritual health
distractions of the human spirit	spiritual potential

EXERCISE 5.1
ROADBLOCKS ON THE SPIRITUAL PATH

The biggest roadblock to spirituality is ego.

—Ancient proverb

If our experience on the human path is indeed our soul's growth process, then the metaphor of roadblocks on the spiritual path can be used to describe a temporary halt to this evolutionary process. Roadblocks on the human path are not necessarily aspects in our lives that separate us from our divine source or mission—even though it may seem like this at times. Rather, roadblocks are part of the human path. And although initially they may seem to stifle or inhibit our spiritual growth, this only occurs if we give up or give in to them and do nothing. In the words of a Nazi concentration camp survivor, "Giving up is a final solution to a temporary problem."

Roadblocks take many forms, including unresolved anger or fear, a sense of unworthiness, greed, apathy, laziness, excessive judgment, and denial, just to name a few. More often than not, these obstacles manifest symbolically as problems, issues, and concerns (and sometimes people). Although the first thing we may want to do when coming upon a roadblock is to retreat and do an about-face, avoidance only serves to postpone the inevitable. Miles down the road, we will encounter the same obstacles. Roadblocks must be dealt with.

Make a list of what you consider to be some of your major (tangible) obstacles on your human journey (e.g., the boss from hell, the ex-spouse from hell, etc.). Take a moment to identify each with a sentence or two.

1. _____

_____

_____

2. _____

_____

_____

3. _____

_____

_____

4. _____

_____

_____

5. _____

_____

_____

   Next, identify what emotions are associated with each of these roadblocks. What emotions do they elicit, and why do you suppose these emotions surface for you as these obstacles come into view?

1. _____

_____

2. _____

_____

3. _____

_____

4. _____

_____

5. _____

_____

EXERCISE 5.2
DISTRACTIONS ON THE SPIRITUAL PATH

Remember—distractions begin as attractions.

—Anonymous

Distractions can best be described as those things that pull us off the spiritual path. Distractions begin as attractions, but their allure can often cast a spell of slumber to the soul's growth process. And although a respite on the human journey is desirable, even necessary at times, a prolonged distraction will ultimately weaken our spiritual resolve. The human spirit, like energy, must flow, not stagnate.

   The lessons of distractions are quite common in fairy tales. Whether it is the story of Pinocchio or Hansel and Gretel, the warnings against distractions are as plentiful as the distractions themselves. The lessons of distractions are common in the great spiritual teachings as well, where they are often called "temptations." Oftentimes attractions that become distractions have an addictive quality to them.

What happens when we become distracted? Metaphorically speaking, we fall asleep on the human path. Like Dorothy and her friends on the way to Oz who stepped off the yellow brick road to smell the poppies and fell fast asleep, we, too, lose our direction and the vision of our mission. Our energy stagnates. The end result is never promising.

Unlike roadblocks, distractions are not meant to be circumvented, dismantled, or even transcended. Rather, they are meant to be appreciated—perhaps from afar; perhaps enjoyed briefly and then left behind. Fairy tales aside, what are contemporary distractions? Common examples of everyday distractions include social contacts, alcohol, television, and the Internet.

Take a moment to reflect on what might be some distractions in your life. Make a list of your distractions and describe each one in a sentence or two. Once you recognize your distractions, list what steps you can take to wake up and get back on the path.

1. _____
   _____

2. _____
   _____

3. _____
   _____

4. _____
   _____

5. _____
   _____

EXERCISE 5.3
MUSCLES OF THE SOUL

Just as a circle is a universal symbol of wholeness, the butterfly is a symbol of transformation. It can rise above what was once considered a limiting existence. Consider the story of a boy who, upon seeing a young butterfly trying to emerge from its chrysalis, tried to help by pulling apart the paper cocoon that housed the metamorphosis. The boy's mother, who saw what he was about to do, quickly stopped him by explaining that the butterfly strengthens its young wings by pushing through the walls of the cocoon. In doing so, the butterfly's wings become strong enough to fly.

If you were to talk with people who have emerged gracefully from a difficult situation, they would mostly likely tell you that the muscles they used to break through their barrier(s) included patience, humor, forgiveness, optimism, humbleness, creativity, persistence, courage, willpower, and love. Some people call these inner resources. I call them muscles of the soul. These are the muscles we use to dismantle, circumnavigate, and transcend the roadblocks and obstacles in life. Like physical muscles, these muscles will never disappear; however, they will atrophy with disuse. We are given ample opportunity to exercise these muscles, yet not everyone does.

Using the butterfly metaphor, write in the wings those attributes, inner resources, and muscles of the soul that you feel help you get through the tough times with grace and dignity, rather than as a victim (you can refer to this chapter's "Muscles of the Soul" section to help you with this exercise if you wish). If there are traits you wish to include to augment the health of your human spirit, yet you feel are not quite there, write those outside the wings and then draw an arrow into the wings, giving your soul a message that you wish to include (strengthen) these as well. Finally, if you have a box of crayons or pastels, color in your butterfly. Then hang it up on the fridge or bathroom mirror—someplace where you can see it regularly to remind yourself of your spiritual health and your innate ability to transcend life's problems, big and small.

© Sergio Hayashi/ShutterStock, Inc.

EXERCISE 5.4a
SEASONS OF THE SOUL

The Earth has four distinct seasons. As we travel on the human journey, we also travel through seasonal changes. If you were to talk to the shamans, healers, sages, mystics, and wisdom keepers of all times and all ages, you would learn that the human soul indeed has four distinct seasons, very similar in nature to the seasons of the Earth. They go by different names, but the process is universal in both scope and style. These are the seasons of the soul:

- *The centering process* (autumn): A time to go within and focus on the self. It is a time of soul-searching, a time of self-reflection when one quiets the mind to calm the soul.

- *The emptying process* (winter): A time to release, let go, and detach from thoughts, attitudes, perceptions, and beliefs that at one time might have served us, but now only seem to hold us back. For some, this may be the dark night of the soul.

- *The grounding process* (spring): A time to seek and process the answers to life's problems and challenges that come to us as we wait patiently. The grounding process is a time to access our intuition and perhaps attain a feeling of enlightenment to get us on the next segment of our human journey.

- *The connecting process* (summer): A season when we come back to our community and share what we have learned on the leg of our most recent experience. This is a time of celebration! The connecting process is based on the premise of love—nurturing our connections with friends, family, acquaintances, and even strangers who might become friends.

What makes life challenging, if not difficult, at times, is that we are experiencing different seasons simultaneously through different aspects (problems) of our lives. For instance, we may be in the emptying process in one aspect of our lives, while smack in the middle of the connecting process in another. Matters become more complex when a loved one experiencing the same situation is in one season while we are in another.

Take stock of your life right now. Are you in the midst of one particular season at the present time? If so, which one? The emptying process is one season we try to avoid only to remain stuck there way too long. Is this a season that you choose to skip? If so, why? Do you take time to soul-search? Of these four seasons, is there one that seems to hold the most importance overall? If so, which one? How would you describe your connecting process? Using the template in **Exercise 5.4b**, take some time to use the mandala of the seasons of the soul to better understand the coordinates of your life.

EXERCISE 5.4b
YOUR SEASONS OF THE SOUL

Centering, emptying, grounding, and connecting constitute the four seasons of the soul. Now is the time to take stock of your life. Are you in the midst of one particular season? Like the planet Earth, we can have many seasons occurring at the same time. Although these seasons occur in a cycle, it is easy to get stuck in one particular season of the soul. The emptying process is one season most people try to avoid only to remain stuck there the longest. Based on the concepts explained earlier in this chapter, take a moment to identify where you feel you are at this time in your life. Please identify what you normally do in each season to get the most out of it. Is there a season you choose to skip? If so, why? Do you take periodic time to do some quality soul searching? Of these four seasons, is there one that seems to hold the most importance for you? If so, why? How would you describe your connecting process?

The Centering Process (Autumn)

_____

_____

_____

_____

_____

The Emptying Process (Winter)

_____

_____

_____

_____

_____

The Grounding Process (Spring)

_____

_____

_____

_____

_____

The Connecting Process (Summer)

_____

_____

_____

_____

_____

◆ ENDNOTES

1. Meyers, P., *K2.* Broadway Production: New York, 1988.
2. John, P., as shared at Larry Dossey's Presentation at the Boulder Bookstore, Boulder, CO, October 12, 1999.
3. Williamson, M., *A Return to Love.* HarperCollins: New York, 1992.
4. Taylor, E., "Our Roots: The American Visionary Tradition," *Noetic Sciences Review,* Autumn, pp. 6–17, 1993.
5. Gilbert, E., *Eat, Pray, Love.* Penguin Books: New York, 2007.
6. Paramahansa Yogananda, as quoted in *Inner Reflections.* Calendar. Self-Realization Fellowship: Los Angeles, CA, 1995.
7. *The Holy Bible,* Psalms: 46:10.
8. Lao Tzu, as quoted in *The Tao of Inner Peace,* by Diane Dreher. HarperPerennial: New York, 1990.
9. Erhmann, M., *Desiderata.* Robert Bell: Melrose, MA, 1927.
10. As adapted from a story recounted in *A Whack on the Side of the Head* by Roger von Oech. Warner Books: New York, 1983.
11. Siegel, B., *Love, Medicine and Miracles.* Perennial Press: New York, 1989.
12. Donne, J., as quoted in *The Promise of a New Day: A Book of Daily Meditations.* Hazelden Books: New York, 1983.
13. Lao Tzu, as quoted in *The Tao of Inner Peace,* by Diane Dreher. HarperPerennial: New York, 1990.
14. Capra, F. *The Tao of Physics* (5th edition). Shambhala Books: Boston, 2010.
15. Capra, F. *The Turning Point.* Bantam Books: New York, 1984.
16. McTaggart, L. *The Bond.* Free Press: New York, 2011.

◆ ADDITIONAL REFERENCES

Chodron, P., *When Things Fall Apart: Heart Advice for Difficult Times.* Shambhala Press: Boston, 1997.

Cochran, T., and Zaleski, J., *Transformations: Awakening to the Sacred in Ourselves.* Bell Tower Books: New York, 1995.

Epstein, M., *Going to Pieces Without Falling Apart: A Buddhist Perspective on Wholeness.* Broadway Books: New York, 1998.

Seaward, B. L., *Stand Like Mountain, Flow Like Water: Reflections on Stress and Human Spirituality.* Health Communications: Deerfield Beach, FL, 2007.

Seaward, B. L., *Quiet Mind, Fearless Heart.* John Wiley and Sons: New York, 2005.

Young-Sowers, M., *Spiritual Crisis.* Stillpoint Press: Walpole, NH, 1993.

CHAPTER **6**

Mind–Body–Spirit Healing

The role of the human spirit is integral to the healing process. It cannot and should not be ignored.

—Rachel Naomi Remen, M.D.

CINDY WAS DIAGNOSED WITH LUPUS at the age of 17. Lupus, an inflammatory autoimmune disease, causes joint pain, skin rashes, organ dysfunction, fatigue, and problems with the blood. It can be fatal. To date, there is no cure, and the treatment is often not very effective. The disease requires regular clinical monitoring. Although the cause of the disease is believed to be organic in nature, it's no secret that stress is a primary factor associated with lupus. Cindy can attest to this as well. I met Cindy at a workshop in Columbus, Ohio, in the fall of 1999. It was after concluding a journal exercise on the topic of forgiveness that Cindy approached me and shared her personal story. She said:

> I can speak firsthand on the topic of the healing power of the human spirit. I was diagnosed with lupus several years ago. I went through the whole mind game of feeling sorry for myself. It wasn't until a few months ago that I made the connection to my disease and a grudge I was harboring against someone whom I felt had really violated me years previously. On top of that, I realized that I had become very judgmental. But as I looked closer at those people I was criticizing, I realized that I was projecting my anger, my fear, and my resentment onto the faces of those people whom I felt uncomfortable around.

Cindy paused for a moment and smiled. "I am happy to tell you that since I have worked through my anger and come to a place of forgiveness, my lupus is under control. In fact," she added with a huge smile, "I just had some clinical tests done and the numbers are way down." In 2011, I made a follow-up phone call to Cindy to see how she was doing. Her voice was beaming over the phone. "In a word, excellent," she said."[1]

On September 1, 1994, Jim was diagnosed with oat-cell cancer, one of the deadliest forms of cancer. Test results revealed two large tumors in his chest; one was wrapped around his vena cava, disrupting the flow of blood back to his heart. His team of physicians gave him 2 weeks with no treatment and at most 4 months with radiation and chemotherapy. "Basically, they told me I wouldn't see Christmas," he said. Although Jim was scheduled for the usual routine of chemotherapy, the prognosis did not look good. Knowing the odds were against him, Jim decided to call in the reinforcements. He contacted Mary Linda, a therapist who was trained in mind–body–spirit healing who taught him meditation, visualization, and guided mental imagery. She also encouraged him to explore all possible options of healing, the most important being the power of faith. And that he did! He quit working for seven months, and, as he said, "I became the captain of my ship."

Jim's curiosity led him to several modalities of healing, including a trip to Tijuana, Mexico, where he stayed at a medical facility for 4 weeks to boost his immune system. His healing regime included diet supplements and herbs, but he takes delight in describing his spiritual awakening as well. When he returned to the Arthur James Cancer Center in Columbus, Ohio, one tumor had completely disappeared and the other, originally the size of a baseball, was now the size of a walnut. Six years later, Jim is the picture of health.

"I get four to five phone calls a week from people with cancer. Most are looking for the magical silver bullet. It wasn't Mexico, or the herbs, or the chemo that did it," he explains. "It was my reconnection to spirituality that did it. Although it was a lot of work, so many positive things have come out of that darkness, I wouldn't have traded this growth experience for anything!" In the fall of 2011, as with Cindy, I made a phone call to Jim to say hello and check in with him. We talked for several minutes about his career, his wife, and his son's summer wedding before I approached the subject of his health. "Couldn't be better," he said.[2]

Lou Gehrig's disease (amyotrophic lateral sclerosis, ALS) is a degenerative disease of the nervous system. Basically, it turns the body to Jell-O. ALS is a crippling disease that steals a person's life away. Like several other chronic diseases, no treatment or cure is available. Evy was diagnosed with ALS at the age of 29. She was given 6 months to live. She found it kind of ironic that for so many years she had wished she was thin, and now she was, but for all the wrong reasons. She had criticized her body for so long, and now it was seeking revenge in a cruel way. One day, sitting in her wheelchair in front of a mirror, she pondered the concept of unconditional love. Pure acceptance, no conditions. That's what she decided to strive for. Evy made a conscious decision that day to open her heart and practice unconditional love, to herself and everyone else she came in contact with. Stricken with ALS, she devoted the rest of her life, however long that might be, to work towards this goal.

Looking in the mirror every day, she told herself that she loved herself. She told herself this, and over several weeks the message got through to her unconscious. And remarkably, as it did, her body began to stop deteriorating. Today, Evy is one of sixteen people noted to have ALS go into remission. Her doctors call it a miracle, but Evy knows what it took to get there. Evy's miracle is based on a foundation of unconditional love.[3]

These are just three of thousands of stories about **mind–body–spirit healing**. The average person finds these stories quite touching. Conversely, the average physician finds these stories wonderful but at the same time disturbing, perhaps even annoying, because these episodes go against everything taught in medical school. There is an expression among doctors that goes like this: if a physician likes the patient's outcome from a disease or illness, he or she calls it a "case history" and sometimes writes it up in a medical journal. If he or she doesn't like or understand it, he or she calls it "an anomaly." Anomalies—those unexplained results that defy the "body as a machine" mentality—also go by other names in the medical profession, the most common being "the ghost in the machine."

The Ghost in the Machine

DESPITE THEIR DENIAL OF THE role of the human spirit in the healing process over the years, Western researchers and physicians do acknowledge this factor, but rather than calling it *spirit* they refer to it as a *ghost*. To be specific, the phrase used in hospital corridors and backroom conference conversations is **the ghost in the machine**.

Because the mechanistic paradigm of health (the body is a machine) has been taught in Western medical schools since the time of Descartes (and still is!), aspects of health and disease that don't fit nicely into this paradigm leave doctors, nurses, and technicians scratching their heads, dumbfounded.

In the mechanistic model of health, consciousness (our ability to think, imagine, reason, dream, etc.) is explained to be the consequence of neuropeptides released from various cells in the brain. Conversely, the holistic model of health suggests that consciousness is a type of energy that uses the brain as its primary organ of choice to do its work. However, consciousness has been rather difficult to quantify scientifically (as has been discussed elsewhere, in Western-style science, that which is immeasurable with the reductionistic/scientific method doesn't really exist). This is often referred to as "thinking inside the box." So when something outside the box (*spirit*) affects something inside the box (*body*), various theories are proposed to explain it. When no logical explanation becomes plausible, then these phenomena fall into the classification of the *ghost in the machine*. Consider the following examples:

Hypnosis: In a relaxed state, the mind becomes receptive to both internal and external directives. As if the walls of the ego are temporarily lowered, thoughts are allowed into the subconscious that might otherwise never enter. Medical researchers who insist that the mind is a result of brain chemistry have no clue as to the dynamics of hypnosis. But research shows that hypnosis (a suggestion to the unconscious mind to heal) is as effective as surgery in treating problems such as warts.[4]

Multiple personality disorder: Why would a person be allergic to orange juice or roses in one personality to the point of anaphylactic shock but show no signs of discomfort in another personality?[5] In at least four documented cases, the color of the patient's iris changed from blue to brown with the respective personalities.[6]

Placebos and nocebos: Why do some people who get sugar water or a sugar pill when they think they are getting a proven medication get well? Why do some people who get sugar water rather than chemotherapy lose their hair? While some placebos have a cure rate of 30%, some are as high as 75%. *Nocebo* is a name given to the situation in which a person gets a proven medication but is told by a doubtful physician that it is just a placebo. With doubtful perceptions of the patient intact, no beneficial results are observed. Is faith (or lack thereof) the real power of placebos? How does one measure faith? The American Medical Association hasn't tried, but the Food and Drug Administration requires that any new drug must have an efficacy rate greater than 30%—the demarcation of the placebo effect or faith healing.[7]

Spontaneous healings: Why do some people who use no medical intervention (radiation, chemotherapy) have their tumors go away, in some cases within days? Patients say they prayed, or forgave someone, or had a change of heart about something. The Institute of Noetic Sciences has collected over several thousand case histories of spontaneous remission. This suggests that they are more than a quirk of nature, yet the medical establishment still regards spontaneous remissions as anomalies. Some even deny them altogether, insisting the patient was misdiagnosed.[8,9]

Distant healings: As if spontaneous healings were hard enough to explain, how does one explain a healing that occurs because someone miles away (sometimes across the globe) sends a healing prayer, intention, or energy and the patient gets better? This evidence was first reported in the now-famous Byrd cardiac-rehab study,[10] but it has been replicated by various researchers from several institutions to the astonishment of many, as reported by Larry Dossey in his book *Healing Word*[11] as well as several other researchers investigating the dynamic relationship between consciousness and healing.[12,13]

Herbert Benson, renowned for Americanizing the concept of Transcendental Meditation (TM), proposes in his newest book, *The Relaxation Revolution*, that consciousness may be able to change (turn on or off) various genes in the DNA strand to promote health and reverse a host of disease processes.[14]

Energy medicine: Not just faith healing, but Qi Gong, bioenergy, therapeutic touch, or Reiki is used on the patient's energy field and the patient gets better—without drugs or surgery.[15]

Cell memory: Perhaps the most amazing of all "ghosts" appears with patients who have undergone an organ transplant (e.g., heart, lungs, liver, or kidneys) who then begin to have actual memories of the person whose organ now resides in his or her body. In one episode, a little girl received a heart from a little boy who was murdered. After the surgery, she recalled the murder in a series of dreams. An arrest was made based on information passed on with the heart. Once confronted, the suspects confessed to the crime.[16]

Before World War II, the greatest cause of illness and death was infectious disease. Most people convalesced in the comfort of their own homes. Physicians made house calls but rarely observed their patients for days on end. With the advent of medical technology and the breakthroughs in antibiotics and organ transplants, more and more people are under the observation of medical staff. This is where the ghost in the machine started to surface quite regularly. One of the most remarkable stories was that of Norman Cousins, the patron saint of humor.

A New Era of Medicine

WHEN PEOPLE HEAR THE NAME "Norman Cousins," smiles come to their faces, because they recognize the man who laughed himself back to health from a fatal illness in 1964. The disease, ankylosing spondylitis, he learned, was associated with stress. The premise of Cousins' healing journey was twofold: first, if negative (stress) emotions can cause the body to become susceptible to disease and illness, is it possible for good emotions to reverse the outcome? He had nothing to lose by trying, and sure enough it worked. Second, each person must take an active role in his or her recovery and not be a passive victim of the healthcare system. Not only did his strategy work, but he also sowed the seeds for what was to become a new direction in medicine, the integration of mind, body, spirit, and emotions into the healing process.[17] As with any great movement, several others were coming to the same conclusion in other parts of the country and in other academic disciplines, including the works of Elmer and Alyce Green with Asian yogis,[18] Carl Simonton and colleagues[19] and Patricia Norris[20] with cancer patients, and Lawrence LeShan with the study of shamanism.[21]

In 1974, Dr. Robert Ader studied the conditioning response of rats (similar to that of Pavlov's work with dogs). In his experiments, Ader looked at the association between nausea induced via a drug injection and sugar water fed to the rats after the injection. The rats soon began to associate the sugar water with nausea, even weeks after the injections stopped. Ader concluded that it wasn't the sugar water but rather the rats' belief about what the sugar water would cause that led to their demise. Ader was convinced that the immune system—which until that time was thought to be independent of the other physiological systems—was directly connected to everything, including the mind's thought processes. By 1981 Ader coined the term *psychoneuroimmunology*, shifting the paradigm of Western medicine towards a more holistic, integrative approach.[22]

Within the field of clinical medicine, the term *psychoneuroimmunology* was used to describe the interconnectedness of the brain, the nervous system, and the immune system. However, several professionals said that it isn't really the brain per se, but rather the role of mind–consciousness in the healing process that needed to be explored. In a time when professionals from various disciplines in human physiology didn't even talk to each other, this proposed collaboration was nothing short of radical. In an effort to explain this collaboration between human physiology and psychology, experts used the term *mind–body medicine*. Researchers such as Herbert Benson, Lawrence LeShan, Carl Simonton, and Patricia Norris championed this liberal theory with a conservative spin, thus leaving any mention of the human spirit as a tacit hint.[23]

Perhaps because the term *psychoneuroimmunology* has so many syllables (it's a mouthful), the abbreviation *PNI* was coined. Outside the field of allopathic (Western) medicine, however, healers employing various forms of **complementary medicine** and their patients referred to this holistic approach as *mind–body–spirit medicine*. Two decades later, the most progressive professionals in the healthcare system also began to use the word *spirit* to complete the mind–body–spirit dynamic. For example, today the Joint Commission that approves accreditation of hospitals in the United States requires that all patients receive a spiritual well-being inventory upon admittance, and many medical schools now introduce the topic of the healing power of prayer in their integrative medicine courses. (Unfortunately, although this information is gradually being introduced at the educational level, those professionals in the field who were trained in a different paradigm are slow to embrace any change.)[24]

To be sure, the medical establishment has not fully embraced the notion of mind–body–spirit healing, mostly because it was not a component of their educational training. In the words of psychologist Abraham Maslow, "If your only tool is a hammer, you'll see every problem as a nail."[25] In terms of allopathic medicine, if a physician's only tools of the trade are drugs and surgery, these are the confines within which he or she will work. However, a growing number of medical professionals have come to the realization that although drugs and surgery may alleviate certain symptoms, they do nothing to address the causes of the lifestyle diseases such as cancer, coronary heart disease, arthritis, and diabetes that are so prevalent today.

Curing Is Not Healing

Lately there has been much confusion in the health field about the terms *healing* and *curing*, so much so that many medical professionals have come to dislike the word *healing*. In fact, in some hospitals the use of the word *healing* is discouraged. *Webster's Dictionary* notwithstanding, it is commonly understood in the medical community, specifically by physicians, that the word ***curing*** means to eliminate or eradicate the symptoms of disease or illness. The two tools of trade in Western medicine are drugs and surgery, and it is these two methods of allopathic medicine that are used to cure disease and illness. Anyone with lower back pain knows that you can take a painkiller to alleviate the pain, but once the prescription runs out the pain returns. The term ***healing***, in contrast, is commonly used by a host of healthcare practitioners (and accepted by the general public, particularly those who use complementary medicine modalities) to express a sense of inner peace and equilibrium throughout the mind–body–spirit continuum.[26]

According to these commonly used and accepted definitions, someone can be cured of a disease or illness but not be healed from it. Similarly, someone can be healed of a disease and die. Of course, the ideal scenario is to be both healed and cured.

Allison Fisher was an undergraduate student of mine at American University in Washington, D.C. After graduation in 1992, she took a position with Channel One, a cable channel for high school programming. Not long after she arrived in California, she discovered a lump in her breast. Allison underwent both surgery and chemotherapy, and it appeared that the cancer was stopped in its tracks; however, a mammography two years later revealed that it had spread to her lungs.

During a trip to Los Angeles, Allison and I met for lunch, during which she discussed her illness. One look at her hair and I could tell she had undergone chemotherapy. She mentioned that she had pretty much given up on Western medicine, mostly because it had given up on her. She was now trying acupuncture, homeopathy, herbal therapy, and her favorite exercises, meditation, and t'ai chi. Allison was all smiles, and there was a wonderful sense of calm about her.

My travels took me back to Los Angeles once again that same year, and Allison and I met for dinner. I had taught her theories about healing and curing. Allison took that knowledge and integrated it with her experience and wisdom, which she then shared with me.

"The doctors said that the cancer has progressed," she said matter of factly. "I realize I may never be cured of breast cancer, but I am happy to say I am healed." She paused for a second, smiled, and then continued. "Let me tell you the difference between healing and curing," she explained with a seat of authority. "Curing merely removes the symptoms of disease. Healing brings one to a sense of inner peace. I am at that place with myself and my disease," she said with an air of utter confidence. "To be healed means to face your fears one by one until they are all gone. I have done that, and I am at peace."

Two months later I received a phone call from a mutual friend. She broke the news gently. On March 9, 1998, Allison died of cancer. I felt remorse but I can say with all honesty that Allison was indeed healed of her disease.[27]

The Human Energy Field: The Interface Between Body and Soul

A LIFE FORCE OF ENERGY SURROUNDS and permeates the physical body. This life force of energy goes by several names, including *chi, ki, prana*, and the *Holy Spirit*. Mystics such as Edgar Cayce[28] and healers, including Caroline Myss, Donna Eden, and Julie Motz, have reported that they can actually see various layers of energy around the body.[29-32] Ancient mystics called this energy the *human aura*. Scientists call it the **human energy field**. Regardless of the name used, the layers of energy that surround and permeate the body pulsate with colorful vibration.

Contemporary healers who can see the human energy field know that the colors within the aura change with respect to changes in thoughts and emotions, which are aspects of consciousness. There has always been an association with one's aura and a spiritual essence. Moreover, aspects of the human energy field, specifically the **chakras** (a Sanskrit word meaning "spinning wheel," identified as a portal of energy into the body), also have this association, most notably the crown chakra that Judeo-Christian culture recognizes as the halo. Many consider the aura itself, a luminescent glow, as the epitome of holiness. Ancient mystics described the aura as a series of undulating layers of consciousness (e.g., intellect, intuition, imagination, emotions, etc.). Clearly, consciousness and spirit are inextricably linked.

Richard Gerber, M.D., a radiologist who has spent several decades researching the human energy field, describes each layer of consciousness as a harmonic vibration.[33] Like keys on a piano keyboard, the frequency of the body's vibration and that of the emotional, mental, and spiritual fields (see **Figure 6.1**) are set at different octaves yet are within the harmonic range of

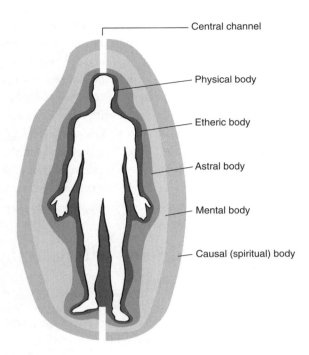

Central channel

Physical body

Etheric body

Astral body

Mental body

Causal (spiritual) body

FIGURE 6.1 The human energy field. Courtesy of Inner Traditions.

each other. If a thought, coupled with an emotion, is left unresolved, it can cause dissonance within the layers of energy in the aura. Distortion first appears outside the body, but over time, through a cascading effect, either through the chakras or meridians, the negative vibration pools within various cell tissues. The result is dysfunction to the related area in the physical body. Dissonance (the opposite of resonance) eventually appears at the cellular level, and the once-harmonic vibration is no longer tuned to homeostasis. This sets the stage for disease and illness. This model of well-being is based on the theory that disease develops outside the body and filters down through the layers of energy. Physical symptoms in the body are not the first signs of illness, but the last.

Stress and Disease

I T WAS WALTER CANNON IN 1912 who coined the phrase "fight-or-flight response," more commonly known today as the stress response.[34] Hans Selye's research in the 1950s clearly indicated that the adaptation to stress can lead to wear and tear on the body's organs, setting the stage for disease, illness, and, quite possibly, death.[35]

It baffles researchers to no end when two people going through the same stressful experience contract completely different illnesses. For example, when two people would lose their jobs during corporate restructuring, one might get an ulcer whereas the other might develop pneumonia or extreme lower back pain. Personality was said to play a role, but to what extent no one could say. The most conservative researchers hesitated to even associate stress and disease, while the more liberal scholars insisted on a direct causal link.

This causal link was identified through the work of Candace Pert and others who showed that, indeed, the immune system becomes suppressed when the emotions of anger and fear linger in the conscious mind too long. Further research proved Norman Cousins right in that positive emotions, such as joy, happiness, and optimism, and feelings associated with humor actually elevate various neuropeptides that enhance the immune system. Considering how connected the immune system is to all other physiological systems, the discovery of this link was a substantial one.[36,37]

Guilt, fear, anger, and envy are just a few of the ways that unresolved issues linger in mind–body–spirit energy patterns, causing disruptions that ultimately can lead to disease. Today, the link between stress and disease is a strong one and is clearly established in the medical literature, which shows that stress can influence the development of everything from the common cold to cancer.[38,39] Some researchers are now looking outside the mechanistic box to investigate a spiritual connection to physical disease, and the trail appears to be headed beyond the conventional mind–body connection toward the dynamics of the human energy field.[40]

In Chinese medicine, the existence of *ch'i* (also spelled *chi*), the life force of energy that runs through the body via twelve major meridians, is commonly accepted as fact. Acupuncture is a treatment used to unblock the congested gates of energy, thereby allowing the current of life force to flow unrestricted once more. What restricts ch'i and causes blocks in the rivers of the life force? If you were to talk to practitioners of classical five-element acupuncture, they would tell you that unresolved emotions, such as anger and fear, and all the many shades of emotions to which these relate, can cause blocks in the flow of our life force. In essence, they impede the flow of our vital life force to the point that they can literally choke it to death.

Cellular Consciousness

In his bestselling book *Quantum Healing*, Deepak Chopra, M.D., cites a very interesting fact of human physiology: every cell in the body regenerates itself, some within days, others within years.[41] Red blood cells, for instance, last approximately 120 days before regenerating. Nerve cells, it seems, take the longest. Consequently, within a seven-year time period, your body has a new body of cells. Chopra says with a Cheshire-cat smile, "I am not the man I used to be seven years ago!"

All jokes aside, Chopra poses a very serious question: cancerous tumors take years, even decades to grow. So why is it then that with a new body we have old tumors? The answer may actually reside in the wisdom of the DNA, and perhaps in the vibrations of consciousness that surround and permeate each and every cell and that are passed from generation to generation of cells through entrainment. *Entrainment* is a physics term used to describe sympathetic resonance between two objects.

Based on the work of Candace Pert and others, Chopra suggests that unlike conventional wisdom, which states that only brain cells hold some level of consciousness, every cell in the body contains a vibration of consciousness. It is this imprint of conscious frequency that is then transferred, via entrainment, from cell to cell, thus allowing a tumor to develop and grow. This is known as **cellular consciousness**. Stories of people who have had organ transplants and then pick up "information" from the organ's original owner have proved quite remarkable to the medical community.

Complementary Medicine/ Energy Medicine

HOMEOPATHY. THERAPEUTIC TOUCH. Reiki. Biofeedback. Ta'i chi. Music therapy. These are all proven techniques to reduce stress and return the body to a sense of homeostasis. These same techniques are included in the host of healing modalities known today as *complementary* or *integrative medicine.* This group of therapies includes literally hundreds of modalities, such as herbal medicines, massage, mental imagery, and humor therapy, which many Americans have adopted as part of their personal healthcare plans.[42,43] Unlike the 7 minutes a patient spends in a physician's office, these sessions of healing and restoration usually last an hour or more. And although they appear to work at the physical level, in actuality they work at all levels—mind, body, spirit, and emotions—because, energetically, there is no separation between these components. All aspects connect.

For the most part, these modalities of healing, which are considered complementary or alternative, are geared to prevent disease and illness and to maintain health and well-being. However, like Allison, a substantial number of people who have met a dead end with Western medicine regarding cancer and other life-threatening diseases have turned toward therapies that integrate, rather than alienate, mind and spirit with the body. Many have made what is known in allied health circles as a "remarkable recovery." Others call it "a miracle." These miraculous healings have made Western medicine stand up and take notice. Although researchers have not, and most likely never will, find the mechanism (machine) in this spiritual healing process, the fact that these recoveries are happening—be they curing, healing, or both—cannot be denied. Research may not explain the how, but it can certainly document outcomes.

French scientist Henri de Vernejoul conducted a validity study in 1985 on the dynamics of acupuncture with a radioactive isotope. He discovered that the trail of the dye did not follow the path of any known physiological system, yet matched identically the meridian charts of ancient Chinese medicine. With this finding, the Western paradigm of medicine underwent a shift in consciousness.[44] This shift continues with data collected on the **distant healing** phenomenon.[45,46]

Although Reiki, acupuncture, and Qi Gong certainly have obvious connections to the human energy field, other complementary modalities, such as mental imagery, meditation, and hatha yoga, are no less dynamic in their efforts to produce a spiritual healing effect. In a survey to determine why people actually use various forms of complementary medicine, the following was reported:

> Users of alternative health care are more likely to report having had a transformational experience that changed the way they saw the world. They find an acknowledgment of the importance of treating illness within a larger context of spirituality and life meaning. The use of alternative care is part of a broader value orientation and set of cultural beliefs, one that embraces a holistic, spiritual orientation to life.[47]

It should be noted that complementary therapies are not superior to allopathic medicine and, in fact, the word *complementary* infers that the best of both can be used together for the greatest result for optimal health.

Healers far and wide have repeatedly stated that their healing work involves transference of energy. Today, though not completely understood by Western science, acupuncture, bioenergy, Reiki, shiatsu, Zero Balancing,

Qi Gong, Tibetan energy healing, Huna energy healing, and t'ai chi are recognized as various forms of energy medicine because they work with layers of consciousness or life force. And, in some manner, the health of the human spirit (also thought to be a form of energy) is restored to wholeness. What these healers say is that they are not actually doing the healing. Rather they are merely a channel for a divine source of healing energy.

One such healer is Susan Ulfelder, a protégé of renowned healer Barbara Ann Brennan.[48] At a young age, Susan could see undulating colors surrounding people's bodies. Several years later, she learned to correlate distortions in the human aura to specific diseases. Susan's rate of accuracy is over 90%. I met Susan in Washington, D.C., where she frequented my personal wellness class at American University as a guest speaker. One day a student walked into my office desperate for help. As a world-class athlete, he was plagued by heart palpitations, urine in the blood, and severe stomach cramping. Although he had undergone scores of clinical diagnostic tests, no physician could find a cause for his condition. At the end of his rope and with his athletic career on the line, he walked into my office for guidance. I recommended that he see Susan. Within two sessions of **bioenergy healing,** my student's symptoms were gone, never to return again.

So Why Doesn't Everybody Get Healed?

So IF THE HUMAN SPIRIT is so high and mighty, if we are truly connected to the divine at all times, if the healing power of prayer is statistically significant, why do people get sick and die? It would appear that the answer is extremely complex and perhaps outside the realm of human understanding. Based on the insights from those who have studied this very aspect of human spirituality, the answer certainly falls outside the domain of both Western science and religion.

In 1992, I attended a conference sponsored by the International Society for the Study of Subtle Energy and Energy Medicine.[49] The mission of this organization is to scientifically validate the healing properties of energy medicine through outcome measures and, ideally, through a yet undetected dynamic (mechanism) that links mind, body, and spirit.

In the main ballroom of the hotel sat approximately 300 conference participants—about one-third of the group were healers from around the world, one-third were scientists (researchers and physicists), and the rest were nurses, physicians, clinical social workers, educators, and a few people from various disciplines who were simply curious about the nature of healing. That afternoon a panel of healers and researchers on the healing dynamics of energy medicine convened. After each panelist spoke, the audience was invited to ask questions. One conference participant, with an air of skepticism, approached the microphone and asked, "If you healers claim to be working with the divine force of the universe, God, angels, etc., why is your rate of healing only 80% and not 100%?" His question was punctuated with silence from the crowd. Then a panel member spoke:

> You are right when you say that healers working with healing energy have an efficacy rate of about 80% to 85%. The answer is not a simple one, and most likely some will have difficulty processing this, but I am in agreement with my colleagues when I say that there are a handful of cases where we are specifically told not to interfere with the disease or illness. I believe the word you are most familiar with is karma.

He went on to explain that in some instances, a person agrees to enter this life with a condition to balance one's karma or, in some cases, to teach others the lesson of love.

Hearing this response brought to mind a conversation with a colleague of mine from India. One day over lunch he inquired about the nature of Christian sainthood. I explained that typically someone of this caliber has had a very difficult life. At some point, there is an undeniable moment of divine intervention. They are reported to have performed miracles both during their time on Earth and after death. "Do you have saints in your culture?" I inquired. His answer was intriguing:

> Yes, but sainthood comes in a different fashion. When people have balanced all the karma in their lives, they reach a state of consciousness known as nirvana, what you might call heaven. Yet there are some who feel this is an empty victory without the companionship of their loved ones. So they volunteer to return to earth one final time for the sole reason to teach the lessons of love. A cripple, a beggar, or a homeless person may really be a saint in disguise. One never really knows. With this in mind, we treat everyone with respect. I believe it is known worldwide as the Golden Rule.

Caroline Myss (pronounced "mace"), renowned healer and author of the book *Why People Don't Heal,* has a different take on the healing/nonhealing phenomenon.[50] After years of counseling people who came to her for readings, Myss began to pay attention to the words clients used to describe their condition. What she discovered is that many people may say they want to be healed, but in reality they don't. In what Myss calls "woundology," people actually find a new identity in their illness. Strange as it may seem, to become healed would be to lose something valuable, that which gives the person attention and notoriety. Moreover, many use their disease to manipulate and control others. It becomes an illusion of power. In reality, she explained, this type of person has given his or her power away—to the disease—and will never be healed in this state of mind. Any healer who works with this kind of person sees that administering an intention of healing is not too different from a physician prescribing a medication. Medications merely mask the symptoms of a deeper problem.

Perhaps the biggest reason why people don't heal is the result of what is known in the field of psychology as the *unconscious resistance*; a series of belief systems embedded deep in the unconscious mind that sabotage one's conscious efforts for optimal well-being. With over 85% of human behavior controlled or influenced by the unconscious mind, healing must include addressing the belief systems and patterns locked deep below the surface of normal consciousness.

Myss' concept of mind–body–spirit is similar to that of Tulku Thondup, author of *The Healing Power of Mind*.[51] Thondup is a Tibetan healer who speaks of healing through the greater mind. In essence, if the lesser mind (controlled by ego) is out of sync with the greater mind (divine consciousness), then true healing will not occur. Healers like Thondup will acknowledge that any true healing is done by the individual who is sick. The healer is merely a cofacilitator of the healing process, an idea similar, if not identical to, that of Norman Cousins, who said that each person must take responsibility for his or her own healing process.

Healings, by any definition, infer the work of miracles. In the popular book *A Course in Miracles*, the following passage reiterates the need to release fear, consciously or unconsciously, and to replace it with love:

> If you wish only to be healed, you heal. Your single purpose makes this possible. But if you are afraid of healing, then it cannot come through you. The only thing that is required for a healing is a lack of fear. The fearful are not healed and cannot heal. This does not mean that the conflict must be gone from your mind to heal. For if it were, there would be no need for healing then. But it does mean, if only for an instant, you love without attack. An instant is sufficient time. Miracles wait not on time.[52]

We still have much to learn about mind–body–spirit healing. Great emphasis and research are being placed on the functions of the brain (i.e., through functional MRIs) with less and less exploration in the realms of the unconscious mind, where so much of personality, belief systems, even healing processes take place.[53]

⚛ SUMMARY

THE CONCEPT OF MIND–BODY–SPIRIT HEALING suggests that the body is not a machine with fixable or replaceable parts. Rather, human beings are a unique combination of spirit and matter. When mind, body, and spirit are considered equally (rather than just the body) in the healing process, it becomes evident that the human spirit plays an integral role in restoring wholeness. Conversely, when health is looked at mechanistically, various phenomena (the ghost in the machine) appear to suggest that this model of health is incomplete. Research into energy medicine provides insight that indeed the mechanistic model is outdated. A new era of medicine, created by experts from many allied fields (e.g., clinical medicine, psychology, nursing, and health) and called psychoneuroimmunology, now honors mind–body–spirit integration. The growing interest in complementary medicine, from acupuncture to prayer, indicates that the American public craves a more humanistic approach to health care as well.

⚛ TERMS AND CONCEPTS

bioenergy healing
cellular consciousness
chakras
complementary medicine
curing
distant healing

ghost in the machine
healing
human energy field
mind–body–spirit healing
unconscious resistance

EXERCISE 6.1
ANATOMY ENERGY MAP

The accompanying figure is an outline of the human body highlighted with the seven primary chakras. The first chakra is called the *root chakra* and the seventh chakra is called the *crown chakra* (also known as the *halo*). Note the body region associated with each chakra, as well as what aspects each chakra is associated with, and then take a moment to identify any health issues or concerns associated with this specific region of your body. Once you have done this, ask yourself honestly if you happen to recognize any connection between the important aspects of the chakra(s) associated with the region(s) in which you have indicated and a specific health concern.

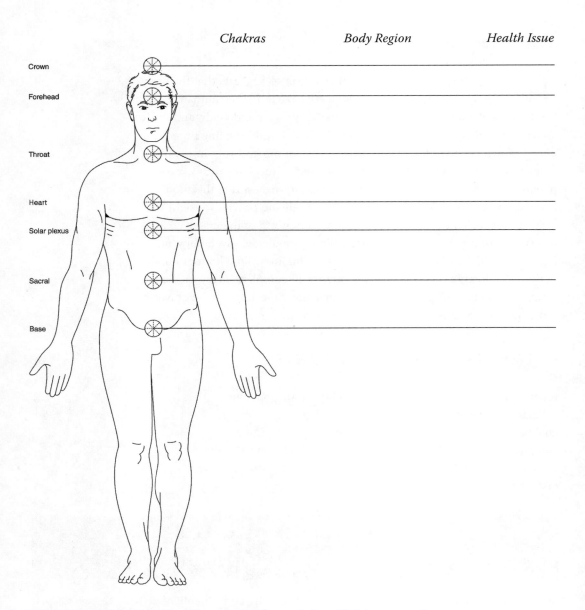

Chakras   *Body Region*   *Health Issue*

Crown

Forehead

Throat

Heart

Solar plexus

Sacral

Base

EXERCISE 6.2
WHEN YOUR BIOGRAPHY BECOMES YOUR BIOLOGY

The cause of illness is ultimately connected to the inner stresses present in a person's life.

—Caroline Myss

In the early 1980s, Robert Ader coined the term *psychoneuroimmunology* to distinguish a new field of study, the field of mind–body medicine. What he and now countless others have discovered is that there is an amazing and profound connection between the mind, body, and spirit. To the contrary of French philosopher René Descartes' reductionistic theory, the mind and body are not separate entities. This means that our minds and the emotional thoughts we produce have an incredible impact on our physiology, for better or worse.

One person to emerge onto the stage of mind–body medicine is Caroline Myss, PhD. A woman with an incredible ability to see what most others cannot, Myss has the gift to view a person's energy field and assist physicians in determining the onset and location of disease as well as the cause of a disease. Myss has remarkable accuracy, especially considering that she can perform a viewing from hundreds of miles away (known as *nonlocal viewing* or *medical intuition*). First intrigued by the concepts of the human energy field and the chakras (spinning wheels of energy positioned over several major body organs from head to spine), Myss has focused her own energy into teaching people about mind–body–spirit harmony.

In one of her first books, *The Creation of Health*, Myss discusses the idea that a life history, in terms of experiences, becomes intertwined with the cells of our physical bodies. From hundreds of documented case studies, she has come to the understanding that symptoms of disease and illness don't start in the body; they end there. Can cervical cancer be rooted in sexual molestation? Can lower back pain be rooted in financial insecurities? Can bone spurs on the heal of the foot be a result of feeling "defeated"? Myss thinks so. Judging by her track record (95% accuracy of diagnosing diseases), she stands on pretty solid ground.

According to Caroline Myss, getting your life story out and examined is one of the first steps toward optimal health. By means of coming to terms with your biography, you can release the negative energies that distort the integrity of each and every cell in your body. So what is your biography? What are some of the most significant (perhaps emotionally painful) events that you now carry in the memories of each cell? Take some time to explore these and perhaps other life-long memories that may now be a part of your biology.

_____

_____

_____

_____

_____

_____

_____

_____

_____

_____

_____

_____

_____

_____

_____

_____

EXERCISE 6.3
ENERGY SYSTEM "VITAMINS"

Donna Eden is a renowned energy healer with a gift for not only observing subtle energies, but also for teaching others how to regulate their subtle energy for enhanced health and well-being. Integrating the flow of energy through the human aura, chakras, and meridians, Donna combines a variety of self-help techniques so that, in her words, "You keep your energies humming and vibrant." The following are ideas and suggestions that Donna teaches in her energy medicine workshops, exercises that she calls "energy system vitamins." She recommends that you do this short routine daily.

1. *Three body taps:* There are various acupuncture/acupressure points that, when stimulated, will help direct the flow of energy, and thus increase your vitality and help boost your immune system.

   - **Chest bone tap:** Known to acupuncturists as K27 (from points on the kidney meridian), gently tap on the top of your chest bone just below where the two clavicles meet for about 15 to 20 seconds using the fingertips of both hands.

   - **Thymus gland tap:** Your thymus gland (an important glad of the immune system) resides between your throat and your heart, but the point to tap is in the center of your chest bone about 2 inches below K27. Once you have found this point, tap on it with your finger tips for about 15 to 20 seconds.

   - **Spleen points tap:** The spleen is an essential organ to your immune system. The spleen points are located on the rib cage, directly below your nipples. Once you have found these two points, tap vigorously with your fingers for about 15 to 20 seconds.

2. *Cross-crawl movements:* To do the cross-crawl, first you must understand that the left side of the brain controls the right side of the body, and vice versa. Many people's energies are

not vibrant or harmonized due to stagnation from the lack of neural energy from the right to the left or the left to the right sides of the brain. Poor energy movement is referred to as a *homolateral pattern* and affects thought processes, coordination, and vitality. Sitting or standing, raise your right knee and your left arm (you can touch knee to elbow if you'd like). Follow this by raising your left knee and your right arm. Twist your torso so that your arms cross the midpoint of your body. Try this movement pattern for about 30 to 60 seconds.

3. *The crown pull:* Placing your hand on top of your forehead and crown of the head, imagine that your fingers are pulling from the center down to your ears in a motion starting from the front of your head and working to the back of your skull. The purpose of this exercise is to move stagnant energy from the top of your head and open the crown chakra. This exercise can be helpful in relieving headaches, too.

4. *Zip up:* The central meridian (in the front of your body) can easily become congested, open, or exposed to others' energy. This technique invites you to close your auric field as a means of health and protection. Start by tapping the K27 point again and then reach down to the top of your thighs with your right (or left) hand, take a deep breath, and pull up as if you were pulling up a zipper, clear up to your chin. Repeat this three times. By pulling up, you trace the directional flow of the central meridian and strengthen the flow of energy. This technique is recommended before making speeches or dealing with someone who is very angry.

EXERCISE 6.4
UNRESOLVED ANGER OR FEAR?

First and foremost, know that neither anger nor fear is a bad emotion. They are survival emotions. They kick in when our lives are threatened. Reflect for a moment on the definition of emotional well-being—the ability to feel and express the entire range of human emotions and to control them, not be controlled by them. Anger and fear are human emotions, yet each is only meant to last long enough to get out of harm's way—only seconds, maybe minutes. Left unresolved, both anger and fear can distort the energy field that surrounds and permeates the physical body, ultimately compromising one's health. Mind–body–spirit healing includes resolving issues of stress (anger and fear) to promote optimal well-being.

1. Do you have any lingering issues of anger or fear hovering over your head like a black cloud? If so, what are they, and why are they left unresolved?

    _____

    _____

    _____

    _____

2. Make a list of the top ten stressors (e.g., issues, problems, concerns) in your life right now. Once you have done this, consider which of the two fight-or-flight responses surface at the thought of each one. Where appropriate, write the word *anger* or *fear* next to each stressor. Remember that both anger and fear can manifest in a great many ways (e.g., impatience, envy, doubt, etc.). Some stressors might induce both anger and fear.

_____

_____

_____

_____

_____

_____

_____

_____

_____

_____

3. If you were to look up the word *remission,* you would find that there is an implicit aspect of forgiveness associated with this word. Forgiveness is an essential aspect of resolving anger. If unresolved anger is a ball and chain on the spiritual path, then forgiveness is what allows us to remove the chains and to be set free. When we forgive, we do it for ourselves, not for the other person. Make a list of those people who have earned a place on your "bad" list. Ask yourself why they are there still. What steps can you take to forgive and move on with your life?

_____

_____

_____

_____

_____

4. Are you suffering from any disease or illness (acute or chronic)? Can you detect a stress component to it? If there is, what is the connection?

_____

_____

_____

_____

_____

5. What are your thoughts on the concepts of curing versus healing? Have you been treated with medications only to have the symptoms reappear once the prescription has run out?

_____

_____

_____

_____

6. Have you considered using complementary medicine (e.g., massage therapy, herbal remedies, energy healing, hypnosis, etc.)? If so, which ones and why? Do you feel a sense of mind–body–spirit integration (inner peace) as you partake of these modalities?

_____

_____

_____

_____

_____

_____

_____

❖ ENDNOTES

1. Cindy L., Personal conversation, Columbus, Ohio, September 27, 1999, and August 7, 2011.
2. Gill, J., Personal conversation, Columbus, Ohio, September 27, 1999, and August 1, 2011.
3. Tamblyn, G., Personal conversation via phone, October 16, 1999. Also recorded as a song by Greg Tamblyn, "Shoot Out at the I'm OK, You're OK Corral," Tune Town Records, 1994.
4. Braun, B., "Psychophysiological Phenomena in Multiple Personality and Hypnosis." *American Journal of Clinical Hypnosis*, No. 26(2): 124–137, 1983.
5. Rogo, S. D., *Infinite Boundary.* Penguin Books: New York, 1987.
6. Zinser, T., Psychologist. Personal conversation, Grand Rapids, Michigan, January 19, 2000.
7. Brody, H., *The Placebo Response.* HarperCollins: New York, 2000.
8. Kent, J., Coates, T., Pelletier, K., and O'Reagan, B., "Unexpected Recoveries: Spontaneous Remission and Immune Functioning." *Advances*, No. 6(2): 66–73, 1989.
9. O'Reagan, B., and Hirshberg, C., *Spontaneous Remission: An Annotated Bibliography.* Sausalito, CA: Institute of Noetic Sciences, 1993.
10. Byrd, R., "Positive Therapeutic Effects of Intercessory Prayer in a Coronary Care Unit Population." *Southern Medical Journal*, No. 81(7): 826–829, 1988.
11. Dossey, L., *Healing Words: The Power of Prayer and the Practice of Medicine.* HarperSanFrancisco: San Francisco, 1993.

12. Oshman, J., *Energy Medicine; The Scientific Basis*. Churchill Livingstone: Oxford, England, 2000.

13. McTaggart, L. *The Field.* HarperCollins: New York, 2002.

14. Benson, H., and Proctor, W., *The Relaxation Revolution.* Scribner: New York, 2010.

15. Krieger, D., "Healing by the Laying on of Hands as a Facilitator of Bioenergetic Change: The Response of In-Vitro Hemoglobin." *Internal Journal of Psychoenergetic Systems,* No. 1:121, 1976.

16. Pearsol, P., *The Heart's Code.* Broadway Books: New York, 1998.

17. Cousins, N., *Anatomy of an Illness as Perceived by the Patient.* Bantam Books: New York, 1979.

18. Green, E., and Green, A., *Beyond Biofeedback.* Delacorte Press: New York, 1977.

19. Simonton, O. C., Matthews-Simonton, S., and Creighton, J., *Getting Well Again.* Tarcher Books: Los Angeles, 1978.

20. Porter, G., and Norris, P., *Why Me: Harnessing the Healing Power of the Human Spirit.* Stillpoint Press: Walpole, NH, 1985.

21. LeShan, L., *The Medium, the Mystic and the Physicist.* Viking: New York, 1974.

22. Ader, R., "Development Psychoneuroimmunology." *Developmental Psychobiology,* No. 10: 251–267, 1983.

23. Seaward, B. L., "Alternative Medicine Complements Standard." *Health Progress,* No. 75 (7): 52–57, 1994.

24. Dossey, L., "Reinventing Medicine." Presentation at Colorado State University, Fort Collins, CO, September 9, 2010.

25. Maslow, A., as quoted in *The Promise of a New Day.* Casey, K., and Vanceburg, M. (editors). Hazelden Books: New York, 1983.

26. McGary, G. T., Keynote Address. "Contacting the Physician Within." The International Society for the Study of Subtle Energy and Energy Medicine. Boulder, CO, June 20–21, 1992.

27. Fisher, A., Personal conversations, June and December 1997.

28. Sugrue, T., *The Story of Edgar Cayce.* A. R. E. Press: Virginia Beach, VA, 1970.

29. Myss, C., *Anatomy of the Spirit.* Harmony Books: New York, 1996.

30. Eden, D., *Energy Medicine.* Harmony Books: New York, 1999.

31. Bartlett, R. *Matrix Energetics.* Atria Books. New York. 2007

32. McLeod, A., *The Path of the Dream Healer.* Viking Canada: Toronto, 2006.

33. Gerber, R., *Vibrational Medicine* (second edition). Bear & Co.: Sante Fe, NM, 1996.

34. Cannon, W., *The Wisdom of the Body.* W. W. Norton: New York, 1932.

35. Selye, H., *The Stress of Life.* McGraw-Hill: New York, 1976.

36. Pert, C., *Molecules of Emotion.* Scribner and Sons: New York, 1998.

37. Pert, C., *Everything You Need to Feel Go(o)d.* Hay House: Carlsbad, CA, 2006.

38. Cohen, S., Tyrrell, D., and Smith, A. P., "Psychological Stress and the Susceptibility to the Common Cold." *New England Journal of Medicine*, No. 325: 606–612, 1991.

39. Temschok, L., "Personality, Coping Style, Emotion and Cancer: Towards an Integrative Model." *Cancer Surveys*, No. 6: 545–567, 1987.

40. Gordon, J., *Manifesto for a New Medicine.* Reading, MA: Addison Wesley, 1996.

41. Chopra, D., *Quantum Healing.* Bantam New Age Books: New York, 1988.

42. Eisenberg, D., et al., "Trends in Alternative Medicine Use in the United States." *New England Journal of Medicine*, No. 280(18): 1569–1575, 1998.

43. The Use of Complementary and Alternative Medicine in the United States. Available at: http://nccam.nih.gov/news/camstats/2007/camsurvey_fs1.htm.

44. de Vernejoul, H. et al., "Etude des Meridiens, D'Acupuncture par les Traceurs Radioactifs." *Bull Acad Natl Med*, No. 169 (Oct.): 1071–1075, 1985.

45. Radin, D., *Entangled Minds.* Parview Pocket Books: New York, 2006.

46. Schwartz, G., *The Energy Healing Experiments.* Atria Books: New York, 2008.

47. Austin, J. A., "Why Patients Use Alternative Medicine." *Journal of the American Medical Association*, No. 279(19): 1548–1553, 1998.

48. Brennan, B. A., *Hands of Light.* Bantam New Age Books: New York, 1987.

49. International Society for the Study of Subtle Energy and Energy Medicine, 2nd Annual Conference. Boulder, CO, June 20–23, 1992.

50. Myss, C., *Why People Don't Heal: And How They Can.* Harmony Books: New York, 1997.

51. Thondup, T., *The Healing Power of Mind.* Shambhala Press: Boston, 1996.

52. *A Course in Miracles*, page 535. Foundation for Inner Peace: Glen Ellen, CA, 1999.

53. Lipton, B., *The Biology of Belief.* Elite Books: Santa Rosa, CA, 2006.

❦ ADDITIONAL REFERENCES

Carlson, R., and Shield, B., *Healers on Healing.* Tarcher Books: Los Angeles, CA, 1989.

Chopra, D., *Reinventing the Body, Resurrecting the Soul.* Three Rivers Press: New York, 2010.

Collinger, W., *Subtle Energy.* Warner Books: New York, 1998.

Dossey, L., *Recovering the Soul.* Bantam New Age Books: New York, 1988.

Goleman, D., and Gurin, J., *Mind Body Medicine.* Consumer Reports: New York, 1993.

Hirschberg, C., and Barasch, I., *Remarkable Recovery.* Riverhead Books: New York, 1995.

Justice, B., *A Different Kind of Health.* Peak Press: Houston, TX, 1998.

McGary, G. T., and Stern, J., *The Physician within You.* Health Communications: Deerfield Beach, FL, 1997.

Wilcock, D, *The Source Field Investigations.* Dutton Books: New York, 2011.

Moyers, B., *Healing and the Mind.* Doubleday: New York, 1993.

Parabola Book. *The Parabola Book of Healing.* Continuing Publishing: New York, 1993.

Siegel, D., *Mindsight: A New Science of Personal Transformation.* Bantam Books: New York, 2010.

Targ, R., and Katra, J., *Miracles of Mind: Exploring Non-local Consciousness and Spiritual Healing.* New World Books: Novato, CA, 1998.

Wallis, C. "Faith and Healing." *Time,* pp. 58–64, June 24, 1996.

Wirkus Bioenergy Foundation. *Bio-Energy: A Healing Art* (video). New World Media: New York, 1992.

CHAPTER

Embrace the Mystery

Eighty percent of reality cannot be observed or detected through the five senses.

—Buckminster Fuller

A LARGE PART OF HUMAN SPIRITUALITY can best be described as *mystical*. This mystical part includes all those experiences and happenings that defy rational or logical explanation in the human mind yet we know they really did happen because we experienced it. If we accept these as expressions of the divine, we call them miracles. If, however, we are somewhat perplexed, or even frightened, we are quick to label these events as hallucinations, tricks—that which is supernatural or paranormal—and quickly wash our hands of them.

Despite the popularity of an occasional bestselling book on the topic of the divine, angels, synchronicities, or psychic mediums, mystical and magical events are not common subjects of everyday conversation.[1,2] So mystical are some experiences, for example, apparitions or crop circles, that the average person, when asked to comment, might pass them off as ludicrous or insane or try to come up with some offbeat logical explanation. More often than not, a form of denial arises when there appears to be no rational explanation. For fear of looking foolish, or worse (e.g., being locked away in a padded room), we dare not tell anyone, save a close friend or two—and even then we might qualify the experience as more strange than wonderful.

These types of happenings make for great Hollywood movie plots, but it's sad to say that they are never discussed with any degree of regularity, seriousness, or intelligence in the scientific community, except by a handful of mavericks![3] Although it is true that paradigms are changing towards a more holistic approach to life, the rate of change appears to be at a snail's pace. Despite the efforts of researchers such as Charles Tart, Elmer Green, Larry Dossey, and Candace Pert, by and large the academic community is still entrenched in the Cartesian method of reasoning, whereby everything is explained scientifically and given a mathematical equation.

Inventor, scientist, and philosopher Buckminster Fuller once said that 80% of reality cannot be observed or detected through the five senses.[4] If, indeed, we base our sense of reality only on those things that we gather from our five senses to the exclusion of the sixth sense of our divine connection, then we deny ourselves a complete and dynamic picture of the reality that constitutes the divine force of the universe. This is known as the *spell of materialism*, in which the Cartesian principle strikes again.

Those who fear the mystical are quick to label such events as trickery, or possibly even evil. Placing faith solely in scientific evidence becomes a defense to the fear of the unknown (a dogma all its own), which arises because we are ignorant of the spiritual domain in which we live. Although we may never know or understand the true intent of various happenings, such as the frequent UFO sightings over Mexico City in 2010 (or for that matter everywhere else), miraculous healings of terminally ill cancer patients, and the apparitions of the Virgin Mary in Medjugorje in Bosnia and Herzegovina and Kuan Yin in China, to deny a view of the big picture at the risk of scientific blinders is nothing less than burying our collective heads in the sand. By projecting our insecurities on only that which we can observe and detect through the five senses, we perpetuate the limitations of our own human potential. To quote St. Augustine, "Miracles do not happen in contradiction to nature, but in contradiction to what we know about nature."[5]

Be a Good Mystic!

A MYSTIC IS NOT NECESSARILY SOMEONE who can see auras, heal the sick, talk to the dead, or predict earthquakes with 100% accuracy. A mystic is someone who opens his or her mind to the realization that the world is more than what meets the five senses, that there is a divine game plan to everything, and that nothing in the universe can merely be chalked up as a random event or reduced to a mathematical equation. Simply stated, anyone who can appreciate the mysterious and mystical events in life qualifies as a good mystic!

It is typical for someone who walks the path of a mystic not only to experience several "bizarre" events, but also, upon sharing his or her experiences, insights, and new understandings, often to be labeled as "crazy" or "New Age" by those rational conformists who walk the line of conventional wisdom. Yet, over time, these individuals tend to gather a following of people, many of whom have experienced similar events but were not as brave to share them publicly. St. Francis is one example. St. Teresa of Avila is another. Paramahansa Yogananda is a third,[6] and there are many, many more. As so often happens throughout the years, a mystic is initially labeled as a pariah, but eventually becomes a hero, helping to change the paradigm of thought through wisdom and self-realization.

A good mystic is someone who not only appreciates the mystery of life but also delights in it. A good mystic is someone who sees the supernatural as being quite natural and the ordinary as being quite extraordinary. The mystical path most certainly includes a sense of curiosity (one of the many muscles of the soul) in the search for clues to make sense of it all. Yes, there is also the inherent realization that no matter how hard you try, you will never have all the answers (shades of Peck's "mystic communal"), and this is all right, too!

Having studied human spirituality for over 25 years, I have discovered that all aspects do not nicely fit into the model of relationships, values, and a meaningful purpose in life that I created in 1990.[7] There was always this one missing piece, the mystical aspect of human spirituality, that I purposely left out for fear of my own expulsion (excommunication) from the academic community. Yet, I knew that at some point down the road it would have to be introduced to complete the framework of spiritual well-being or the legacy of René Descartes would taint this aspect of optimal wellness also. Lately some colleagues have even begged me to give this greater emphasis in the bigger picture of spiritual well-being. To reiterate a very important point: human spirituality is inclusive in nature; to ignore the mystical side would not only paint an incomplete picture, but would also be a gross injustice to the whole topic.

No Short List of Mysteries Here!

I F ALL THE MYSTERIES OF the world were to be written down, there would not be enough books to contain them. Yet, if none was documented, then those who speak of these events would be stigmatized as being "one of those people." History is punctuated with mystical happenings, from Moses' parting the Red Sea to St. Teresa of Avila, who levitated when she prayed,[8] to Marshall Stewart Ball, a developmentally challenged 6-year-old whose ability to communicate through elaborate poetry is far beyond his age.[9] In fact, in every age, in every culture, mystical experiences are not uncommon.

The truth is that we all have mystical experiences, but only some of us choose to share these more openly than others. Michael Talbot, in his book *The Holographic Universe,* is one such person.[10] The collection of stories and experiences, ranging from miracles at Lourdes, France, to psychic phenomena, is one such attempt to align human spirituality and science together under a holographic theory of energy. Paul Pearsall, in his book *The Heart's Code,* has done much the same thing with patients who have undergone organ transplants and then feel the spirit of the person whose organ now lives inside them.[11] The stories are nothing less than remarkable.

I, myself, have had numerous experiences that I see as windows into the divine, events that I call **holy moments** (Abraham Maslow called these "peak experiences"). From my conversations with others, I know I am not alone. I share these four stories here so that they may serve as a catalyst for conversation, reflection, and new ways of thinking and perceiving.

Holy moment 1: I am sitting in the living room of a healer in Washington, D.C. Originally from Poland, Mietek Wirkus has lived in the United States for years. Both he and his wife, Margaret, conduct four-month courses in bioenergy healing in their home. Mietek has the ability to see auras and so does his wife. More specifically, he has the ability to see disease (congestions and distortions) in the aura before it manifests in the physical body, and he is able to heal it. His accuracy rate of detection, 95%, is better than a CAT scan (this in itself is a mystery).

Tonight's class hasn't begun yet. I wander around his living room where the class is being held and look at various works of art on the walls. Among them is a photograph of the Virgin Mary. A photograph mind you, not a painting. As I look at the image, Mietek comes up and explains how he acquired this. "A student of mine went to Medjugorje last spring to see the church where three children, now teenagers, saw the apparition of the Virgin Mary. My friend took several rolls of film, aiming her camera at what she thought the children were looking at. All of the rolls of film showed nothing but a blank wall, save this one photo."

Holy moment 2: It is summer in 1996. I have been invited to the Yankton Sioux Indian reservation for a conference on extraterrestials,[12] which the American Indians call their "space brothers." Among the many mystical experiences that occurred (and there were many), I attended a sweat lodge hosted by two American Indian elders. Included in the group was a terminally ill cancer patient. The elders, speaking Lakota to their spirit guides, continued to throw cold water on the hot stones, chanting prayers, singing songs, and speaking healing words. Hours later they exited the lodge. Hot, tired, and sweaty, I departed as well.

Two years later in an airport in Chicago, I saw the man who sat beside me in the sweat lodge—the one who had cancer. He said that the heat in his body that night in the sweat lodge was intense. The next day his pain was gone. Upon examination by his physician the next week, who had pretty much written him off as dead, there were no signs of tumors anywhere in his body. He was healed and doing quite well, he explained with a smile from ear to ear.

Holy moment 3: I met Ron Russell at the New Science Conference in Fort Collins, Colorado, in the fall of 1998. I had just given a presentation on mind–body–spirit healing. Ron's presentation was directly after mine, and because he was about to show slides on the latest crop circle sighting in England, I quickly decided to attend. Ron works for NASA as an artist, and it was the detailed artwork of the crop circles that initially got him interested in the topic. He takes frequent trips to England to photograph new crop circle sightings. In a conversation with Ron, I learned that these crop circles form at night in as little as three to five seconds, and the electro-magnetic energy given off in the center of the circles is outside the normal limits. Wheat and barley stalks bend yet do not break as they fold to make unique and complex patterns. No one is exactly sure how or why they form, although there is much speculation. One thing is for sure. They are not the creations of college students pulling a fraternity prank. In fact, human efforts to replicate these circles fail every time.

Holy moment 4: It is February of 1994. I have been asked to organize a retreat for the board of directors of a Midwest hospital that is looking to integrate various forms of complementary healing. Rather than meet out-side Chicago, it is suggested that we meet in Arizona. Rather than stay in a stuffy hotel, one member of the group offers her house. Everyone agrees. We arrive just after noon. We find a key under the mat and a note saying "make yourself at home." So we did. In the course of waiting for Caroline, I scope out the house. I see a large montage of photographs, a history of the host family: Carolyn; her husband, Tony; their son, Jerry; and their daughter, Lori. Carolyn comes home at five o'clock, and we head out for dinner. We come back four hours later and everyone goes to bed early. That night I have a dream. I dream that I walk into the kitchen to get a glass of water, and I see a man by the fridge. He is tall, about six feet. He has long brown hair and brown eyes. He appears to be about 30 years old. He sticks his hand out to shake and says his name is Larry. He tells me to pass a message along to his mom Carolyn. The message is that he is okay, not to worry. In fact, he says, he is great.

The next morning I awake to hear Carolyn fixing breakfast in the kitchen. The moment I walk into the kitchen, I am reminded of the dream. I share the dream with Carolyn, as much as I can remember. I add a com-ment that the guy sure doesn't look like your son in the photo montage. Carolyn takes a deep breath and sits down. Then she proceeds to tell me that her first son died of SIDS (sudden infant death syndrome) 30 years ago at the age of 6 months. He had brown hair and brown eyes and indeed his name was Larry.

Without a doubt, my journey has led me on a magical mystery tour of sorts from explorations of the human energy field, to miraculous healings, to shamanistic journeys, to the mysteries of DNA. It was a book on DNA that helped me pull together so many missing pieces. With an ear to the ground of human spirituality, I came across a great many people who saw/felt that humanity was on the verge of an exciting evolutionary leap—not physical, mental, emotional—but spiritual. This concept goes by many names, includ-ing *homochristos, homouniversalis,* and *homospiritus,* where each and every person is consciously aware of his or her divine connection. Several people suggest that the link to evolution seems to be contained in the activation (waking up) of a spiritual energy that mystics say resides within each of us. This energy goes by the name of *kundalini,* a serpentine energy coiled at the base of the spine—a symbolic energy that radiates enlightenment of our true spiritual selves. There are those who associate this energy with the potential properties of our DNA. This leg of my journey began with a book called *The Cosmic Serpent: DNA and the Origins of Knowledge* by Jeremy Narby.[13]

The Mystery of DNA

JEREMY NARBY, AN ANTHROPOLOGIST BY training, set out from his home in the Swiss Alps for Peru in 1985 to study the work of shamans, particularly the hallucinogenic drugs they used, their chemical properties, and what he calls "plant communication." He was amazed to discover that the wisdom (in this case, the medical properties of plants) that shamans brought back from their "trips" was identical to the scientific data revealed in research studies of these plants years later. What intrigued Narby was that these shamans had virtually no formal educational training. Somehow they were tapping into a deep-seated wisdom that science had yet to explain. Soon, Narby was on the trail to something big.

In reviewing his research notes back in Switzerland, Narby was puzzled by this mystery. He wrote: "They talk of a ladder, or a vine, a rope, a spiral staircase, a twisted rope ladder that connects heaven and earth, which they use to gain access to the world of spirits." Narby said he began to trust the literal descriptions of his mentors even though he didn't quite comprehend their source of knowledge.[14] When told by one shaman to study the form (e.g., stairs, ladders, twisted vine, and so on), Narby's intuition stepped in and he began to see a connection between the ladder, the pool of knowledge frequently accessed, and **DNA**. Could it be that these shamans used the hallucinogenic drug ayahuasca as a gateway to unlock the secrets stored in DNA?

Intrigued, Narby began to research what was known about the double helix of life. What he discovered connected the dots to form a new understanding of the human mystery. For instance:

- DNA, a double-stranded molecule of twenty amino acids and sugar, is a reservoir of immense data.
- DNA is referred to both as a chemical compound and as a language of instruction. Narby goes so far to say that DNA has consciousness.

- Whether contained in animals, plants, or humans, DNA contains a code of four letters, A, G, C, T, that correspond to four chemical compounds: adenine, guanine, cytosine, and thymine, respectively.

- Only 3% of DNA is deemed active, whereas 97% is labeled junk (it's not really "junk," but as Narby states, it is a stupid label by arrogant scientists).

- Genes make up only 5% of our DNA.

- The smallest known bacteria genome contains 58,000 DNA letters, comparable to the information found in a telephone book. The Human Genome Project to determine the human DNA code has recently been completed.

- If a strand of DNA were stretched out end to end, it would be a thread two yards long and only ten atoms wide.

- If all of the strands of DNA in your body were extended end to end, it would reach 125 billion miles, long enough to circle the Earth 5 million times.

- DNA emits photons of light in a narrow band of visible light.

- DNA emits light like a laser with luminescent colors.

- DNA has crystalline properties that act as both transmitters and receivers.

- DNA appears not only to be an information molecule but a text as well.

Narby poses the following question: "How can one analyze a text if one presupposes that no intelligence wrote it?"[15] Narby suggests that there is indeed a supreme intelligence at work as the author of this text. Moreover, the clues he assembles in search for his answers lead back to another mystery, a spiral of energy called the *kundalini.* Could these be related as well?

The Kundalini Effect

SINCE THE DAWN OF HUMANITY, mystics have spoken of a coil of energy located at the base of the spine. Some call it the *serpent energy*, still others call it the **Kundalini energy**, but everyone who speaks of it acknowledges that it is a powerful, mystical force of energy that is our connection to the divine. As one awakens to his or her spiritual nature (an increase in consciousness usually achieved through the practice of meditation), this energy rises up, like a cobra, to where it reaches the crown of the head (the crown chakra, the portal of divine energy) in illumination. Those who have learned to access the kundalini energy are said to be enlightened.

If you pursue the question of spiritual well-being with any kind of passion, at some point you will come face to face with the concept of the "ascension process." *Ascension* means many things to many people, but wisdom keepers speak of this as a significant advancement *up* the spiritual spiral—an elevation of consciousness, a significant soul-growth process. Implicit for some in the concept of ascension is a fall, as in the "fall from grace." Though there are many interpretations of "the fall," simply stated, the fall occurs every time the shadow of the ego eclipses the light of the soul. For some people, this is a pretty deep decent into darkness. Conversely, the ascent is described by others as the ascension of divine energy up the spine (also known as the *kundalini energy*). As this energy rises, from the root chakra to the crown chakra, the cleansing process in each chakra region can be emotionally painful (as one learns to release old thoughts, feelings, and perceptions that no longer serve one's well-being).

Carl Jung addressed the concept of the ascension process, tacitly, as the union of the conscious and unconscious minds, where the wisdom of the unconscious and collective (divine) consciousness rises up to a conscious level. As consciousness rises, we evolve spiritually, acting less from a motivation of fear and more from love. The ascension process is a shift (upward) from the darkness of fear toward the light of love and compassion. In many ways, this is a small step up through the "doors of perception," yet for many with ego attachment the abyss is nothing short of a quantum leap up.

Step outside your "guarded self" today and observe how often your thoughts and actions are fear-based. As you do this, take inventory on what expectations weren't met. What aspect of your life didn't seem in control? Take inventory of the ego's shadow. Then assess how to release these thoughts, feelings, and perceptions so you can move toward a motivation of love and compassion. Love's rainbow has many colors (e.g., patience, forgiveness, optimism, courage, tolerance, persistence, faith, humor, creativity, and, of course, compassion). Rather than taking one step forward and two steps back (and losing ground), take two steps forward, one towards the doors of a new perception and the second through the door—towards the light.

In his book *Stalking the Wild Pendulum,* physicist Itzhak Bentov discusses the energetic nature of the kundalini effect,[16] documenting several cases. Yet he implies that due to its mystical nature Western science has yet to recognize this phenomenon. This denial of the spiritual nature of humanity is often called a *blind spot.*

Science's Blind Spot

AFTER DISTILLING THE INFORMATION he collected, Narby came to the conclusion that these shamans carefully used sacred medicinal herbs as a way to access a source of information that he attributed to DNA. His presentation of facts is impressive. There has long been an association between specific hallucinogenic drugs and nirvana. (Please note that I am not advocating the use of drugs for spiritual experiences.) Narby contends that there seems to be an active ingredient in various hallucinogenic compounds that allows one access to the wisdom found in DNA. However, he notes that access can occur without the aid of these compounds. Yogis seem to do it through meditation and come back with remarkable wisdom.

Narby points out a critical factor in his search for truth. Science, which has for centuries turned a deaf ear to the spiritual connection of life, also appears to be wearing blinders—a form of denial that clearly separates science from spirituality, what many people call blatant arrogance. In essence, this arrogant attitude in science perpetuates a paradigm of thought mixed with one's beliefs that is quite difficult to change, as noted by Thomas Kuhn in his book about paradigm shifts titled *The Structure of Scientific Revolutions*.[17] "Biology," Narby states, "has a blind spot of historical origin."[18] Narby isn't the only one to mention science's myopic vision. Larry Dossey, M.D., has been saying this for years.

Prayer, Distant Healing, and the Nonlocal Mind

LARRY DOSSEY IS A PHYSICIAN, author, and executive editor of the medical journal *Alternative Therapies*, a peer-reviewed journal that studies the various modalities of complementary medicine. Dossey states that Western medicine is on the vanguard of a new era, what he calls "**Era-III medicine**," in which human consciousness will be regarded as an essential aspect of the healing process.

In his book *Reinventing Medicine*, Dossey explores the aspects of what he terms the *nonlocal mind*, consciousness that is not merely contained in the brain, but that seems to travel at the speed of light around the globe.[19] He uses prayer as an example. Researchers at Duke University Medical Center are conducting a double-blind, clinically controlled study in which prayer is a treatment for cardiac patients. Names of patients are given to prayer groups around the world—Buddhist monks in Tibet, Carmelite nuns in Baltimore, Jews in Israel, and Baptists in North Carolina—a diverse group so no one religion can take all the credit. Preliminary results are impressive, showing that those subjects who were prayed for had statistically significantly fewer complications with coronary care. Dossey has compiled these and hundreds of studies, stories, and case histories about **prayer**, leading to a critical mass that cannot be ignored by Western science.[20]

Healing with prayer is intriguing, but no more fascinating than that of **distant healing**. Elizabeth Targ, M.D., a medical scientist in northern California, codesigned a study in 1996 to examine the effects of distant healing on patients with advanced AIDS. Healers from around the country were assigned patients by name. Whether by intention, prayer, or healing energy, as done through Reiki, bioenergy, or Qi Gong, results revealed that the treatment group had a statistically significant rate of reduced symptoms associated with AIDS than the control group that received only the benefits of standard Western medicine. This and other studies have prompted several physicians and scholars nationwide to include the study of spiritual matters in medical school training.[21]

One study by Herbert Benson found no effect of the prayer phenomenon whatsoever, making the cover of *Newsweek* magazine, yet upon close examination of the methodology used, the study has been dismissed and nearly forgotten.

Dossey contends that there is an ocean of quality data to support the reality of the human spirit as a healing agent in medicine, yet old habits (denial) die hard, particularly in a healthcare system that is stressed to the max and begging for reform. Ever the optimist, Dossey is assured that as medicine evolves from **Era-II medicine** (mind–body) to Era-III medicine (mind–body–spirit), wonderful advances in healing will take place.

⚛ SUMMARY

A LARGE COMPONENT OF HUMAN SPIRITUALITY falls under the domain of divine mystery—that which cannot be explained through the rational mind but nonetheless is very real. Experiences that are mystical in nature are not for a chosen few. Rather, these moments—some call them *holy moments*—are available for everyone, but it takes an open mind to be receptive to their meaning. As science and religion search for universal truths, an appreciation for that which cannot be easily explained becomes evident, even if the explanations are elusive. The search for truth appears to extend to the farthest reaches of the universe as well as to the complex building blocks of life, DNA. Could the secrets of our DNA be related to what sages and mystics call the kundalini energy, located at the base of our spine? Perhaps! Some scientists looking through a myopic lens may indeed have a blind spot, yet there are others who stand at the vanguard of current understanding, bushwhacking a trail to new levels of consciousness and wisdom.

⊪ TERMS AND CONCEPTS

distant healing	holy moments
DNA	kundalini energy
Era-II medicine	prayer
Era-III medicine	

EXERCISE 7.1
ON BEING A GOOD MYSTIC

In a recent Harris poll, over 70% of those questioned admitted to having a mystical experience. It's likely the number is even higher. There are many types of mystical experiences, many of which defy description, but by not attempting to articulate them into a comprehensible language we begin to forget details of fragments that initially lingered in the mind. By writing them down we make the intangible slightly more tangible, the supernatural a little more natural, and the ordinary a little more extraordinary.

1. Beyond the five senses, what experiences have you had that you consider to be of a mystical, divine nature? Please take a moment to describe two or three of the most memorable ones here.

   _____

   _____

   _____

   _____

   _____

2. The renowned psychologist Carl Jung spent the better part of his professional career exploring the mystical nature of the mind. Much of his research involved dreams and dream analysis. He was of the opinion that not only are we capable of precognitive dreams and premonitions, but that these are common occurrences. Do you recall any dreams that foretold future events? Please explain them here.

_____

_____

_____

_____

_____

3. Carl Jung used the word *synchronicity* to describe two seemingly random events that come together with great significance. More than just a coincidence, synchronistic events are often thought to be divine messages when we take the time to decode them. As the expression goes, "There is no such thing as a coincidence. It's God's way of remaining anonymous." What unusual coincidences have you had that are worth noting?

_____

_____

_____

_____

_____

4. Abraham Maslow coined the term *peak experience* to convey a sense of oneness with the universe. People who experience this sensation describe it as "touching the face of God." Although these experiences are often beyond description, describe, as best you can, through metaphor, simile, or analogy, what this experience was like.

_____

_____

_____

_____

_____

5. To be a good mystic means to appreciate the mystery of life. M. Scott Peck, author of the acclaimed book *The Road Less Traveled*, stated that the highest stage of spiritual growth was to explore the mystery of life, but to never lose one's appreciation for it. To some, the mystical side of life, those things that cannot be explained rationally through the framework

of Western science, is baffling. It leads to a sense of frustration rather than a sense of appreciation. Where do you fall on this continuum?

_____

_____

_____

_____

_____

EXERCISE 7.2
MORE THAN JUST INTUITION!

Have you ever thought of a good friend or family member hundreds of miles away and the next moment the phone rings and, guess who? It's the person you were thinking of right there on the phone. Coincidence? Perhaps not. Have you ever missed your bus or plane only to find out that the one you tried so hard to get on was involved in a serious accident? How about a time when you had a premonition about a certain situation only to find out that, without any way of knowing, you knew what was going to happen?

Life is full of countless experiences that defy the rational mind's ability to come up with a satisfactory answer. Science may attempt to come up with an answer, yet most likely months later even it has been rebuked. Being a good mystic doesn't mean you have the answers for these extraordinary moments; it just means you can appreciate them for what they are: extraordinary reminders that our daily reality far exceeds the five senses. Premonitions, clairvoyant thoughts, insightful dreams, and synchronistic moments are all very natural and part of the human experience. Yet it's easy to pass these off if we are afraid of them. In fact, fear can even diminish our memories of them. Reflect for a moment and see if you can recall any extraordinary moments that might fall into the following categories:

1. Premonitions (thoughts about someone or something that actually happen the next day or so):

_____

_____

_____

2. Insightful dreams (dreams in which a solution to a problem came to you, or some image appeared that appeared again later in a wakeful state):

   _____

   _____

   _____

3. Clairvoyant thoughts (psychic thoughts, feelings, or intuitive thoughts that come true in the future):

   _____

   _____

   _____

4. Synchronistic moments (more than just a coincidence; a moment when two events come together, and there is a message there for you):

   _____

   _____

   _____

5. Other mystical moments (visions, apparitions, voices, altered states of consciousness, etc.):

   _____

   _____

   _____

6. What is your comfort level with these types of experiences, and why do you feel this way?

   _____

   _____

   _____

EXERCISE 7.3
ONE: A HOLY MOMENT

Have you ever experienced a moment in your life where you became one with the universe? A special, if not rare, moment—a natural high or a singular sensation that took your breath away and filled your heart with so much joy and wonder that you wanted to reach out and grab the world and hug it? Most likely you have had a few singular sensations, more if you are really lucky!

Psychologist Abraham Maslow called these moments "peak experiences." Stress researcher Joan Borysenko calls them "holy moments," and indeed, they are very special. Like Maslow, Borysenko is of the opinion that not only do we need to be more receptive to these experiences, but that we also need to occasionally remind ourselves of these events to help lend emotional balance to the negative experiences we encounter throughout our lives. Search your memory bank. What holy moment comes to mind at the thought of this suggestion? Perhaps it was seeing a deer jump into a thicket of woods while you were jogging on a dirt road. Perhaps it was watching the birth of your first child. Perhaps it was standing on a mountaintop watching the sun reflect its crimson colors on a blanket of clouds near the horizon or swimming with dolphins. Maybe it happened while making personal contact with a long-lost friend, or hugging your favorite dog or cat after a really bad day.

Close your eyes for a moment and think back to a very special moment when you felt a profound, if not divine, connection to the universe—a moment that transcended time and space as well as your everyday thoughts, feelings, and responsibilities. Try to recall the emotional sensation that you experienced with this event. Then open your eyes and try to recapture the event on paper in as much detail as possible.

_____

_____

_____

_____

_____

_____

✦ ENDNOTES

1. Redfield, J., *The Celestine Prophecy.* Warner Books: New York, 1996.

2. Walsch, N. D., *Conversations with God.* G. P. Putnam's Sons: New York, 1996.

3. Harvard professor and psychologist John Mack has done extensive research on clients who claimed to have been abducted by aliens, and he nearly lost his tenure position at Harvard for this research. The reason cited was that it was unworthy of academic study.

4. Fuller, B., as quoted in *The Aquarian Conspiracy* by Marilyn Ferguson. Tarcher Books: Los Angeles, 1980.

5. St. Augustine, as quoted in *Alternative Medicine.* Future Medicine Publishing: Puyallup, WA, 1993.

6. Yogananda, P., *Autobiography of a Yogi.* Crystal Clarity Publishing: Nevada City, CA, 1946 (rereleased in 1994).

7. Seaward, B. L., "Spiritual Well-Being: A Health Education Model." *Journal of Health Education,* No. 22(3): 166–169, 1991.

8. Medwick, K., *Teresa of Avila: Progress of a Soul.* Random House: New York, 1999.
9. Ball, M., *Kiss of God: The Wisdom of a Silent Child.* Health Communications: Deerfield Beach, FL, 1999.
10. Talbot, M., *The Holographic Universe.* HarperSanFrancisco: San Francisco, 1991.
11. Pearsall, P., *The Heart's Code.* Broadway Books: New York, 1998.
12. Star Knowledge Conference, Yankton Sioux Reservation, South Dakota, June 21–23, 1996.
13. Narby, J., *The Cosmic Serpent: DNA and the Origins of Knowledge.* Tarcher/Putnam Books: New York, 1999.
14. Narby, J., *The Cosmic Serpent: DNA and the Origins of Knowledge.* Tarcher/Putnam Books: New York, 1999.
15. Narby, J., *The Cosmic Serpent: DNA and the Origins of Knowledge.* Tarcher/Putnam Books: New York, 1999.
16. Bentov, I., *Stalking the Wild Pendulum.* Destiny Books: Rochester, VT, 1988.
17. Kuhn, T., *The Structure of Scientific Revolutions.* University of Chicago Press: Chicago, 1981.
18. Narby, J., *The Cosmic Serpent: DNA and the Origins of Knowledge.* Tarcher/Putnam Books: New York, 1999.
19. Dossey, L., *Reinventing Medicine: Beyond Mind–Body to a New Era of Healing.* HarperSanFrancisco: San Francisco, 1999.
20. Dossey, L., *Healing Words.* HarperSanFrancisco: San Francisco, 1993.
21. Sicher, F., et al., "A Randomized Double-Blind Study of the Effect of Distant Healing in a Population with Advanced AIDS: Report of a Small-Scale Study." *Western Journal of Medicine,* No. 169(6): 356–363, 1998.

◀ ADDITIONAL REFERENCES

Altan, H., and Koppel, M., "The Cellular Computer DNA: Program or Data?" *Bulletin of Mathematical Biology,* 52(3): 335–348, 1990.

Carey, K., *Starseed: The Third Millennium.* HarperCollins: San Francisco, 1992.

Coelho, P., *The Alchemist.* HarperCollins: New York, 1993.

Dossey, L., "Decoding the Human Genome: Second Thoughts." *Alternative Therapies,* 6(5): 10–14, 63, Sept. 2000.

Pollack, R., *Signs of Life: The Language and Meaning of DNA.* Viking: New York, 1994.

Rattenmeyer, M., et al., "Evidence of Photon Emission from DNA in Living Systems." *Naturwissenschaften,* No. 68: 572–573, 1981.

Seaward, B. L., *Stressed Is Desserts Spelled Backward.* Conari Press: Berkeley, CA, 1999.

Sylvia, C., *A Change of Heart.* Little, Brown & Co: New York, 1997.

Twyman, J., *Emissary of Light.* Warner Books: New York, 1996.

CHAPTER

The Art of Meditation

Meditation. It's not what you think!

—Anonymous

T HOSE WHO FOLLOW THE SPIRITUAL journey in earnest will eventu- ally come upon a sign on the road that reads: "Meditation begins here." Ancient cultures that have documented their past with their own scriptures speak of such a practice to quiet the mind and, in doing so, comfort the soul. **Homeostasis** does not merely describe a state of physical calmness. Tranquility is desired at all levels, including the human spirit. Meditation provides such a state.

For millennia, meditation has been looked upon with skepticism in the West. The influence of René Descartes has been so great that intangible abstracts like the mind are difficult to quantify, thus meditation has not been an easy topic to study. In the 1960s and 1970s, researchers, including Elmer Green at the Menninger Institute[1] and Herbert Benson at Harvard,[2] began to study effects of meditation on the body. The data revealed what mystics have been saying for millennia—a quiet mind calms the body. Medi- tation decreases one's resting heart rate, blood pressure, respiration, and so on. The American Heart Association was so impressed with the findings that it now advocates meditation for anyone prone to or diagnosed with coronary heart disease.[3]

Meditation is not a science; it's an art. Meditation experiences are as varied as the people who meditate. And those who practice the art of medi- tation will tell you that it is as essential to the health of the human spirit as food and water are to the physical body.

Recent research in the field of meditation by Richard Davidson and col- leagues suggests that when the mind engages in a repeated practice of medi- tation (specifically mindfulness meditation), the act of calming the mind actually rewires the brain synapses in a process called *neuroplasticity*.[4–7] Taking neuroplasticiy one step further, author Matthew Alper believes that the brain was designed specifically with a divine connection, in what Alper calls the "God part of the brain." This part of the brain shows a higher rate of activity during MRI scans when people are instructed to think about the concept of God or to feel one with the universe through prayer or medi- tation.[8] Others believe that the mind needs a special vehicle to access the higher realms of consciousness, including psychotropic drugs like peyote and ayahuasca.[9]

Though misconceptions about meditation have diminished in recent years, it is best to reiterate here that meditation is not a religious practice even though many religions incorporate meditation into their rituals (e.g., prayer, reflection, contemplation, etc.). Simply stated, meditation is a health practice to bring integration, balance, and harmony to the mind, body, spirit, and emotions.

Many different definitions of *meditation* have been offered, but reduced to its simplest terms it is best described as increased concentration that leads to increased awareness. Meditation first requires the discipline of focused attention. With practice, the focused, quiet mind opens up to insights and ideas that, until that time, remained a mystery. A wonderful Chinese proverb about meditation states, "When the pupil is ready, the teacher will come," inferring that we are both the student and the teacher. Meditation is a practice that ultimately promotes access to the profound wisdom of what Carl Jung called the "collective unconscious."[10]

Cleansing the Mind

IN GENERAL, WESTERN CULTURE DOES not motivate people to turn their thoughts inward for self-reflection. Rather, people are constantly encouraged to direct their attention outward through the five senses, seeking information and satisfying curiosity of all that exists in our immediate surroundings.

More than ever before, we have an abundance of external stimuli to entertain and distract the mind, with technology taking the lead in mental distractions—smartphones, text messages, tweets, Wi-Fi, YouTube, laptop computers, the Internet, the World Wide Web, and the vast array of social networking venues, to name just a few (all of which lead back to information overload). As a result of this bombardment of information, first the mind and then soul suffer from what can only be described as sensory overload. Moreover, with so many marketers vying for consumers' attention, advertisements have become shorter and shorter to keep our attention from drifting away. The epitome of this phenomenon is the diagnosis of ADD (attention deficit disorder), which is no longer just for fidgety kids in grade school.

First and foremost, the mind craves balance. As important as information gathering is, so, too, is the purging of nonessential information. Whereas the unconscious mind is limitless, the conscious mind appears to have storage limitations. Like a computer, which is really an imitation of the mind, the conscious mind must at some point delete various facts, feelings, and such before the space is overloaded and stress ensues. Balance is restored to the conscious mind when outside stimuli are significantly decreased; the intensity of ego-chatter is reduced; and thoughts, feelings, attitudes, and beliefs that no longer serve us are resolved, released, or deleted.

Because of the abstract nature of the mind, metaphors are often used to describe how meditation works. Assume for a moment that your mind is like the floor in your garage with dust or dirt scattered about. Meditation is like a broom that sweeps away the debris, leaving a clean space. Another metaphor describes meditation like this: if your mind is like the ever-expansive sky, extraneous thoughts are like big billowy clouds that tend to obstruct the view of the heavens. Meditation is like a soft wind that gently blows the clouds away, leaving a clear view of the heavens.

Perhaps because of its associations with Eastern traditions, the practice of meditation has been castigated by some Western religions as the work of the devil. This includes the notion that if you open your mind crazy thoughts might enter and drive you insane or, worse, take possession of your mind. In fact, this fear-based approach is what meditation works to dispel. A story by Christian theologian C. S. Lewis brings home the point quite clearly. In his classic book *The Screwtape Letters*, a dialogue between the devil and his apprentice takes place. The devil says, "It's funny how mortals always picture us putting things into their minds: in reality, our best work is done by keeping things out."[11]

Of Ego and Soul

WHEN ONE THINKS OF EGO, the first response is often a negative one, but the ego is not entirely bad (after all, a healthy ego is very much related to high self-esteem). In the grand view, the ego plays a necessary role as the bodyguard for the soul. Like a king who dismisses his guards when he retires to the evening chamber, meditation provides a chance for the soul to consciously reconnect to the divine source without the censorship of the ego. To paraphrase the wisdom of Catholic scholar and author Ron Roth, we do not have a soul—we are a soul dressed in a physical body that allows us to wander freely to explore this earthly existence.[12] Knowing all the potential dangers one could face, it makes sense for the soul to have a bodyguard. In a partnership quickly taken advantage of, the ego confuses caution for control, thus weaving the veils of illusion. The soul is always aware of its divine connection (its higher self), and although it knows it is never alone, this recognition and memory are often eclipsed by the shadow of ego. In a period of darkness, the soul falls asleep. The image of a slumbered soul brings to mind this quote from Dr. Albert Schweitzer:

You know of the disease in Central Africa called sleeping sickness. . . . There also exists a sleeping sickness of the soul. Its most dangerous aspect is that one is unaware of its coming. That is why you have to be careful. As soon as you notice the slightest sign of indifference, the moment you become aware of the loss of a certain seriousness, of longing, of enthusiasm and zest, take it as a warning. You should realize your soul suffers if you live superficially.[13]

It is the soul's desire to travel lightly, whereas the ego is a renowned pack rat. For better or worse, the soul is responsible for all the actions of the ego and, consequently, it gets weighed down with the ego's possessions (perceptions, fears, frustrations, etc.). Because the ego collects these for security, both ego and soul are equally encumbered. Meditation is a sure way of releasing the ego's perceptions, beliefs, and attitudes so that the load may be lightened and the promise of the journey ensured.

Domesticating the Ego

HAVE YOU EVER had a dog? If so, then you know how important it is to house train it so that you don't have "poop" all over the place. To successfully train your puppy, you catch it in the act and take it outside so it begins to associate this behavior with the outdoors. Domesticating the ego works much the same way. With your mind analogous to a clean house, you train the voice of the ego to be silent.

Long before Sigmund Freud coined the term *ego,* sages and wisdom keepers far and wide spoke of an aspect of consciousness that acted as a censor to thoughts and information seeking entrance to the conscious mind. As a bodyguard to the soul, the ego's primary role is to protect us from danger. Yet, in its thirst for power, the ego cordons off the far reaches of the mind in what perhaps can be described as a *coup of consciousness.* The ego conspires to control and manipulate the soul on a daily basis. Nowhere is this more evident than in the conscious dialogue of the mind, where the ego holds a perpetual conversation of incessant chatter.

The purpose of meditation is to pause the idle chatter long enough so that the mind can become calm. This allows any insights from the depths of the unconscious to bubble up to the conscious mind so that you can acknowledge them and let them help you navigate safely on the path of your journey.

A Free Spirit Must Be Disciplined

THERE IS A SIDE OF human spirituality that appears wild and carefree, yet the complete picture is one that honors responsibility as well. Nowhere is this more evident than in the practice of meditation, in which discipline is paramount to spiritual growth.

If the average person were asked to sit quietly for 30 minutes, most likely he or she would begin to fidget within the third minute. By the fifth minute, the person would be climbing the walls. Let there be no doubt, the practice of meditation takes great discipline. Discipline is a hybrid of desire and commitment that grooms the soul for any circumstance and any adventure. To discipline the mind, one must begin by taking small steps. Some advocate starting with as little as 5 minutes per day. As one works with this goal to quiet the mind, more time can be added. It is not uncommon for people to begin with a 5-minute interval and slowly build up to about 30 minutes per session. This same quality of discipline is no different from that needed by musicians and athletes who work hard to hone their specific skills.

A friend of mine, Greg, studied in Japan to learn firsthand the martial art of jujitsu. His master began each day with three hours of meditation. The purpose was to domesticate the ego and to discipline the mind, because only when the mind is totally disciplined can the mind and body act in unison. Students in this class sat on their heels, back straight, chin up, and eyes forward for three uninterrupted hours. The master would walk down the rows of students, holding a reed in his hand. If he observed a student letting his or her mind wander rather than staying focused per the instructions, he would whack them with great force on the back of the head with the stick. Greg said he learned really quickly to stay focused.

Although this method of his teacher's practice was rather draconian, and unlike any other I have heard of, typically the discipline of meditation comes with no punishments, only rewards.

Types of Meditation

ALTHOUGH THERE ARE MANY WAYS to meditate, they generally fall into one of three categories: exclusive meditation, inclusive meditation, and mindfulness meditation. Let's take a look at each one.

Exclusive Meditation

Exclusive meditation is a style of meditation in which you sit still, close your eyes, and focus your awareness on one particular thought to the exclusion of all the others. For example, you begin by focusing your attention on your breathing—the inhalation, the exhalation—repeating this for the duration of the meditation period. Should a distracting thought surface that competes with the focus of your attention, allow the thought to leave your mind as you exhale.

Some people use a verbal mantra when doing this style of meditation. Rather than focusing on the breathing, you would repeat a word or phrase, such as "love," "peace," or "calm." Visual objects of focus can also be used, such as a mandala or a candle flame, where the focus of your vision is undisturbed for the duration of your meditation session. Repetitive sounds are also used, such as the sounds of ocean waves, a trickling stream of water, or Tibetan bells. The most common form of exclusive meditation is Transcendental Meditation (TM).

Inclusive Meditation

Inclusive meditation is often referred to as Zen meditation, and unlike exclusive meditation, in which the mind's focus is very narrow, here the mind's focus is as wide as possible. Every thought is allowed equal access. In this style of reflection, one sits still with the back straight and the eyes wide open. As you sit still, you observe your thoughts, any and all thoughts. Keeping in mind that meditation requires domesticating the ego, all thoughts are observed without judgment. It's as if you are watching yourself think. A common image is to imagine that your thoughts are like free-flowing logs floating down a stream. If you find yourself with a judgmental thought (e.g., "my boss is an idiot"), you allow that thought to float down the stream, too. You are the observer, sitting on the shore watching your thoughts go by. **Ultimately inclusive meditation** is where you observe yourself observing your thoughts. This state of detachment is considered the highest level of oneness while maintaining a sense of compassion. As your mind clears itself of extraneous mental chatter, the mind becomes a clean blank screen, the epitome of inner peace.

Mindfulness Meditation

Mindfulness meditation is similar to inclusive meditation in that the focus of one's attention is limited to the here and now, not the past or future, but to the present moment. Inclusive meditation is typically done sitting still, yet mindfulness meditation is not limited to a time of day or one room in the house. Mindfulness meditation is a mind-set that is carried with you wherever you are—washing dishes, eating an apple, or driving a car. Like inclusive meditation, you are asked to pass making judgment on any and all thoughts. Vietnamese Buddhist monk Thich Nhat Hanh is renowned for his teachings in mindfulness meditation,[14] as is Jon Kabat-Zinn.[15]

Several different meditation exercises are presented at the end of this chapter. Try these at your leisure and see which, if any, produces a calming effect.

Reaching Enlightenment?

Renowned American psychic Edgar Cayce once said, "When we pray, we talk to God, when we meditate, God talks to us."[16] The purpose of meditation, as teachers of Zen say, is to enlarge the smaller mind. The smaller mind, which we call the conscious mind, is enshrouded in a tapestry of veils woven by thoughts, perceptions, attitudes, beliefs, opinions, and philosophies that constitute our identity as dictated by ego. But this complicated tapestry shields us from our greatest potential. Meditation allows us to pull back these veils to view a whole new reality, a conscious connection to the divine source.

Is it possible in the absolute stillness of one's mind to draw the thinnest of veils that separates the small conscious mind from the expansive unconscious mind to reveal a wealth of knowledge there for the asking? Most definitely, yes!

Enlightenment comes in several ways. Most often it appears as simple thoughts, images, concepts, or ideas that hold a profound significance when they are acted upon. A quick study of the history of ideas and inventions reveals that some of the greatest advances in humanity—from Einstein's theory of relativity and Edison's phonograph to Picasso's Cubist masterpieces and Mozart's sonatas—occurred in a relaxed, lucid state in which the veils of illusion were opened.[17]

Today it is often said that only a few chosen people (Jesus and the Buddha) have ever reached a perpetual state of enlightenment. Although this may be true, countless people have been able to reach up and pull away the veils of illusion, and, in doing so, they are forever changed. Surrounded in a stream of brilliant light and love, it is an unmistakable feeling that can only be experienced, for no book on meditation can begin to describe this transcendent light and love.

As spirits on a human path, we experience enlightenment as neither a place of supreme residence nor the end point of a long journey. It is a bank of wisdom that we are able to draw upon in the course of daily events. And this bank of wisdom is open to everyone. However, you should be aware of two important aspects of meditation. First, bursts of intuitive thought, flirtations with nirvana, and grandiose insights do not come to the unprepared, undisciplined mind. Second, insights that make themselves known are to be shared, not hoarded, for greed is not a spiritual value. So be prepared to share whatever you learn with those who are the most likely to benefit.

Although the mind and brain are not one and the same, the mind uses the brain as its primary organ of choice. There is a wonderful correlation between the conscious and unconscious minds and those attributes associated with what is now understood to be the cognitive functions of the right and left hemispheres of the brain. The left hemisphere, noted for skills that draw upon judgment, analysis, and rational thinking, is quite active in times of stress. Conversely, the right brain, which houses the attributes of holism, receptivity, intuition, and imagination, seems to be more accessible in a relaxed, meditative state.[18] Perhaps it is no coincidence that these traits are similar to those cited by those people who have made a trip to hell and back and have come through the experience gracefully.

There is a story of a young man who conversed with an old monk who was reputed to be the most enlightened person for miles around. The young man, who aspired to be as wise as his mentor, one day asked him, "Old man, how does one reach enlightenment?" The old monk looked deep into the eyes of the young lad, and, with a pause, he answered, "Chop wood, carry water." Then he walked away.

The young man walked away without smiling, for he knew that the goal he desired required much discipline and determination but most of all a strong mind. He also knew that enlightenment doesn't come solely from sitting contemplating one's navel for eternity. One must be an active participant in life.

After several years of diligence in meditation, the now middle-aged man approached his mentor and said, "Old man, what does one do after one reaches enlightenment?" The old monk looked deep into the eyes of the middle-aged man, and, without pause, said, "Chop wood, carry water." The moral of the story is one of humbleness, for even when you get to this point of clarity you must continue to live your life.

Steps in Meditation

Years ago, meditation practices were considered important only by those actively on the spiritual path, but today with the constant bombardment of sensory stimulation from our high-tech gadgets meditation is now advocated by many in the field of psychology as a necessity for everyone. Research now reveals that people surrounded by a flood of information (and choices of information venues) are showing signs of what has come to be called "brain freeze."[19] Taking time to clear the mind of excess sensory stimulation as well as domesticating the ego (and its addictive tendencies) is now considered essential for mental health as well as spiritual well-being.

Although there are no hard and fast rules to meditation, the following suggestions may help guide you through the oftentimes arduous process:

1. **Find a quiet place.** Pick a place at home or work where you can sit or lie comfortably for a while and not be bothered. If you have one specific place that is dedicated to this practice, it helps minimize distractions.

2. **Schedule a regular time each day.** The preferred time to meditate is at the start of each day. Although it is not necessary to rise before the sun, it is suggested that you dedicate the same time each day (e.g., 7:15 A.M.). In doing so, this practice is budgeted into your daily schedule, whereas a random time each day soon loses its priority and never happens.

3. **Minimize any distractions.** Before the mind can focus to minimize the mental chatter of the ego, it must first minimize outside noise that can also serve to distract the mind. Do your best to create a place of silence by turning off radios, televisions, phones, beepers, fax machines, computers, and anything else that robs your attention. Distraction can also include people. In this regard, it is important to have good boundaries. Diplomatically tell anyone who may walk in that an interruption is a violation of your personal time and ask that they honor your request not to interrupt.

   Purists choose to have total quiet, but you may find that some background (white) noise is in order to balance things out. The most popular choice is soft melodic, even repetitive, music (without lyrics). If this helps, give it a try.

   A note about food and eating: it is recommended that you do not try to meditate after a snack or meal, because the physiology of digestion can be a distraction, particularly when more blood is directed to the stomach and less to the head, which can cause drowsiness.

4. **Find a comfortable position.** The most important aspect of comfort is a straight spine. Sitting with a straight back is the preferred method of meditation. Leaning against a wall may help, as might sitting on a pillow to raise the tailbone off the floor. Sitting with your legs crossed (e.g., the lotus position or half-lotus position) may help to promote a straight spine as well. While lying flat on the floor certainly can promote a straight spine, it also lends itself to a loss of consciousness (sleep), which is not the same thing as meditation (being fully awake).

5. **Create an object of focus.** Many devices can be used to focus the mind. In exclusive meditation, the device is called a **mantra**. The purpose of the mantra is to help cleanse the mind by focusing exclusively on one thought, which, in turn, helps erase all the extraneous thoughts that beg for attention. There are many types of mantras—a word

that is endlessly repeated, sounds that are listened to, beads that are touched, or the cycle of the breath that is observed. Because breathing is something that everyone does naturally, focusing one's attention on the breath, both inhalation and exhalation, serves as a simple mantra.

For those with a penchant for Zen (inclusive) meditation, a mental device that allows the mind to expand beyond its normal limits of ego is helpful. Images such as watching logs floating down a stream, clouds floating across an afternoon sky, playing with a koan, and stating an unanswerable question can all serve to liberate the mind from ego attachment.

6. **Establish the duration of meditation.** For those just starting, to sit quietly for 5 minutes may seem like an eternity, but 5 minutes is a good start for just about anybody. For those in a rush, 5 minutes is good, too. Those who make a practice of meditation find that time flies while sitting still, and it is not uncommon to spend 30, 40, or even 60 minutes in solitude. Every person is different, so find a length of time that works best for you.

7. **Keep a pad of paper nearby.** It's a good idea to keep a pad of paper and pen/pencil nearby so that if you have a thought that must be written down to be remembered, you've got the means to do so. This also helps clear the mind, because once you've written it down you can let it go. So people sit with a pen and pad of paper, close their eyes, and as important thoughts bubble up to the surface, down they go onto paper, with lists, ideas, and reminders (and emotional baggage to be discarded!).

8. **Relieve the boredom factor.** One of the most common complaints about meditation is the boredom factor. The conscious mind, once so actively engaged in sorting out sensory information, feels underrepresented, but this will soon pass with time. Some ways to relieve boredom are to pick from an assortment of music while meditating or to vary the meditation themes from day to day (there are eight different meditation exercises at the end of this chapter). Another way to begin your meditation is to read from a meditation book (e.g., the Bible, *Earth Prayers*, etc.), and then use the meditation reading as a theme to contemplate on.

⬖ SUMMARY

THE PRACTICE OF MEDITATION, clearing mental chatter to gain clarity of thoughts and feelings, is an ageless health practice found in nearly every culture on the planet. The ego is thought to be responsible for this mental chatter, and the expression "domesticate the ego" refers to this calming of psychological defenses. In doing so, you gain greater clarity on various aspects of your life. Some people refer to this clarity as enlightenment, a deep-seated wisdom that can only be accessed through a quiet mind. There are hundreds of ways to meditate, but they generally fall into three categories: exclusive, inclusive, and mindfulness. One cannot meditate just once to gain the benefits for a lifetime. The practice of meditation requires discipline. The reward of discipline is inner peace.

✹ TERMS AND CONCEPTS

enlightenment

exclusive meditation

homeostasis

inclusive meditation

mantra

mindfulness meditation

ultimately inclusive meditation

EXERCISE 8.1
MEDITATION CHECKLIST

Here is a checklist to get you started in the practice of meditation:

1. Where can you find a quiet spot in your house, apartment, or office to meditate?

   a. Primary location: _____

   b. Backup location: _____

2. What time of day is best for you to meditate?

   a. Primary time: _____

   b. Backup time: _____

3. What steps do you need to take to make clear boundaries for peace and quiet (phones, television, people, animals, etc.)?

   a. _____

   b. _____

   c. _____

4. What items, if any, do you need to create the most conducive atmosphere for meditation?

   a. Music: _____

   b. Visual object: _____

   c. Pad of paper: _____

   d. Meditation books: _____

   e. Candles: _____

   f. Incense: _____

5. Anything else you need?

    a. _____

    b. _____

    c. _____

✺ MEDITATION EXERCISES

The following eight exercises are meditation exercises that may be used as a means to quiet your mind and to bring a sense of peace to your heart and soul. As has been mentioned numerous times, the practice of meditation is a cornerstone to spiritual wellness and optimal well-being.

There is no one way to meditate, which is why this section offers a host of different exercises. As you will see with these eight visualization techniques, each meditation is varied in its scope, yet the underlying premise is to calm the mind and, in doing so, to bring peace to all aspects of your being. Please feel free to adapt the specifics of these images and suggestions found within these exercises so that they are most beneficial to you. The eight exercises are as follows:

Exercise 8.2: Breathing Clouds Meditation

Exercise 8.3: Open Heart Meditation

Exercise 8.4: Crystal Cave Meditation

Exercise 8.5: Seven Veils Meditation

Exercise 8.6: Body Colors and Healing Light Meditation

Exercise 8.7: Rainbow Meditation

Exercise 8.8: Energy Ball Meditation

Exercise 8.9: DNA Meditation

EXERCISE 8.2
BREATHING CLOUDS MEDITATION

The purpose of this meditation is to focus on your breathing and, at the same time, to help clear the mind of distracting thoughts and unresolved emotions that no longer serve you. This meditation is one that can be used to initiate the emptying process. As with all meditations that use mental imagery, please feel free to augment these suggestions in your own mind to promote the greatest sense of comfort and peace.

In this meditation, two images are combined with your breathing. The first is an image of a clean white cloud that you focus on as you inhale; the second is a dark, dirty cloud of air that you focus on as you exhale. The clean white cloud of air is symbolic of cleansing the mind. It is pure and fresh, with the intention of cleansing the mind, body, and spirit. The dark cloud of air symbolizes any or all thoughts and feelings that we wish to release and let go of, including fears, frustrations, grudges, physical pains, or any unresolved issues that we need to resolve by first letting go. The inhalation is symbolic of invigoration; the exhalation is symbolic of cleansing and detoxification.

You can do as many breathing clouds cycles as you wish. Ten is a good number to start with. The idea behind this meditation is that at some point in this breathing clouds cycle (which will vary from person to person) the air you breathe out will become as pure as the air you breathe in, and, in doing so, you become relaxed and peaceful.

1. Begin by closing your eyes and focusing on your breathing. Place all of your focus on your breathing.

2. Now, as you take your next breath—slowly and comfortably—inhale through your nose and imagine that you are inhaling clean fresh air, like a white puffy cloud. Feel the air circulate up through your sinuses, up to the top of your head, and down the back of your spine.

3. As you begin to exhale, slowly and comfortably, exhale through your mouth. As you exhale, visualize that the air you breathe out is a dark dirty cloud of air. As you exhale, bring to mind a thought or feeling that no longer serves you and let it go as you exhale.

4. Again, inhale clean, fresh air through your nose. Let it circulate to the top of your head and down the back of your spine to where it resides in your stomach.

5. Exhale very slowly through your mouth and, as you do, think of a moment of frustration or feeling of resentment that you have been carrying around for a long time. Now is the time to let it go; as you exhale, visualize the dark, dirty air you breathe out carrying this toxic thought as it leaves with the breath.

6. Slowly inhale clean fresh air in through your nose and feel it circulate to the top of your head and down the back of your spine. As it circulates, feel it invigorate your entire body.

7. Exhale slowly through your mouth and once again bring to mind a thought or feeling of unresolved stress that begs to be resolved. Letting go is the first step in doing so, and as this cloud of dark, musty air leaves your mouth, give yourself permission to release this stress by letting go as you exhale.

8. Repeat this cycle of breathing clouds—fresh air in, dark, dirty air out—until you come to a greater sense of calm. As you do, notice that the air you exhale becomes as clear as the air you inhale, symbolizing homeostasis between mind, body, and spirit.

EXERCISE 8.3
OPEN HEART MEDITATION

We all know how important the heart is. It is a crucial component of human physiology. However, heart disease is the number one killer in the United States, taking the life of one person every 30 seconds. The association between clogged arteries and heart disease is well proven, but in addition to cholesterol buildup is the consequence of hardened arteries from plaque buildup, in essence, a *hardened heart.*

Before we knew all about the dynamics of anatomy and physiology, we trusted our body wisdom, which told us about feelings from the heart. As it turns out, every aspect of gross anatomy is paired with symbolism. Placed over our physical heart is a symbolic heart. In Eastern culture, this is referred to as the *heart chakra*—a spinning wheel of energy—that allows energy to flow into and out of the anatomical heart. Ageless wisdom tells us that our emotions are closely tied to the heart chakra; the heart chakra expands with the expression of love and compassion and constricts or closes in times of fear and anger.

We have all heard the expression of "a hardened heart." We speak of it in terms of being mean, nasty, hateful, rude, aggressive, stoic, inconsiderate, or indifferent. Symbolic messages can have very real physiological consequences. Stress caused by unresolved feelings of anger and fear is now thought to be the single most important risk factor for coronary heart disease. Recently, cardiologist Dean Ornish discovered that when cardiac patients were introduced to meditation, there was clear evidence of a reversal of the blockage of the coronary arteries.

Ornish, who spent time studying in India, is no stranger to the concept of the heart chakra. The expression of love through the heart is the strongest healing power known. And we each have the ability to receive, share, and be an instrument for this love. Opening the symbolic heart, the heart chakra, comes from the depths of ageless wisdom, and its message is one that we must put into daily practice.

1. Sit quietly for several minutes and focus on your breathing. Feel the air come into your nose or mouth, down into your lungs, and your stomach begin to expand, only to return as you start your exhalation. Repeat this seven times, and as you exhale repeat the phrase "My body is calm and relaxed" to yourself.

2. After the seventh breath, focus your attention on the center of your upper chest, the area over your heart. If you desire, you can imagine that over this area is an image of a heart, or flower, or whatever symbol you associate with love and compassion. If you use a flower (e.g., a lotus, rose, chrysanthemum, etc.), imagine that it is opened up fully toward the sun.

3. For the next seven breaths, imagine that you are breathing air into your lungs through your symbolic heart. Follow each inhalation with an exhalation back out through the symbolic heart.

4. Using your imagination, picture someone whom you care about in front of you and allow yourself to picture a rainbow of light, a beam of light, or some manifestation of loving energy from your heart to the heart of this person.

5. It is important that you not only think the thought of love, compassion, and bliss, but that you actually feel it as well. Feel love in every cell of your body and then express the intention and desire to share this feeling with that person whom you have chosen to connect with.

6. Sending love to people toward whom we feel a sense of fondness is easy. Sending feelings of love and compassion to people whom we dislike, by whom we feel violated, or with whom we are not at peace is a much greater challenge, but it's not impossible. Bring to mind a person with whom you are not at peace. Using your imagination, re-create a beam of light, a rainbow of love, from your heart to this person's heart. If this seems too hard

at first, then merely place an image of this person(s) in front of you and send a message of acknowledgment of his or her human spirit—for even though we may not like the person's behaviors, the divine presence in each person is a reflection of the divine presence in ourselves.

7. Continue this meditation by refocusing on the image of a dear friend or family member to whom you wish to communicate a bond of compassion. Take seven breaths, each time renewing the thought and feeling of love and compassion as you focus on this image.

8. Close with one final, slow, deep breath—sending a ray of loving light to yourself.

EXERCISE 8.4
CRYSTAL CAVE MEDITATION

Have you ever had a problem to which you knew the answer at some deep level but just could not seem to get to? In some cases, talking with friends and acquaintances comes close yet never really hits the mark. It's like there is a barrier between you and what you need to know. The following meditation has been used by people who have been searching for answers to problems or who are trying to resolve issues that beg for attention. Some remarkable stories have emerged from this exercise with great triumph. This meditation helps to remove the barrier and helps you to come to resolution with insights, allowing you to move on with your life.

The premise behind this meditation is that we have the answers within us at some deep and profound level. We also have assistance from guides who remain unseen but are there to help us when we put out the intention for help. This meditation is based on the Jungian concept of archetypal images and the collective unconscious.

1. Imagine that you are standing at the bottom of a short set of stairs of about ten steps. At the bottom, where you are, it is rather dark, but at the top of the stairs you see a radiant light.

2. You feel compelled to walk up the stairs toward the light, but you find that you can only take one step at a time. As you take the first step, you begin to feel a sense of inner peace within yourself. On the second step, you feel a sense of inner peace among you and your family members. On the third step, you gain a sense of peace and resolution with friends and acquaintances. The fourth step brings a sense of calm and serenity with you and your higher self. With each step, you feel your body becoming lighter and more relaxed. With this sense of lightness and peace, you almost feel yourself floating up the remaining steps—toward the top.

3. As you appear on the top step, you find yourself surrounded in a brilliant white light. Soon thereafter, you feel yourself floating up into the light, and each cell in your body radiates this brilliant white loving light. After a moment, you sense that you cannot distinguish yourself from the light, and you feel an incredible sense of love, support, and nurturing from this source of light.

4. Surrounded in light, you feel yourself floating down a hall of crystal glass, and the light that resides in you and around you shines through the crystal glass so that rainbows appear everywhere. The colors of these rainbows make you smile and feel a sense of wonder and awe.

5. As you continue to float through this hall of crystal glass, you come upon a big room, also constructed of crystal glass prisms. As various colors of the rainbow filter through the room, you see an area that has a sunken floor, and you soon find yourself sitting on a comfortable step. As you look around, you notice the beauty of this room, like a grand living room, comfortable and cozy. And as you look around, you notice sitting there next to you one of your spiritual guides. It may be someone you recognize, or it may be someone you have never seen before. Look at his or her face and into his or her eyes, and as you do feel a sense of comfort and compassion coming from this person.

6. Spiritual guides are with us all the time and they are here to guide and guard us, when we take the time to listen. If there is a question you would like to ask of your guide, feel free to do so now. All you need to do is think the question, and your voice will be heard. Then listen very carefully for the answer. It will come as one of your own thoughts, but at a deep level you will know that your guide has answered you.

7. When you feel ready, thank your guide, and as you do, you then find yourself floating back through the hall of prism glass with multicolored rainbows and then through the passage of brilliant white light to where you now sit or lie. Take a deep breath and relax, contemplating the message you have received.

EXERCISE 8.5
SEVEN VEILS MEDITATION (LIFTING THE VEILS OF ILLUSION TO BE ONE WITH THE SOURCE)

It is said that the spiritual path cannot be measured in miles, years, experiences, or possessions. Some say that the distance cannot be measured at all. Yet there are others who say that the entire distance is no more than 12 to 15 inches. Really, you ask? I believe it is so—the distance from the head to the heart—for the spiritual journey is one where we learn the trials and bliss of love, unconditional love.

Stress is perhaps best defined as the "perceived disconnection" from our divine source. Although we are never truly separated, feelings of alienation can seem very real—feelings of fear generated from ego. The greatest obstruction on the spiritual journey is fear (and its mirror image, anger). It has been said that both fear and anger are projections of the ego. In its finest measure, the ego is the bodyguard for the soul; at its worst it is the greatest impediment to spiritual growth. Fear and anger are nothing more than illusions. They are exaggerations of ego to move into a position of emotional control. In Eastern culture, it is said that once these veils of illusion are removed, we are in the total presence of the divine.

The following meditation is a soul-searching exercise to lift these veils of illusion and to return to the source, the source of unconditional love. Assuming that there are seven veils, use this meditation exercise to change any lingering perceptions of disconnection to form a harmonious union with the divine, however you conceive this to be. (Please note that it may take several times with this meditation to feel its full effects, as some veils may be too heavy to lift the first time around. Also, if you should choose to use a different metaphor, such as a door, please feel free to do so.)

Sit quietly in a comfortable position with your spine in complete alignment. Close your eyes and focus your attention on your breathing. Take several slow deep breaths and come to a place of calm stillness. As you sit, become aware that in front of you are several veils, layers of consciousness that you wish to slowly pull back, for what lies beyond these veils is a view of unparalleled beauty and profound wisdom. This beauty, this wisdom, beckons you, but first the veils, one at a time, must be drawn.

1. The first veil to dissolve is the veil of fear—fear of the unknown, the fear of failure, fear of rejection, and, perhaps most commonly, the fear of death. Fear manifests in a great many ways. Take a moment to search your mind to identify what elements of fear obscure your vision. Ask yourself, "What aspects of my life fall prey to fear?" Take a moment to identify one specific fear that surfaces to your conscious mind. Slowly bring yourself face to face with it. In this place of comfort, ask yourself "Why am I afraid?" What is it in you that hangs on to this fear? Take a deep breath and relax. As you do this, let this thought and feeling of fear escape as you exhale. In the place of fear, feel a sense of courage. Then see the veil of fear as translucent until it completely disappears, either dissolving into thin air, parting in two, lowering to the ground, or evaporating like fog in sunlight. To encourage this process, once more take a deep breath and repeat the phrase, "I am at peace with my fear; I now release my fear and bring love to my heart once more."

2. The second veil is the wall of anger. Anger manifests in a great many ways, from impatience to rage and hostility. Guilt, envy, jealousy, and indignation are also aspects of anger. Search your mind to identify what aspect of anger presently obscures your vision. What aspects of your life fall prey to anger? Take a moment to identify one current episode of anger. Slowly, bring yourself face to face with it. In this place of comfort, ask yourself, "Why am I angry?" What is it in you that keeps hanging on to these feelings of anger? Take a deep breath and relax. As you do this, let this thought and feeling of anger escape as you exhale. In the place of anger, feel a sense of confidence reside there now. Then see the veil of anger as translucent until it completely disappears, either dissolving into thin air, parting in two, lowering to the ground, or evaporating like fog in sunlight. To encourage this process, take a deep breath and repeat the phrase, "I am at peace with my anger; I now release my anger and bring love into my heart, once more."

3. The third veil is the roadblock of greed. Greed initially arises out of need, but the ego, expressing insecurity, senses that there is never really enough. As such, the feeling of

greed feeds upon itself to keep searching and acquiring more and more possessions, more accolades—more anything, to provide a sense of security. In truth, we are the source of our security. No amount of possessions, money, or compliments will ever fill the void of insecurity. Search your mind to identify what aspect of greed presently obscures your vision. What aspects of your life fall prey to greed? Take a moment to identify one current episode of greed in your life. Bring yourself face to face with it. In this place of comfort, ask yourself what it is in you that feels the need to acquire security through external sources. Take a deep breath and relax, letting this thought and feeling escape as you exhale. In the place of greed, feel a sense of security and stability. Then see the veil of greed as translucent until it completely disappears, either dissolving into thin air, parting in two, lowering to the ground, or evaporating like fog in sunlight. To encourage this process, take a deep breath and repeat the phrase, "I am at peace with my sense of greed as the source of my security. I now release any feelings of greed and bring love into my heart once more."

4.   The fourth veil is the obstruction of laziness. Laziness is a stop in the flow of the life force of spiritual energy. Although it may be nice to stop on the spiritual path and take in the view (this is actually encouraged), a pause that refreshes is not meant to be a 20-year nap. Inertia builds upon itself, making it harder to start moving again should we rest too long. Laziness appears most commonly in the face of addictions, for what begins as an attraction soon becomes a distraction. Some say that humans, by our very nature, are susceptible to addiction. However, this needn't be the case. The spiritual journey is walked in the balance of freedom and discipline. So often we forget the latter. Search your mind to identify any aspects of laziness, from low motivation to the shadow of an addiction. What aspect of laziness presently obscures your vision? What aspects of your life fall prey to inertia? Take a moment to identify one current episode of laziness or lack of discipline in your life. Bring yourself face to face with it. In this place of comfort, ask yourself what it is in you that has allowed this inertia to persist. Take a deep breath and relax, letting this thought and feeling escape as you exhale. In the place of laziness, feel a sense of inspiration. Then see the veil of laziness as translucent until it completely disappears, either dissolving into thin air, parting in two, lowering to the ground, or evaporating like fog in sunlight. To encourage this process, take a deep breath and repeat the phrase, "I am at peace with my sense of laziness, yet I vow to keep the life force of energy moving. I now release any feelings of laziness and bring love into my heart once more."

5.   The fifth veil is the curtain of desire. Desire is a tether that encumbers dreams and wishes, never letting them get off the ground. Desire is the hand that holds the arrow of intention yet refuses to let go as the string of the bow is pulled for fear of loss of control. Desire begins as a feather but quickly becomes a rock, pulling even the strongest inspiration down. The opposite of desire is detachment, letting go. The Buddha said that of the four noble truths, desire was the cause of the most suffering. Take a moment to search your mind to inquire where desire resides. Is there a spark of desire that presently obscures your vision? What aspects of your life—relationships, values, or purpose in life—reside in the shadow

of desire? Identify one personal goal that is tethered to the chain of desire. Bring yourself face to face with it. In this place of comfort, ask yourself what it is in you that allows this desire to keep this dream in bondage. Take a deep breath and relax, letting this thought and feeling escape as you exhale. In the place of desire, feel a sense of faith that all will turn out as it should in the divine game plan. Then see the veil of desire as translucent until it completely disappears, either dissolving into thin air, parting in two, lowering to the ground, or evaporating like fog in sunlight. To encourage this process, take a deep breath and repeat the phrase, "I am at peace with my desire, and in recognition, I release my desire with my wishes and dreams and bring love into my heart once more."

6. The sixth veil is the mask of pride. Mistake not happiness for pride, nor jubilation in the glory of one of life's many fine moments. Pride is the insatiable ego dominating the limelight of the soul's present moment. Pride is approval-seeking, an addiction all to itself. Pride is self-love turned sour. Pride is a consuming need for adoration—if some is good, more is always better. Pride is not self-esteem or worthiness. Pride is conceit on its way toward arrogance. Take a moment to search your mind to identify any aspects of pride that obscure your vision. What aspects of your life fall prey to pride? Take a moment to identify one current episode of pride in your life. Bring yourself face to face with it. In this place of comfort, ask yourself what it is in you that has allowed modesty and humbleness to take a backseat to praise. Take a deep breath and relax, letting this thought and feeling escape as you exhale. In the place of pride, feel a sense of godliness that seeks no praise. Then see the veil of pride as translucent until it completely disappears, either dissolving into thin air, parting in two, lowering to the ground, or evaporating like fog in sunlight. To encourage this process, take a deep breath and repeat the phrase, "I am at peace with my sense of pride, yet I vow to turn the passion of pride to humbleness, to serve rather than be served. I now release any feelings of pride and bring love into my heart once more."

7. The last veil is the thinnest of veils: conditional love. Conditional love is often mistaken for unconditional love; this is why it is the last of the seven veils to be dissolved. Let there be no mistake, the ego desires love. But in an effort for reciprocation, the ego places restrictions and limitations on love. Ifs and whens are the loopholes for love's retraction. The ego places restrictions on the expectations of love as a protection in the event that the goods are not delivered. So we hold love in reserve, just in case. And, like cut flowers, love soon wilts because the source of sustenance is missing. So common are acts of conditional love that they often go unnoticed. Some say that humans are incapable of unconditional love, yet any mother can tell you how possible unconditional love is. Love is not ours to give so much as it is ours to share. We are conduits for divine love when our hearts are open. Search your heart to identify any conditions placed on the love you share with others, including family, friends, pets, and even strangers. What conditions of love presently obscure your vision of the vista that lies beyond this last veil? What aspects of your life fall prey to conditional love? Take a moment to identify one current episode of conditional love. Bring yourself face to face with it. In this place of comfort, ask yourself what it is in you that has allowed

these conditions to persist. Take a deep breath and relax, letting this thought and feeling escape as you exhale. In the place of control, feel a sense of compassion. Then see the veil of conditional love as translucent until it completely disappears, either dissolving into thin air, parting in two, lowering to the ground, or evaporating like morning fog in sunlight. To encourage this process, take a deep breath and repeat the phrase, "I am at peace with my sense of conditional love, yet I now vow to share my love unconditionally, freely. I now release any feelings of control and bring unconditional love into my heart once more." Now open your eyes and observe what you see with each person you meet today.

EXERCISE 8.6
BODY COLORS AND HEALING LIGHT MEDITATION

The human spirit has an inherent healing quality to restore wholeness whenever possible. When the mind and heart are aligned, anything is possible. Much attention has been brought to people who have experienced what is now commonly called a spontaneous remission of disease. When questioned about behaviors that promote healing, many people speak of a change of attitude or perception. Some call it taking responsibility for their own health. Others speak of prayer, meditation, visualization, and mental imagery. The following meditation is based on the concept of combining all of these aspects together to bring the physical body back to a state of wholeness.

1. Find a comfortable place to sit quietly for a few moments with no distractions. Close your eyes and focus on your breathing.

2. Next, imagine that you are standing in front of a mirror looking at your body. What you see is a silhouette. But rather than a black silhouette, you see a white silhouette of your body image.

3. As you look at this image, search your body for any areas that seem to be in a state of stress—perhaps a headache, backache, a cancerous tumor, joint pain, or just a racing mind. Wherever you feel pain, imagine that that pain is represented by a strong flashing red light in the corresponding area of the silhouette image. Allow the pulse of the red light to match the level of discomfort you feel. Repeat to yourself the phrase, "My body is healing, my body is whole."

4. As you look at this image, take five slow deep breaths and imagine that you are breathing (inhaling and exhaling) through this area. With each slow deep breath, allow the pain to decrease as you exhale, and notice that the color and intensity of the light pulse decreases, changing from a bright intense red to light orange. Again, repeat to yourself the phrase, "My body is healing, my body is whole."

5. As you focus your attention on the orange pulsing light within the white silhouette, send a thought of peace and tranquility to the area of attention. Take five slow deep breaths, and as you exhale notice that the color and intensity of the orange light pulse decrease. At the

same time, the color in this area changes from light orange to yellow. Once again, repeat this phrase to yourself, "My body is healing, my body is whole."

6. Now, take a slow deep breath and as you exhale feel a sense of peace throughout your body. Focusing your attention on that body region that merits attention, take five more slow deep breaths. Each time you exhale notice that the pulsing yellow light now turns to a white light and, in doing so, blends completely with the entire silhouette.

7. As you imagine this image, feel a sense of peace throughout your whole body. Take a nice slow deep breath and repeat this phrase to yourself as you exhale, "My body is whole, and I am at peace."

8. Take a moment to sense how your body feels, as well as how the region you have placed your attention on feels. Using your mind's eye, feel a gentle, pulsing golden white light emanate from your body, as much as 6 feet in each direction. This gentle vibration of light is symbolic of homeostasis and inner peace. This image, combined with the white silhouette of your body, sends a message to your unconscious mind that begins to restore homeostasis to mind, body, and spirit.

© Paramount Wellness Institute. Inspiration Unlimited. Reprinted with permission.

EXERCISE 8.7
THE RAINBOW MEDITATION

From a metaphysical perspective, the body has seven regions that need to be constantly revitalized with universal energy to maintain optimal wellness. These seven areas correspond to the seven major endocrine glands. Perhaps not uncoincidentally, there are also seven notes to the harmonic scale and seven colors to the rainbow. This mental imagery exercise brings to mind these seven areas and the colors associated with them. Each area is represented as a circular window through which energy passes. This window goes by the name of *chakra*, a Sanskrit word used to describe a spinning wheel. With each color, you will repeat a series of meditational phrases to yourself as you visualize this image. When first learning this exercise, it is best to try it lying down, if possible. And, as with any guided mental imagery exercise, feel free to modify these suggestions to augment the strength of the image for you.

1. **Base of the spine—red.** Imagine a laser beam of red light emanating from the base of your spine. The area and color are metaphorical symbols representing your being grounded to the Earth. To be grounded means to feel stable and securely rooted in your environment—both physically and emotionally. Take a slow deep breath, and as you exhale see this beam of red light and say the phrase to yourself, "I feel grounded." Take one more deep breath and repeat this phrase again.

2. **Two inches below the belly button—orange.** Now focus your attention to the center of your body. If you are like most people, this point is approximately 2 inches below your belly button. Imagine that from this point emanates an orange beam of light outward toward infinity. This area of your body represents both the literal and figurative center of your body. To become centered means to focus inward and maintain personal balance. To be centered also means to feel self-confident and worthy of high self-esteem. Think what it is like to have a strong sense of self-confidence and self-esteem. Now take a slow deep breath, and as you exhale see this beam of orange light and say this phrase to yourself, "I feel centered" or "I have confidence." Take one more deep breath and repeat this phrase again.

3. **Upper stomach—yellow.** Bring your attention to your upper stomach. This area is often referred to as the solar plexus. From this area, imagine a beam of brilliant yellow light emanating outward toward infinity. This area and color are symbolic of several factors, including self-empowerment and the ability to receive love—love from family, friends, and all elements of the universe. Like the previous area, it, too, is related to self-esteem. Take a slow deep breath, and as you exhale focus on this beam of yellow light and say to yourself, "I feel loved." Take one more deep breath and repeat this phrase again.

4. **Center of the upper chest—green.** The upper chest houses the heart, perhaps the most important organ in the body. The heart is symbolic of the emotion love, for it is through the heart that we share compassion with our fellow human beings and creatures of the planet, even the planet itself. Like a window, the metaphorical heart can be opened to share love or it can be closed. The latter is often compared to a "hardened heart." Open the window of your heart and imagine an emerald green beam of light shining forth toward infinity. This region of your body and this color represent your ability to share your feelings of warmth, happiness, compassion—those aspects that comprise the emotion of love. Take a slow deep breath, and as you exhale focus on this color green and say to yourself, "I choose love." Take one more deep breath and repeat this phrase again.

5. **Throat—aqua-blue.** Bring your attention to your throat. Imagine a soft aqua-blue beam of light emanating from your throat area and extending toward infinity. This area and this color represent your meaningful purpose in life or your life mission. For a moment, ponder what you think this might be for you right now. It may be very general, yet profound, or it may be a short-term goal you wish to accomplish. Think of the willpower and the drive necessary to accomplish this mission. Know that you have this resource within you. Focus on this mission and at the same time focus on the color aqua-blue. Take a deep breath, and as you exhale repeat this phrase, "I have a meaningful purpose to my life." Take one more deep breath and repeat this phrase again.

6. **Center of the forehead—indigo.** This area of the forehead is sometimes referred to as "the third eye." It is this area that symbolizes wisdom and intuition. More clearly, it symbolizes wisdom from the balance between the right and left hemispheres of the brain and the conscious and unconscious minds. Clarity in this region suggests the ability to access all

mental faculties. Focus your attention on this area, just above your nose, in between your eyes. Using your imagination, see the color indigo emanate as a laser beam of light shooting straight toward infinity. As you see this color blue, think of your ability to balance your thinking skills to access your deepest wisdom. Take a slow deep breath, and as you exhale repeat the phrase to yourself, "I feel balanced" or "I have inner wisdom." Take one more deep breath and repeat this phrase again.

7. **Crown of the head—violet.** From the crown of your head imagine a beam of light of the color violet or lavender. Regardless of which position your head is resting, flat on a pillow or upright on your shoulders, this beam of light always directs itself upward towards the heavens. This chakra, as represented in the Renaissance period, was depicted as a halo over the head. This body region and the color associated with it represent your connection to the divine consciousness of the universe. To feel connected is a very important aspect of one's well-being. Focus on this color and think what it is like to feel a sense of connectedness and belonging. To be aware of this connection is to feel at one with the universe, to feel at peace with yourself. Take a slow deep breath, and as you exhale visualize this color and say to yourself a phrase that reinforces a feeling of connectedness. It might be something like "I am one with the world," "I am at peace with myself," or "I am one with God." Take one more deep breath and repeat this phrase again.

8. Finally, allow all these beams of light to grow in all directions so that they all merge together and you find yourself surrounded in a ball of brilliant golden light.

EXERCISE 8.8
ENERGY BALL MEDITATION

This relaxation technique was taught to me by the renowned bioenergy healers Mietek and Margaret Wirkus. I have adapted and taught this technique many times in classes and workshops throughout the country with great success. Although it was introduced to me as a healing technique, first and foremost it is a relaxation exercise.

1. Begin by sitting comfortably with your legs crossed and your back straight. You may wish to sit up against a wall. In this exercise, it helps to keep your back straight. Close your eyes and focus your attention on your breathing. Take a moment to clear your mind of distracting thoughts and feelings, and place your attention on your breathing. If it helps to have some soft acoustic/instrumental music in the background, then try this as well.

   Sometimes it helps to think of a happy moment in your life, one when you were filled with joy. Allow this feeling to resonate with every cell in your body. Then take a slow comfortable deep breath.

2. Unlike belly breathing, which is typically taught in relaxation workshops, this particular exercise requires that you focus your attention on the upper lobes of your lungs. Take a moment

to place your hands on your upper chest to become fully conscious of your upper lungs. Then take five breaths, breathing comfortably, slowly, and deeply into your upper lungs.

3. Once you have completed this, then place your hands on your knees or thighs and repeat this breathing style by taking five slow, deep breaths. As you exhale, repeat the phrase, "My body is calm and relaxed." As you say this, feel a sense of relaxation throughout your body with each exhalation.

4. Next, fully conscious of your hands resting on your knees or thighs, take five more deep breaths, but this time as you exhale each breath, repeat this phrase, "I am my hands." With each breath, place all your concentration, all your attention, on your hands. Sense what your hands feel like. Are they warm? If so, where? On the palms, fingertips, the backs of the hands? Do your hands feel heavy? If so, how heavy? What other sensations do you feel? Again remind yourself, "I am my hands."

5. Using your imagination, picture a small window, about the size of a dime, in the center of each palm. Imagine now that as you breathe air not only comes into your nose or mouth, but into your hands as well. If you prefer, you may use the image of light coming into the palms of your hands. Imagine that as you inhale, air or light enters your palms and moves up your arms to the center of your chest. As you exhale, feel the energy return from where it came through your hands. Try repeating this several times, again taking slow deep breaths and repeating to yourself, "I am my hands."

6. Next, slowly lift your hands off your knees or thighs so that they rest comfortably, suspended in front of your chest, with the palms face open toward the ceiling.

7. Next, fully conscious of your hands, take five more deep breaths. Again as you exhale each breath, repeat this phrase, "I am my hands." With each breath, place all your concentration, all your attention, on your hands. Again, sense what your hands feel like. Are they warm? If so, where? On the palms, fingertips, the backs of the hands? Do your hands feel heavy? If so, how heavy? What other sensations do you feel? Again remind yourself, "I am my hands."

8. Now, keeping your hands about 10 to 12 inches apart, allow the palms to face each other. Again, using your imagination, imagine that between your hands is a large sponge ball. As you hold the ball, slowly press in and then release. What do you feel as you do this? Again, bring your hands close together without touching. Then begin to separate them farther apart. Ask yourself, what do you feel?

9. Now, placing your attention on the palms of your hands with your hands about 12 inches apart, imagine that there is a beam of light from palm to palm. Take a slow deep breath, and as you exhale slowly compress the beam by bringing your palms together without touching. Then, during the next inhalation, allow your hands to separate again. What do you feel? Is the sensation between your hands stronger when you inhale or exhale?

10. Again return to the sensation between your hands. Between your hands is a ball of energy, the healing energy ball. Take this ball of energy and place it into a region of your body that

feels tense or stressed. If you are completely relaxed, then try placing it in your heart. Take five slow deep breaths, and repeat the phrase to yourself, "My body is calm and relaxed." Feel a sense of relaxation throughout your entire body. Take one final slow deep breath and enjoy this sensation again.

11. When you are done, slowly place your hands back on your knees or thighs. Recognize that although you feel relaxed, you also feel energized. When you feel ready, open your eyes to a soft gaze in front of you. Make yourself aware of your surroundings, and smile.

© Paramount Wellness Institute. Inspiration Unlimited. Reprinted with permission.

EXERCISE 8.9
DNA MEDITATION

It has often been said that we have a wealth of knowledge inside us. What was once a cute poetic proverb now seems to be a surprising reality. As scientists explore the wonders of our DNA, it appears that the two spiraling strands of sugar and protein molecules contain a vast source of information that would make even the National Library of Congress envious.

Research indicates that we use only 3% of our DNA; the rest seems to be inactive (scientists call the inactive part "junk"). Like a string of lightbulbs that has not been plugged into a socket and is therefore deemed useless, it would appear that our DNA needs some attention to become activated or, as mystics have said, "to be woken up." Current research, as highlighted by Herbert Benson and colleagues, suggest that consciousness can change (turn on or off) specific genes that may set the stage for disease or illness. Simply stated, the DNA has become the new frontier of science, and perhaps the nexus where science and spirit meet inside the human body.

This meditation is an exploration into the wonders of the DNA. Again, it requires the use of your imagination. And remember, please feel free to change these suggestions to make this meditation most comfortable for you.

1. Place yourself in a comfortably seated position, back straight, with your eyes closed. To become more relaxed, take a few deep breaths, and as you exhale remind yourself that you are becoming calmer and more relaxed.

2. Now, imagine that you have the ability to look within your heart muscle. Traveling to your heart, focus on one specific cell and enlarge it so that an image of it is directly in front of you.

3. Next, look deep into the cell and find the nucleus. Focus your attention on the nucleus. Enlarge it so that an image of the nucleus is directly in front of you. Once you have the image, find the double helix, the spiral strand of DNA within the nucleus.

4. Focusing all your attention on the DNA, enlarge this structure so that it is directly in front of you. Depending on your perspective, the strand of DNA may look like a ladder or a twisted bridge. Looking straight on, it may even resemble the Taoist yin–yang symbol. Take a moment to look at this DNA strand from every possible angle, rotating it in your mind.

5. As you look and study this double helix and all its many complexities, imagine a string of lights with a hundred bulbs, of which only three are actually lit. Using your imagination, create a light switch that when turned on makes all the lights shine. Not only does each bulb extend a brilliant brightness but, upon closer examination of the double-stranded helix, there also appears to be a beam of light that the two strands surround and actually embrace. The light from the DNA emanates out to the edge of the nucleus and then continues toward the cell membrane itself.

6. Again, using your imagination, think that just as this one cell contains a vibrating DNA of light, so do all cells. Every cell in the body now contains a double helix of DNA that emanates light, with all parts active.

7. Now allow this image to fade from your mind's eye, but retain the feeling of light. Pay attention to the wisdom that comes to your conscious mind as you travel through the course of your day. Remember, repetition with this visualization will begin to enhance the access of deep-seated wisdom within you.

⚜ ENDNOTES

1. Green, E., and Green, A., *Beyond Biofeedback.* Delacorte Press: New York, 1977.
2. Benson, H., *Timeless Healing.* New York: Scribner, 1996.
3. American Heart Association, National Center, 7320 Greenville Ave., Dallas, Texas, 75231.
4. Davidson, R., and Lutz, A. "Buddha's Brain: Neuroplasticity and Meditation [In the Spotlight]." *IEEE Signal Processing Magazine,* 25(1): 176–174, 2008.
5. Davidson, R. J., et al. "Alterations in Brain and Immune Function Produced by Mindfulness Meditation." *Psychosomatic Medicine,* 65(4): 564–570, 2003.
6. Begley, S. *Train Your Mind, Change Your Brain.* Ballantine Books: New York, 2007.
7. Schwartz, S., "Meditation – The Controlled Psychophysical Self-Regulation Process That Works." *Explore,* 7(6): 348–353, 2011.
8. Alper, M., *The God Part of the Brain.* Source Books: New York, 2008.
9. Hagerty, B., "The God Chemical, Brain Chemistry, and Mysticism." http://www.npr.org/templates/story/story.php?storyId=104240746.
10. Jung, C.G., *Man and His Symbols.* Anchor Press: New York, 1964.
11. Lewis, C. S., *The Screwtape Letters* (revised ed., p. 20). Collier Books: New York, 1961.

12. Roth, R., Institute of Noetic Sciences Annual Conference, Boca Raton, FL, July 12, 1996.

13. Schweitzer, A., as quoted in *Handbook for the Soul* (p. 85) by Richard Carlson and Benjamin Shield. Little, Brown: Boston, 1995.

14. Hanh, T. N., *The Miracle of Mindfulness: A Manual on Meditation* (revised edition). Beacon Press: Boston, 1987.

15. Kabat-Zinn, J., *Wherever You Go, There You Are: Mindfulness Meditations in Everyday Life.* Hyperion Books: New York, 1994.

16. Sugrue, T., *There Is a River: The Edgar Cayce Story.* A.R.E. Press: Virginia Beach, VA, 1973.

17. von Oech, R., *A Whack on the Side of the Head.* Warner Books: New York, 1983.

18. Ornstein, R., *The Psychology of Consciousness.* Penguin Books: New York, 1972.

19. Begley, S., "I Can't Think." *Newsweek*, March 7, 2011: 28–33.

✦ ADDITIONAL REFERENCES

Benson, H., *Beyond the Relaxation Response.* Berkeley Books: New York, 1985.

Boorstein, S., *Don't Just Do Something, Sit There: A Mindfulness Retreat.* HarperSanFrancisco: San Francisco, CA, 1996.

Farhi, D., *The Breathing Book.* Henry Holt & Co.: New York, 1996.

Hanh, T. N., *Peace Is Every Step.* Bantam Books: New York, 1991.

Kornfield, J., *A Path with Heart.* Bantam New Age Books: New York, 1993.

Levey, J., and Levey, M., *Simple Meditation and Relaxation.* Conari Press: Berkeley, CA, 1999.

Pritz, A., *Pocket Guide to Meditation.* Crossing Press: Freedom, CA, 1997.

Health of the Human Spirit

To know and not to do, is not to know.

—Ancient proverb

*S*KIING DOWN A MOUNTAIN OF champagne powder on a crystal-clear day. Sitting on a deserted Hawaiian beach watching the sunrise over the Pacific Ocean. Holding a newborn baby. Lying outside on a summer night looking at shooting stars. Clapping your hands at a concert to the fourth encore of your favorite rock group. These are the events we take delight in, experiences that make us feel euphoric, that make us want to yell at the top of our lungs with gratitude, "It doesn't get any better than this!" Each experience is a slice of heaven on earth when we know, if only for a moment, how divine life can be.

To be sure, there is a side of human spirituality that reflects the epitome of joy and happiness in life. Equally so, there is a side of human spirituality that speaks of healing our inner wounds, including grieving, forgiveness, and acceptance. Human spirituality is about finding balance in our lives through both joy and sadness, and this, as anyone can tell you, is a lifelong process. This balance can also be found in both the time spent alone in reflection and the time spent in the company of great friends. Balance is the key to life.

First and foremost, human spirituality is experiential. Although information gathering may help ignite a spark in the soul, to limit the spiritual journey exclusively to smartphone apps, websites, books, and seminars about prayer, miracles, healing, and ecstatic journeys is merely an exercise in mental well-being, not spiritual well-being. And although some may think that human spirituality is purely that which comes from the heart rather than the head, true balance requires the use of both assets. To follow the sage advice of the ancient proverb, "To know and not to do, is not to know" is not an easy task.

To be sure, engaging in acts of spiritual well-being, from forgiveness to compassion in action, is demanding work. If you think doing aerobics and following a low-fat diet is tough to maintain, exercises in human spirituality require even more willpower, stamina, and passion. Yet anyone who has been there will tell you it is surely worth it. As they describe their journey, there is not a trace of regret, remorse, or animosity. Jim Gill is one example.

Jim is a cancer survivor, and a remarkable one at that. As someone who defied the odds to live years beyond the 2 months his doctors gave him, Jim now gets several phone calls a week from people who have been diagnosed with cancer. He told me that many times they are looking for a magic bullet, a quick fix to make their cancer go away—a miracle drug, a renowned healer in the Philippines, or some crystal amulet to wear around the neck. But healing is not about quick fixes, he explains. "If they haven't hung up by that time, I then say to them that if they want to be healed, they have to work at it. Not everyone wants to hear this, but it's the truth."

Medicine for the Soul

THOSE WHO KEEP A CONSTANT eye on the welfare of the collective human spirit, the pulse of humanity so to speak, are a bit concerned these days, and for good reason, not just for an individual here and there, but for the human race as a whole. Although apathy, laziness, and greed have always been a part of the human condition, at no time in the past does it seem that people have felt more disconnected and separated from their divine source. It is not uncommon to hear the expression "spiritually adrift" used to describe this condition of lost souls. Adrift is only one metaphor; there are many others.

Addressing the issue of the health of the human spirit has taken on new relevance as we begin the new millennium. Ours was once a planet of many nations and cultures, but the trend toward globalization of commerce combined with high technology appears to be eroding the spiritual foundations of a great many people worldwide. Episodes of fear and greed are all too common in the daily news headlines (e.g., Wall Street banking scandals) despite what appears to be simple common sense. Individuals seek continually to fill a void that cannot be satisfied with material possessions, such as flat-screen TVs, iPads, and smartphones. As with a boa constrictor that tightens its hold around its victim with each breath, the collective spirit of humanity is getting choked, not only by material possessions, but also by the unresolved anger and fear that drive our behaviors. At the personal level, we can metaphorically choke ourselves with an imbalanced lifestyle coupled with unresolved anger and fear, where the dominating ego eclipses the spiritual soul. To use another metaphor, imagine, if you will, that the human spirit is like a river that flows through your body. Now imagine that unresolved issues of anger or fear act like dams to block the flow of this life force. Add stress as an external force, and the scene looks extremely compromised.

Americans have often been criticized for seeking happiness through external means (e.g., new cars, Netflix subscriptions, snow boards, and video games). Furthermore, it has been suggested that we buy these things to fill our hungry soul, yet before long we find ourselves feeling hollow and begin the whole process of consumer addiction all over again. It becomes a never-ending cycle. And although it may do wonders for the economy, it sends us spiraling downward deeper into darkness, which manifests as depression, a midlife crisis, or even chronic disease.

Medicine for the soul is a common term used by counselors, therapists, life coaches, and healers to describe various ways to nurture the soul's growth process toward the direction of the divine—the light, not the darkness. More than "spiritual triage," medicine for the soul is a prescription for inner peace. The concept of medicine for the soul begs the question: is the soul really sick? Scholars, theologians, psychologists, and healers from various disciplines are in agreement that, indeed, there is a malady of the soul that is ever present in our global society. Whenever apathy, greed, prejudice, anger, or anxiety becomes the driving force behind our behavior, then our souls suffer. Anthropologist Angeles Arrien describes medicine of the soul as one's inner resources, including, but not limited to, faith, humor, honesty, and love.[1]

Theologian Matthew Fox put it best this way:

> Since the time of Descartes, the human soul has been shrinking, reduced to the pineal gland of the brain. Simply stated, the soul is boundless. It is expressed in your passions, your convictions, your hopes, even your suffering, your joy, your thoughts—wherever they go and whomever they touch. This is your soul. Our bodies become instruments of our soul. We don't have a soul in a body, we have a body in our soul. The medicine of the soul is to grow the soul, through courage, compassion and love. Medicine for the soul means to understand our cosmology, the big picture, the whole and our purpose in it.[2]

Fox also notes that a healthy soul is also one that enjoys the mystery of life and is full of curiosity, wonder, and awe, something that children have but adults tend to lose as they grow older. To reclaim these attributes is not impossible and, in fact, is quite necessary for spiritual well-being.

Keeping the Human Spirit Healthy

THERE ARE LITERALLY HUNDREDS OF ways to promote optimal spiritual well-being. Some speak to the nature of joy, whereas others speak to the aspect of healing. Still others remind us of the dance between ego and soul. Each one underlies the importance of balance. You might notice that all of these ideas underscore the strength of muscles of the soul, and there is a good reason for this. A healthy human spirit makes good use of these muscles. In an article that highlighted the lives of several centenarians, each person was asked what contributed to his or her health and longevity. Their answers were quite similar, but perhaps Bostonian Constance Poirier, age 102, said it best when she replied, "Live the best way you know how. Try not to talk ill of your neighbors. And be charitable."[3]

The following are some of the more common ideas that lend balance to the health of the human spirit. As you read through these ideas, note that each suggestion directly supports the premise of spiritual well-being through relationships, values, and a meaningful purpose in life. A closer look at these ways to enhance the health of the human spirit shows the importance of the muscles of the soul, including, faith, patience, and compassion. No less important than the muscles of the soul for spiritual health are the seasons of the soul: centering, emptying, grounding, and connecting. It is quite easy to first think of spiritual health in the connecting process—the "Disney World" euphoric sensation—yet the human spirit needs as much nurturing in the emptying process. As you read through each idea, first ask yourself how each suggestion supports the model for spiritual well-being, and then ask how you can best incorporate these behaviors, habits, and activities into your life.

The Art of Self-Renewal

There was a time not long ago when Sunday (the Sabbath) was truly considered to be a day of rest. Stores were closed. Offices were closed. For the most part, people stayed home and renewed their personal energy. Today the common expression is "24/7," indicating that everything is running at full pace 24 hours a day, 7 days a week, every day of the year! The result is a lifestyle that is anything but relaxed. Moreover, between text messages, apps, smartphones, and iPads, people are literally plugged into a web of communication, always accessible. Being plugged in all the time has its price.

The **art of self-renewal** speaks to the ideas of healthy boundaries, solitude, and recharging one's personal energy; it is the stepping stone to the centering process. In an age of constant accessibility, healthy boundaries are essential. Solitude, a quiet place, is paramount for rejuvenation. This is one reason why getting out in nature—free of the congestion of technology, work, and social interactions—is looked upon as "healing." Recharging one's personal energy can take many forms, but the first step is to quiet the mind.

Although we are not machines, this one metaphor does quite nicely to explain the importance of self-renewal. The day I bought my first cordless phone I was excited to have complete mobility around the house. I could even walk outside without losing the connection. As I read the instructions, I noticed a warning: this phone must be placed back in the cradle to recharge for 10 hours or it won't work. Naively, I thought they were exaggerating. Perhaps it was really only 6 or 8 hours. Nope! It was 10 hours. I found out the hard way. I was talking on the phone and a red light came on with a high-pitched beep, warning me that the battery was low. Sure enough it was. It had not charged for 10 straight hours.

Humans do not have red lights that flash on their heads when their personal energy is low (although it would be nice if they did). Instead, the signs for low personal energy manifest as rudeness, arrogance, impatience, cynicism, and other unsociable behaviors.

Like the cell phone that needs to recharge to work properly, we, too, need to go back to "the cradle" and recharge our personal energy. In this busy world of rapid change, however, you need to make a concerted effort to disconnect from the world long enough to do it. Honoring healthy boundaries with technology is not only important; it is essential in today's high-tech world. Unlike the cell phone, humans do not need 10 hours. Recharging your personal energy can be done in as little as 10 minutes a day. Finding both a time and a space where you will not be interrupted is essential.

The Practice of Sacred Rituals

Did you ever hear the expression, "Nothing is sacred anymore"? Although at times it may certainly seem this way, what we consider to be sacred is really a perception. Actually anything can be regarded as sacred, if we give it that meaning. Sacredness is a value. What do you consider sacred? How do you honor this?

In a world with much violence and what appears to be lack of morals, there is still plenty of sacredness, as long as we feel it in our hearts. It is up to us to assign importance to various aspects of life that we deem important. In doing so, we become empowered, which is the antithesis of how you feel when you say, "Nothing is sacred anymore"!

The **practice of sacred rituals** means engaging in habits and traditions that remind you that life is indeed sacred. By and large, religions are very good at this (e.g., candles, ceremonies, burning incense, etc.), but sacred rituals can be done outside of buildings of worship as well. What are some examples of sacred rituals? Watching the sunrise, calling a distant friend, reading poetry on Wednesdays, watching birds at the bird feeder, or being of service to the elderly—anything that reminds us of how sacred life really is.

It makes no difference what your ritual is, as long as it serves as a reminder of your divine connection.

One problem with rituals is the boredom factor. Because the mind is always looking for new stimulation to cross its threshold of excitement, day after day, year after year, repetitive rituals tend to lose their luster of meaning. What might become practices of comfort can result in a spiritual rut. They become habits that can eventually turn into empty gestures. What was once hallow soon becomes hollow, and the mind begins to drift elsewhere.

There is an expression that says, "If you get bored with your rituals, throw them out and create some new ones." What this means is that if what you have done traditionally, either in ceremony with others or in the privacy of your own heart, has lost its significance and left you feeling rather empty, find something new to ignite the spark of inspiration that will breathe new life into your soul. In this fast-paced world, where the rate of change can make one feel dizzy and disconnected, we hold the responsibility to remind ourselves of life's sacredness. The practice of sacred rituals is a necessary part of spiritual well-being.

Sweet Forgiveness

To hold someone in contempt of an action that has violated you is to give your personal power away. To hold a grudge against someone who has victimized you is also to give your personal power away. Although anger is a human emotion and part of the continuum of emotions that make up the whole, anger was never meant to last longer than seconds. To hold a grudge against someone for days, weeks, months, or years is to be held captive by the thoughts of anger. In doing so, personal power is given away. As stated earlier, unresolved anger chokes the human spirit. **Sweet forgiveness** is a way to loosen the grip of anger and to relax the hold completely. To loosen and let go is the premise of the emptying process.

Many people think that to forgive someone for a personal violation, whether it be a minor rift or an unthinkable act, is to get walked over twice: first when you felt violated and again when forgiveness is enacted. But the act of forgiveness is not to let someone off the hook. Engaging in acts of forgiveness helps you to move on with your life. If the person(s) involved benefits from the forgiveness process, great! But this is not what forgiveness is all about. Forgiveness is done so we can get unstuck from a position of victimization and move on gracefully with our lives.[4] To forgive someone, or ourselves, is not an easy task, and it takes much work (the ego likes to hang on to anger for control). Yet despite the work involved, the reward is expansive freedom, and it feels great!

Embrace the Shadow (Domesticating the Ego)

We all have a dark side to our personality. It is the side that is judgmental, the side that is sarcastic, cynical, even rude, the side that is less than perfect; this is the shadow. These are the traits most commonly associated with the ego, an overblown protection factor that puts the self first, often at the expense of everyone else. Everyone has a shadow side, the side of prejudice, greed, and envy. Some people have learned to embrace their shadow by acknowledging their selfish, judgmental thoughts and actions and moderating these so that they are intercepted by the conscience and never make it past the mouth. There are others who exploit their shadow side and capitalize on their negativity. As you begin to cultivate the relationship with your inner self, you encounter the face of the dark side. As you continue to cultivate this internal relationship, embracing the shadow becomes easier.

Carl Jung once said, "That I feed the hungry, forgive an insult and love my enemy—these are great virtues. But what if I should discover that the poorest of beggars and most imprudent of offenders are all within me, and that I stand in the alms of my own kindness; that I myself am the enemy who must be loved. What then?"[5]

Embracing the shadow means first to become aware of those thoughts that are produced by an overactive ego and then to deactivate them so that they do not hijack conscious thoughts and actions. In Eastern culture, this exercise is known as "domesticating the ego." It speaks to the nature of cultivating our thoughts and actions through a filter of love and compassion toward others and forgiveness toward ourselves.

Acceptance

There is a large part of life that we have absolutely no control over. Try as we might, there are some things we can never change. Although it is admirable to exhaust every option until success is achieved, it is wise to know that success is as much letting go of things we cannot control as it is hanging on to that which we can. **Acceptance** is acknowledging the situation and adapting to it. The opposite of acceptance is judgment, a very strong attribute of the ego. Although judgment is certainly necessary in some instances, constant judgment is a toxin to the human spirit.

A large aspect of acceptance is tolerance. Tolerance is not necessarily an agreement with others in their beliefs, attitudes, or actions. Rather it is an acceptance of your individuality. Like acceptance, tolerance is a value that you choose to adopt into your value system. Acceptance is not easy, but when coupled with patience, the two prove to be a formidable force to a negative ego.

The Serenity Prayer, by Reinhold Niebuhr, serves as an excellent reminder of acceptance: "God, grant me the serenity to accept the things that I cannot change, the courage to change the things I can, and the wisdom to know the difference."

Keeping an Attitude of Gratitude

In the fast-paced world in which we live, it is easy to jump to the next event before we have finished the last one, no matter how fantastic. Like a child tearing through a stack of Christmas presents, opening the next before fully processing the last, we often pass through an experience without taking a moment to acknowledge its meaning, significance, or splendor. In moments of stress, moments of gratitude are rare and far between. To hold an **attitude of gratitude** means to keep a healthy perspective on our lives. An attitude of gratitude speaks to the nature of giving thanks. Whether this be done formally in prayer or informally in conscious acknowledgment, whether it be said to a family member, friend, or a higher source, gratitude is a way of honoring the many gifts in life that come our way.

In her book *Attitudes of Gratitude,* Mary Jane Ryan says:

> Gratitude births only positive feelings—love, compassion, joy and hope. As we focus on what we are thankful for, fear, anger and bitterness simply melt away, seemingly without effort. A few of my basic assumptions about gratitude: I've learned over time that it helps to take the long view, to choose to see our lives from a spiritual perspective. I know we are here to grow our souls, to heal our wounds, or at least bless our woundedness—and become loving, fearless and hopeful. The longer I live, the more I recognize that cultivating an attitude of gratitude is the key to living from an open heart; that is, living in a spirit of joyful expectation. Gratitude is not just the key. It's the magical key.[6]

In times of crisis and calamity, it is not uncommon to hear someone say, "count your blessings." This phrase serves as a subtle reminder that even in the worst of times, we can find something to be grateful for.

Keeping the Faith

Faith, it is said, can move mountains. To anyone who has ever experienced a miracle, escaped a horrible ordeal, or made a graceful exit from a trip to hell, faith indeed moves more than mountains. Faith is the cornerstone in the foundation of human spirituality. Ask anyone who faced insurmountable odds and came out the victor, and you will hear faith mentioned every time as that which got them through the ordeal.

Faith is a unique muscle of the soul. It is more than just a belief that we are a small part of something much bigger in the universe. **Keeping the faith** is an inherent knowledge that no matter how bad things might seem, all will be okay in the end.

The alchemy of faith is quite unique. It is one part optimism, one part trust, one part love, one part intention, and two parts mystery. Indeed, there is an element of mystery involved with faith. No one knows for sure how a thought, when combined with a divine intention, can manifest into a promising result, but it happens.

The biggest obstacle to faith is doubt. Doubt is the tool of the ego. While caution is good in situations of danger, doubt can act as a strong tether that holds one back from taking action. Doubt is the most benign aspect of fear. Metaphorically speaking, if fear is smoke from a fire, faith is the water that puts it out. If fear is like a sinking ship, faith is a ring buoy to keep you afloat till you get to shore. How does hope differ from faith? Hope is a desire that carries with it some aspect of doubt. "Hope," as the expression goes, "is a good snack, but it doesn't make for a great meal." It is common to see that where there is hope, there are expectations and conditions. Faith is unconditional.

It may seem like our faith is tested at times, but perhaps a more accurate expression is that it is exercised. We are invited to exercise our faith regularly. And with each workout, our faith grows stronger.

Walking with a Light Heart

Have you noticed that by and large, most people take themselves extremely seriously these days? Look at people's faces and you can read a personal history of determination, seriousness, and even pain. In the balance of life experiences, it was never meant for us to miss out on the lighter side of life—the humorous side. Indeed, life can have its hilarious moments. We just need to be open to them.

Research in the topic of humor therapy reveals that the average child laughs and giggles between 300 and 500 times a day. The average adult laughs about 15 to 20 times—if that! Somewhere between childhood and adulthood we let our funny bone atrophy. The consequence of this behavior is not healthy. A quote in the book of Proverbs speaks to this wisdom, "A merry heart does good like medicine, but a broken spirit drieth the bones."

Walking with a light heart is an expression to convey laughter and mirth. This can be done in a hundred different ways, from finding daily examples of life's irony to laughing at ourselves when expectations are less than what we had hoped for. There is a real healing power in humor to mind, body, and spirit. We just have to be open to it. Those people who have made a trip to hell and back gracefully will tell you that they could not have done it without a sense of humor.[7]

Here is an idea to give the funny bone a good workout. Start collecting cartoons, photographs, greeting cards, e-mail jokes, and anything else that has proven to put a smile on your face. Start pasting these into a tickler notebook—your own private collection of funny things. Not only will making a tickler notebook keep you on the lookout for items that help you walk with a light heart, but it will also provide a great resource of humor for those times when you find yourself down in the dumps and in need of a pick-me-up.

Compassion in Action

There are a great many people who speak to the theoretical nature of love, but love is so much more than a theory. A theory without application holds little merit. You cannot just think love; you have to feel it. And to feel love means to be moved to act on it. If love is just an idea in your head, it really isn't much. For love to be real, it must be acted upon. **Compassion in action** is love in action. Compassion in action is making ourselves available for service. In fact, compassion in action can be explained in one word: service. Service is the epitome of engaging in dynamic interpersonal relationships.

It should be understood that service is not the same thing as helping. Helping holds a connotation of inequality: the one who helps is better off than the one who is being helped. Service is based on the principle of equals, where an exchange (giving and receiving) is made in the offering—both people benefit when service is performed. Helping involves a sense of judgment, whereas service is performed for the highest good of all concerned.

The concept of service, where all people benefit, can best be seen in the following story. An elderly woman died and found herself walking up to the pearly gates of heaven. She was greeted by St. Peter, who gave her a warm hug. He said to her, "I will take you inside, but I thought you might like to see what hell is like first, just for the purposes of comparison."

In the blink of an eye, the woman found herself in a very large room the size of a football field. The room was packed with people. She could not help but hear the moaning. Upon closer examination, she saw people seated at what appeared to be picnic tables. As she looked around, she saw that bowls of delicious hot stew were placed before each person. Alongside each bowl was an extra-long spoon. For some strange reason that she could not understand, the people seated were not able to bend their elbows and hence could not use the long spoons to eat the stew. As she observed this taking place, the cries of hunger grew deafening. The woman looked at St. Peter quite puzzled. Saying she had seen enough, she asked to leave.

In less than a nanosecond, the woman was in another room much like the first. This time, however, she could hear laughter and giggles. There was a very festive atmosphere. Already she liked the place. Upon closer examination, she noticed the same bowls of delicious stew and the long spoons as well. These people also had arms that would not bend at the elbows. But instead of being frustrated, each person used the long spoon to feed the individual directly across the table, thus allowing everyone to eat, drink, and be merry. The moral of the story is that service is that which benefits everyone!

Compassion in action is nothing less than the manifestation of unconditional love, without conditions or expectations. Compassion in action begins with ourselves. This is why self-renewal is so crucial. If we don't take the time to replenish our own personal energy, then whatever we offer in service is compromised. In fact, when we do not take time to recharge our personal energy, frustration and animosity build to the point that the quality of our service is jaded. Compassion in action and the art of self-renewal are the actualization of the Golden Rule: loving your neighbor as yourself.

My favorite stories of compassion in action are based on random acts of kindness, when a good deed is done anonymously. With acts of service that are random in nature, the ego may beg for attention, but it has to take a back seat to a big heart instead. Placing money in a parking meter that is about to expire, helping someone who has fallen, or letting someone go ahead of you at the grocery store checkout line are examples of random acts of kindness.

In the words of the Dalai Lama: "Love and compassion are necessities, not luxuries. Without them humanity cannot survive. With them, we can make a joint effort to solve the problems of the whole humankind."[8]

Can one person really make a difference? Most definitely, yes! The book *Stone Soup for the World* is a collection of over a hundred stories of people who, with love in their hearts, made a pledge of service and changed the world—one person at a time.[9]

Bryce, a nontraditional student at the University of Northern Colorado, quit school at 20 when he was offered a job with a huge salary. He explained to me one day that after a few years of racking up wealth and adult toys, the paycheck became a shallow victory. So he quit his job and started offering his carpentry skills to Habitat for Humanity, a service organization that builds homes for the underserved population. Now back in school to finish his bachelor's degree, Bryce spends occasional weekends working in a soup kitchen in Denver. "Life is not about making money," he said. "It's about being there to help others in whatever way you can be of service—from a generous smile to the gift of a few hours of your time."

In the theme of compassion in action, Martin Luther King, Jr., once said, "Every person can be great, because everyone can serve."

Live Your Joy!

Watching a tiger-swallowtail butterfly land on your hand. Feeling the hands of a massage therapist kneading your aching muscles. Scuba diving off the deep blue shores of Bora Bora. These are life's simple pleasures. And they bring joy to the heart and soul. Life is a balance of both good times and bad times. If we are lucky, the good and bad times balance out. Although we may not be responsible for the chaos we find ourselves in, we are responsible for participating in the simple pleasures in life. It is up to each and every one of us to seek them out and engage in them. **Living your joy** is being fully conscious of your blissful connection to the divine presence of the universe.

In the acclaimed book *Healthy Pleasures,* authors Robert Ornstein and David Sobel describe a concept called the "pleasure principle," a universal innate guide to health. And while research shows that joy promotes an abundance of healthy neuropeptides to enhance the immune system, joy, happiness, and bliss are essential nutrients for the human spirit as well.[10]

For many people, joy and happiness are hard to grasp. Rather than focusing on the present moment, they tend to be absorbed with past or future events. Living your joy means to live in the present moment, not the past, nor the future, but the present moment. Some people call this the "Disney World" effect. You know—beautiful sunsets, warm fuzzy puppies, and tall ice cream sundaes on a hot day. Living your joy does not have to be expensive either. The best joys in life are free!

These are just a few of the more significant ways to promote and sustain a sense of inner peace. There are many others. What matters most is not which strategy (or collection of approaches) you take, only that you continue to strive for balance. As you engage in your strategy, you will find ways to improve and fine-tune each aspect so that this internal balance of mind–body–spirit is indeed a successful means for inner peace.

The Divine Paradox

As you continue to explore the spiritual path, you will discover that there are many paradoxes—juxtaposing ideas that seem to contradict old ways of thinking or basic perceptions that used to provide a sense of comfort through familiarity. These are examples of the **divine paradox,** an illusion of sorts. The goal, at this point of the spiritual journey, is to rise above the limitations that deny us a bigger view of the divine reality, one in which we are very much a part. One step in the spiritual growth process, and considered by many to be a cornerstone to the health of the human spirit, is to be able to hold two contradictory thoughts in your head at the same time—and not be threatened by either. Spiritual luminaries the world over will tell you that dogma, one of the first and important steps of the spiritual journey, must eventually be cast aside as you progress so that you may see the bigger picture. For some, these paradoxes may seem incomprehensible. For others, they may seem trivial and merely a matter of semantics. Nevertheless, to live in the balance of the divine paradox is one of the highest pinnacles of spiritual well-being. The following are five hallmark paradoxes you may encounter if you continue to augment the health of your human spirit.

1. **You are God, but you are not God!** Throughout the ages, mystics from all cultures and spiritual practices remind us that within us is a spark of divinity. This spark goes by several names including the *soul*, the *Tao, Pranayama,* and *Atman.* It is this spark that makes us divine. For this reason, spiritual luminaries remind us that we are God. However, before you get cocky and try to walk on water or heal lepers, remember this important fact: you are not God! You have countless limitations (or do you?). The Serbian proverb says it best: be humble, for you are made of earth. Be noble, for you are made of stars.

2. **You are insignificant, but you are essential to the universe**! With seven billion people on the planet, it might seem easy and commonplace to feel insignificant. Seven billion people is a LOT of people. Googling your name only to find out that there are several people with the identical name as you can emphasize the fact that, indeed, you are not as unique as you once thought. Becoming lost in the sea of humanity is easy at times (despite all the means for social networking). Additionally, when you stop to ponder all the hundreds of planets discovered from the Hubble space telescope in the past decade, not to mention all the galaxies in the cosmos, it all becomes very humbling. Yet despite the immensity of it all, each and every one of us is essential to the universal game plan. We cannot sit out on the sidelines or act like a wallflower. Each and every one of us has a purpose. if nothing more than to add light on the planet. Remember, you are essential to the universe. Don't take this responsibility lightly.

3. **You are your body, but you are not your body**! The next time you walk by a mirror, stop and take a good look at yourself. Yup! That's you! Your face, your shoulders, your hands, your feet . . . That is you in that body, so take good care of it. You *are* your body. You cannot live in somebody else's body. You can only inhabit your own. But remember this, you are not your body. You are so much more than your body. Your body has an expiration date (roughly about 100 years), but your spirit is ageless. You are light that inhabits your body, but your light shines on forever. So take good care of your body, you will need it for the entire journey on planet Earth. But remember you are not your body!

4. **You are separated from, but connected to everything!** The next time you get up from sitting down in a chair, become aware that the chair doesn't get up with you when you walk across the room. It stays there. In this physical world we are separated from everything outside of our skin. But are we really? Quantum physics reminds us that everything is energy, including us. At the quantum level, everything is connected. This, the luminaries say, begins to help explain premonitions, synchronicities, and much of what we call the mystical aspect of human spirituality. It's an illusion, they say, that we perceive everything as separate from ourselves. We are connected to everything and everyone. The realization of this is expressed in the saying, "To be at one with the universe." So enjoy your separateness, but, at the same time, embrace your connectedness.

5. **God is invisible, yet God is visible everywhere**. This paradox may be nothing more than a matter of semantics (and depending on your belief system, not a paradox, or not worthy of being a paradox at all). Our first introductions to the concept of the divine is often a personification with human characteristics. Falling back on the Cartesian principle, we tend to trust only that which we can validate through our five senses. This habit becomes magnified under stress. Yet the spiritual luminaries invite us to go beyond the five senses to perceive the divine, making use of our sense of compassion, our sense of creativity, and our sense of humor. As the expression goes, if you look closely enough, you will see God in everything (and everyone).

◈ SUMMARY

THE WAYS TO NURTURE, INVIGORATE, and enhance the health of the human spirit are countless. If there is a common theme among these ideas, perhaps it can best be stated like this: tame the ego and open the heart. A subtle yet equally powerful theme is how one engages the muscles of the soul: forgiveness, compassion, patience, optimism, and faith, regardless of what season of the soul you are in. Each suggestion, activity, behavior, or habit listed in this chapter is grounded in the premise of the three pillars of spiritual well-being: relationships, values, and a meaningful purpose in life. Metaphorically speaking, the human spirit is like a river of energy that surrounds and permeates every cell of our being. A healthy spirit is one in which this river of life flows evenly. This river has paradoxes that take time to explore and understand. Through it all we stand a little higher with a greater understanding and appreciation of the bigger picture.

✢ TERMS AND CONCEPTS

acceptance
art of self-renewal
attitude of gratitude
compassion in action
divine paradox
embracing the shadow

keeping the faith
living your joy
medicine for the soul
practice of sacred rituals
sweet forgiveness
walking with a light heart

EXERCISE 9.1
HEALTH OF THE HUMAN SPIRIT

Imagine, if you will, that there is a life force of divine energy that runs through your body. This life force is what we call the human spirit. We are a unique alchemy of humanity and divinity. Like a river, spirit runs through us with each breath. And it is spirit that invigorates the soul. A lack of spirit can starve the soul of its most important nutrient. The ways to nurture the soul are countless, yet each way ensures a constant flow of this essential life force. Unresolved anger and fear are two ways to choke the human spirit.

The following are some ways to enhance the health of the human spirit. As you read through these ideas, make a list of ways you can engage in these activities and, in doing so, enhance the health of your human spirit.

1. **The art of self-renewal.** List three ways in which you can find time to renew your personal energy—alone. Pick the activity, the day, and the time of the day.

    a. _____

    b. _____

    c. _____

2. **The practice of sacred rituals.** List three rituals you take part in on a regular basis to remind yourself of the sacredness of life.

   a. _____

   b. _____

   c. _____

3. **Sweet forgiveness.** List three people who currently have made it to the top of your "bad" list. First write down why you feel violated, and then write down how you can let it go and move on—to forgive and start moving again freely.

   a. _____

   b. _____

   c. _____

4. **Embrace the shadow.** List three aspects of yourself that you find less than flattering. How can you begin to come to peace with these aspects of yourself?

   a. _____

   b. _____

   c. _____

5. **Acceptance.** Identify at least three issues in your life that you have absolutely no control over. These issues are begging for acceptance. Are you listening?

   a. _____

   b. _____

   c. _____

6. **Keeping an attitude of gratitude.** List three things in your life for which you are extremely grateful. When you are down in the dumps, think back to them and count your blessings rather than your miseries.

   a. _____

   b. _____

   c. _____

7. **Keeping the faith.** Remind yourself of three times when the call of faith was answered. Then think of a problem you are dealing with now. Imagine that 7 years have passed and your prayers are answered again.

   a. _____

   b. _____

   c. _____

8. **Walking with a light heart.** List three things that are sure to make you laugh. They could be jokes, memories, photographs, bumper stickers, embarrassing moments, or cartoons.

a. _____

b. _____

c. _____

9. **Compassion in action.** List three things you can do to express your compassion in action. Is it a random act of kindness? Is it a generous gesture? Or perhaps it is just being there—without feeling a sense of obligation—really being there! Next, set out to do all three of these.

a. _____

b. _____

c. _____

10. **Living your joy.** Name your joy! What gives you happiness, real unconditional happiness, without any sense of regret afterward? List your top three pleasures. When was the last time you did each of these? How soon can you do them again?

a. _____

b. _____

c. _____

EXERCISE 9.2
THE DOORS OF PERCEPTION

If the doors of perception were cleansed, everything would appear as it is—infinite.

—William Blake

On average, we walk through an open doorway 15 to 20 times a day, perhaps many more. Symbolically, the thresholds we cross are far fewer, much to the detriment of our curiosity, and hence to our spiritual growth and human potential. From a metaphorical perspective, doors are portals to the unexplored aspects of our lives, many of which reside below the waters of the conscious mind. The mind has countless rooms, courtyards, and dimensions that beg for exploration—and understanding. Each room, each space, has a threshold, represented by a door, a stairwell, a tunnel, an arch, a gateway, or a portal. Each threshold serves as an invitation to exploration. Some even offer the chance for resolution and closure. We are repeatedly called to this exploration and evolve our soul growth process. Simply stated, this is "health of the human spirit."

If we were to use a door as a powerful archetypal symbol, then perhaps fear is best described as the locked handle that bars our passage across the threshold; one from stagnation to liberation, from ignorance to wisdom, from darkness to illumination. Crossing the threshold requires answering the "call to adventure," as Joseph Campbell put it. Once you have crossed the threshold you will never see the world the same way. This is what esteemed philosopher William Blake called the "doors of perception." Blake called the treasure beyond the door "infinity." Joseph Campbell might have called it "bliss." Carl Jung would have used the term "enlightenment."

What does it take to place your hand on this symbolic handle, open the door, and walk through? For some it's courage. Others require forgiveness or acceptance. Still others need a gentle shove in the form of inspiration. Only you can know for sure, yet immobilization is never a good option. Paradoxically, doorways offer both an entrance and an exit. Sometimes we have to cross the threshold several times before we know which is which, and on which side to reside, even to make a stand. Doors can also grow old with moss and rust. The hinges can become frozen in time by fear and anger. Blake reminds us to "cleanse" these doors so that we may see the infinite, experience bliss, or become enlightened. The choice is ours.

Here are some questions to ask yourself as you reflect on this soul-searching journal theme.

1. What symbolic door have you closed that keeps you in darkness or immobilized in your life?

   _____

   _____

   _____

   _____

2. What threshold do you stand behind, called by curiosity, but frozen in fear to take that next step?

   _____

   _____

   _____

   _____

3. What adventure awaits you? What new threshold are you ready to cross so that you can begin a new chapter in your life?

   _____

   _____

   _____

   _____

In the spirit of open doors, bon voyage and welcome home.

EXERCISE 9.3
SWEET FORGIVENESS

You cannot shake hands with a clenched fist.

—Indira Gandhi

Every act of forgiveness is an act of unconditional love. If unresolved anger is a toxin to the spirit, forgiveness is the antidote, and where anger is a roadblock, forgiveness is a ladder to climb above and transcend the experience. For forgiveness to be complete and unconditional, you must be willing to let go of all feelings of anger, resentment, and animosity. Sweet forgiveness cannot hold any taste of bitterness, because they are mutually exclusive. Victimization is a common feeling when one encounters stressors in the form of another person's behaviors. When we sense that our human rights have been violated, feelings of rage can quickly turn into feelings of resentment. Left unresolved, these toxic thoughts can taint the way we treat others and ourselves. To forgive those who we feel have wronged us is not an easy task. Often it's a process, and at times a very long process at that.

Turning the other cheek does not mean you have to let people walk all over you. Forgiveness is not a surrender of your self-esteem, nor is it a compromise of your integrity. When you can truly forgive the behavior of those whom you feel violated by, you let go of the feelings of control and become free to move on with your life. Resentment and grudges can become roadblocks on the human path. Forgiveness turns a hardened heart into an open passageway to progress on life's journey. Think for a moment of someone who might have violated your humanness. Is it time to let go of some toxic thoughts and initiate a sense of forgiveness?

To begin this journal entry, write the name of that person or those persons toward whom you feel some level of resentment. Beside each name write down what action or behavior it was that offended you and why you feel so violated. What feelings arise in you when you see this person, or even hear his or her name? Next, make a note of how long you have felt this way toward this person. Finally, search your soul for a way to forgive the people on your list, even if it means just to acknowledge their human spirit. Then practice the act of forgiveness as best you can, and let the feelings of resentment go.

_____

_____

_____

_____

_____

_____

_____

_____

_____

_____

_____

_____

_____

_____

_____

_____

_____

_____

_____

_____

_____

_____

_____

_____

_____

EXERCISE 9.4
CREATIVE ALTRUISM: THE POWER OF UNCONDITIONAL LOVE

Love, it is said, is the glue that holds the universe together. The expression of love can be made manifest in a great many ways. The following questions encourage you to explore the concept of unconditional love as an alternative to the motivation of fear.

1. Write your best definition of *love*.

    _____

    _____

    _____

2. If love is the energy that moves the human spirit, then fear is the metaphorical brake that stops love in its tracks. How does fear impede your ability to express love?

    _____

    _____

    _____

3. The slogan "random acts of kindness" was coined by a woman who was searching for a way to make the world a better place in which to live. She created this catchphrase as a means to express heartfelt altruism. The idea of performing a random act of kindness means to give anonymously without the expectation of receiving anything back. Compose a list of five ways to "give" altruistically and identify at least three ways that don't involve money.

    a. _____

    b. _____

    c. _____

    d. _____

    e. _____

4. Service! One cannot speak on the topic of altruism without speaking of the concept of service, yet service is an idea that has fallen on deaf ears lately. It's hard to feel sorry for yourself when you are helping others who are less fortunate. Over the past decade, the Institute of Noetic Sciences has given the Creative Altruism Award to those unique individuals who demonstrate the spirit of selfless service. If you could create an altruistic nonprofit organization to help others, what would you do? Explain it here:

    _____

    _____

    _____

EXERCISE 9.5
THE DIVINE PARADOX

Based on the information that attempts to explain the divine paradox of life (and all its nuances), take a few moments to reflect on the following five possible paradoxes and write down your thoughts and perceptions. Feel free to add any additional paradoxes you have come across as well. Be sure to include how it feels to hold two contradictory thoughts in your mind as well.

1. You are God, but you are not God.

   _____

   _____

   _____

2. You are insignificant, but essential to the universe.

   _____

   _____

   _____

3. You are your body, but you are not your body!

   _____

   _____

   _____

4. You are separated from, but connected to everything!

   _____

   _____

   _____

5. God is invisible, yet God is visible everywhere.

   _____

   _____

   _____

6. Additional paradoxes.

   _____

   _____

   _____

✦ ENDNOTES

1. Arrien, A., Keynote Address, Institute of Noetic Sciences Annual Conference, Boca Raton, FL, July 8–12, 1996.
2. Fox, M., Keynote Address: "What Is Medicine for the Soul?" Body and Soul Conference, Boston, September 30, 1994.
3. Poirier, C., as interviewed in "The Secret of Their Success." *Natural Health,* November/December 1999.
4. Casarjian, R., *Forgiveness: A Bold Choice for a Peaceful Heart.* Bantam New Age Books: New York, 1992.
5. Jung, C. G., as quoted in *The Laws of Spirit,* by Dan Millman. HJ Kramer: Tiburon, CA, 1995.
6. Ryan, M. J., *Attitudes of Gratitude: How to Give and Receive Joy Every Day of Your Life.* Conari Press: Berkeley, CA, 1999.
7. Klein, A., *The Healing Power of Humor.* Tarcher Books: Los Angeles, 1989.
8. H. H. Dalai Lama, *The Power of Compassion.* Thorson Books: San Francisco, 1995.
9. Larned, M., *Stone Soup for the World: Life-Changing Stories of Kindness and Courageous Acts of Service.* Conari Press: Berkeley, CA, 1998.
10. Ornstein., R., and Sobel, D., *Healthy Pleasures.* Addison Wesley: Reading, MA, 1989.

✦ ADDITIONAL REFERENCES

Bender, S., *Everyday Sacred.* HarperSanFrancisco: San Francisco, 1995.

Ellen, M., *Expect Miracles.* Conari Press: Berkeley, CA, 1999.

Dyer, W., *Your Sacred Self.* HarperCollins: New York, 1996.

Kundtz, D., *Stopping: How to Be Still When You Have to Keep Going.* Conari Press: Berkeley, CA, 1998.

Muller, W., *Sabbath: Restoring the Sacred Rhythm of Rest.* Bantam Books: New York, 1999.

Remen, R. N., *Kitchen Table Wisdom.* Riverhead Books: New York, 1996.

Ryan, M. J., *An Attitude of Gratitude.* Conari Press: Berkeley, CA, 1999.

Salwak, D. (Editor), *The Wonders of Solitude.* New World Library: Novato, CA, 1998.

Seaward, B. L., *Stand Like Mountain, Flow Like Water: Reflections on Stress and Human Spirituality.* Health Communications: Deerfield Beach, FL, 1997.

Seaward, B.L., *Quiet Mind, Fearless Heart.* John Wiley and Sons. New York. 2005.

Simon, S., and Simon, S., *Forgiveness: How to Make Peace with Your Past and Get on with Your Life.* Warner Books: New York, 1990.

Storr, A., *Solitude: A Return to the Self.* Ballantine Books: New York, 1988.

Walsh, R., and Vaughan, F., *Paths beyond Ego: The Transpersonal Vision.* Tarcher/Putnam: New York, 1993.

CHAPTER 10

The End Is Just the Beginning

The time will come when, after harnessing space, the wind, and the tides, we harness for God the energy of love, and that day for the second time in the history of the world, we shall have discovered fire.

—Teilhard de Chardin

THIS TEXT, LIKE YOUR OWN sojourn through life, has been an exploration into the ideas, philosophies, and theories of human spirituality. What can be difficult to put into words is sometimes more easily felt in the heart. This text has been an attempt to speak to both mind and heart, serving as a lighthouse, a reminder to attend to the health of the human spirit as you would other aspects of personal health.

We began with a "call to spirit," a recognition that, indeed, spirituality is not only a part of the human experience, but an essential part of daily existence as well. It is agreed by many leaders from all walks of life that perhaps more than ever before we are living in a time when there is a great spiritual hunger, a yearning for a closeness to the divine—however we might call it or define it. As the world spins faster into the brave new world of science and technology, with growing concerns for the future of humanity, perhaps this yearning is justified. Regardless, the call to spirit is a necessary step at any time, not only for our personal health but also for our personal evolution. As mythology scholar Joseph Campbell suggested, we must each answer the call, for no one else can do it for us.

A large part of this text highlights perspectives from many sages and wisdom keepers, from Jean Houston to Jesus of Nazareth, from Carl Gustav Jung to His Holiness, the Dalai Lama, each luminary contributing a significant morsel of wisdom to nourish our souls on the human journey—what many refer to as the *spiritual path.* Topics in this text ranged from spiritual potential and spiritual health to mind–body–spirit healing, all of which underscore the premise that spirituality is both a subtle and dynamic force in every aspect of our lives, whether we are aware of it or not.

And although we may not always understand the mystical nature of spirituality, as we come to appreciate both the subtle aspects (unbelievable synchronicities) and dynamic events (miraculous spontaneous healings) we become mystics ourselves. There is no one way to ensure the health of the human spirit; forgiveness, gratitude, self-renewal, and compassion all play an equal role in spiritual health, each taking its turn as the need arises. Poor spiritual health ignores the call when the need arises. Knowing that all aspects of health are connected, poor spiritual health cascades into poor mental, emotional, and physical health as well.

The concepts that you have read about in this text are based on real-life experiences, from literally hundreds, if not thousands, of people around the globe over centuries and centuries of time. The intention of this text and the many ways it is used (courses, workshops, and so on) is to act as a guide, a compass as you continue on your own odyssey. This may be the last chapter of the text, but in another sense it is really just the beginning of the next stage of your life journey. No matter what age you are, no matter what experiences you have accrued to date, the human spirit never stops growing, nor do the challenges we face.

It's very likely that some of the ideas and concepts you have read and perhaps discussed with others are hard to relate to because the course of your journey has brought you to a different place. The paths of our lives, however, take interesting and unpredictable twists and bends, no matter how hard we might choose to move otherwise. Because of this, you may wish to revisit some of these ideas months or even years later. And if you are like me, you may find that what at one time was just a theory takes on a whole new relevance with a new relationship, a new job, or a life-changing event years later.

As you have learned in several chapters, the language of spirituality is one of metaphor, simile, and allegory. To use a final metaphor, may these concepts, ideas, philosophies, and theories, like seeds, take root and germinate as the need arises, and may you discern the significance as you continue and cultivate your own wisdom.

As a college professor, corporate consultant, and workshop facilitator, I know that information in books, lectures, seminars, and workshops takes time to germinate. The following is a letter I received the day I returned from a visit with Elisabeth Kübler-Ross. It speaks to the timing of seeds as they take root so they may bear fruit when needed. I thought it was a nice way to finish the book. I think you'll agree.

Dear Luke,

Ahoy from the peaceful shores of Seattle! This is a long overdue letter from one of your American University students, class of '93, your last semester I believe. I should have written much sooner; there's been something I've been meaning to tell you. Remember when you told us that the things you were teaching might take on greater significance as we aged and matured (or failed to mature)? That was a major understatement! In fact, you may have saved my life. This is my story:

I'm an alcoholic. I've been one since I was in my teens, and I was headed for more advanced stages when we crossed paths. I had a DWI and was charged with another misdemeanor before I reached 20. And that's when they caught me. But my legal difficulties were the least of my problems. I was becoming a vicious, animalistic monster, the very antithesis of who I really was. I was alienating everyone I loved and lost all self-respect. But try to tell me that back then and you would've been treated to the work of a master manipulator with true genius toward rationalization and self-deceit.

And then, I had the beginnings of what I now see to be a spiritual awakening. It was suggested that I go to Alcoholics Anonymous. I went and my first instinct was to run out the door. They used words like *God* and *spirituality*. What the hell did God and spirituality have to do with my problems? I am sure you know the answer to this question better than I. But of course my ego told me that these people were freaks thinking that spirituality was the answer for them.

When was the last time I heard of talk like this? It was from you. And you certainly weren't a freak. You possessed a sincere inner calm. You helped people, and I believed you were behind the concepts you taught. I remembered how impressive some of your presentations were. How you could get a group of students to open their minds and try meditation. I remember when you had an American Indian shaman visit the class and how impressed I was with what he shared. I remembered when you told us that drugs and alcohol did not enhance spiritual development; they put up walls. I did feel a spiritual link back then for all my faults and I saw some of the things you covered in the Twelve Steps. So maybe there was something to this spiritual angle they talked about in AA, I thought. And I stayed.

I celebrated 4 years of sobriety and am still sober as I write this letter. I have gained a deep and very personal appreciation for the concepts you introduced me to and promised would become important further down the road. Thank you.

Sincerely,
Steven M.

The end is just the beginning. Happy Trails.

The Winds of Grace

Disturbing the winds of change,
As they produce growing pains.
Oh God, I seek a safe port
To harbor my fears and worries.
Grant me courage,
To endure the winds of change.

Comforting are the winds of grace,
As they instill a sense of faith.
Oh God, fill my sails with love
On this journey of self-exploration.
Grant me the insight,
To enjoy the winds of grace.

Blessed are the winds of grace,
As they invigorate my human spirit.
Oh God, I seek to know my purpose
In the community we know as "one people."
Grant me the strength,
To do my work.
The winds of change *are* the winds of grace.

—Brian Luke Seaward

Index

Note: Italicized page locators indicate figures.

A

Abbott, Jim, 78
Acceptance, 236–237, 245
Acupuncture, 167, 169, 173
ADD. *See* Attention deficit disorder
Addictions, 131–132
Ader, Robert, 162, 163, 175
Ageless Body, Timeless Mind
    (Chopra), 66
Agnostics, 10, 104
Alcoholics Anonymous, 7, 44, 256
Alcoholism, 131
Algonquins, 52
Ali, Muhammad, 103
Allopathic (Western) medicine, 163
Alper, Matthew, 202
Alternative healing, 168–170
Alternative Therapies (Dossey), 192
Altruism, 4–5, 249–250
American Association for the Advancement of Science, 33
American Heart Association, 202
American Indian Nation, 7, 52, 54
American Medical Association, 161
Amyotrophic lateral sclerosis (Lou Gehrig's disease), 159
Anatomy energy map, 173, *174*
Anderson, Sherry, 18
Angelou, Maya, 12
Anger, 12, 217
    loosening grip of, 235
    unresolved, 177–179
    wall of, 218
Apollo Space Project, 7
Archetypes, Jungian, 42
Armstrong, Lance, 13
Arrien, Angeles, 232
Art of self-renewal, 233, 244
Ascension process, 191
Ascent to Truth, The (Merton), 82
Association for Global New
    Thought, 64
Astral body, *166*
Atheists, 10, 104
Attention deficit disorder, 203
Attitude of gratitude, 237, 245
Attitudes of Gratitude (Ryan), 237
Augustine, St., 185
Auras, 165, 187
Auschwitz, 15, 77, 78, 132
Autobiography of a Yogi (Yoga-nanda), 85

Avoidance, 129, 143
Ayahuasca, 189, 202
Ayurvedic medicine, 65

B

Balance
    human spirituality and, 230
    restoring, 203–204
    wellness and, 26, 27
Ball, Marshall Stewart, 186
Baum, L. Frank, 138
Benson, Herbert, 57, 161, 163, 193, 202, 226
Bentov, Itzhak, 71, 191
Berendzen, Richard, 34
Bergen, Edgar, 80
Bhagavad Gita, 63, 66
Bible, 63, 66
Bioenergy, 161, 193
Bioenergy healing, 170
Biography, as part of your biology, 175–176
Black Elk, 52, 54–55
Black Elk Speaks (Neihardt), 52
Blake, William, 66, 246, 247
Blind spot, 191
Blitzer, Roy, 10
Bly, Robert, 62
Body Colors and Healing Light
    Meditation, 221–222
Body taps, 176
Bolen, Jean Shinoda, 109
Bond, The (McTaggart), 148
Borysenko, Joan, 57–59, 133, 198
Brain
    meditation and, 202
    mind *vs.*, 209
Brain freeze, 209
Brave New World (Huxley), 101
Breathing Clouds Meditation, 213–214
Brennan, Barbara Ann, 170
Brief History of Time, A (Hawking), 34
Buddha, 67, 208
Buddhism
    Golden Rule and, 84
    physics and, 71

C

Campbell, Joseph, 61–64, 80, 81, 87, 89, 93–95, 140, 247, 254
Cancer, 132, 159, 164
Cannon, Walter, 166
Capra, Fritjof, 71, 148

Carey, Ken, 59–60, 83
Carter, Gari, 14
Cartesian principle, 31, 34
Castaneda, Carlos, 107
Causal (spiritual) body, *166*
Cayce, Edgar, 165, 208
Cell memory, 161–162
Cellular consciousness, 167–168
Centering process (autumn), 139, 140, *141*, 141–142, 149, 154, 155
Central channel, *166*
Chakras, 165, *166*, *174*, 175
Change, grace and, 10–11
Chaotic antisocial stage, 49
Character, spirit and, 12–13
Chi, 75, 101, 165, 167
Chief Seattle, 52, 147
    letter from, 53–54
China, Tibet invaded by, 7, 60
Chogyam Trungpa Rimpoche, 8
Chopra, Deepak, 65–68, 89, 167
Christianity, 82, 84, 107
Clairvoyant thoughts, 196, 197
Clark, William, 1
Climate change, 8
Closed heart, 9, 11
Collective unconscious, 10, 42–42, 70, 71, 203, 216
Columbine High School, shootings at, 6
Comfort zones, 10, 11
Commonweal Cancer Help Program, 44
Compassion, 17, 61, 64, 72, 74, 112, 135–136, 191, 230, 244, 254
    in action, 239–241, 246
    gratitude and, 237
Complementary medicine, 163, 168–170, 173
Conditional love, 220–221
Confucianism, Golden Rule and, 84
Connecting process (summer), 139, 140, *141*, 147–149, 149, 154, 155
Conscience, 20–21
Conscious evolution, 65
Conscious Evolution (Hubbard), 64
Consciousness
    cellular, 167–168
    turning point in, 6–8
Cooke, Alistair, 3–4
Copernicus, Nicolaus, 30
Coronary heart disease, 164, 202, 215

Cosmic Serpent, The: DNA and the Origins of Knowledge (Narby), 189
Courage, 17, 112, 135
Course in Miracles, A, 83, 172
Cousins, Norman, 162, 167, 172
Covey, Stephen, 13
Creation of Health, The (Myss), 175
Creation spirituality (Fox), 72–74
Creative altruism, 249–250
Creativity, 136
Crop circles, 187–188
Cross-crawl movements, 176–177
Crown pull, 177
Crystal Cave Meditation, 216–217
Cultural Creatives, 5, 18
Curing, healing *vs.*, 164–165
Curiosity, 135
Cyclical growth principle, 76, *76*

D
Dalai Lama, 60–61, 89, 114, 240, 254
Davidson, Richard, 202
de Chardin, Teilhard, 80, 108, 253
Departure
    hero's journey and, 62–63
    your mythical journey and, 94
Descartes, René, 30, 31, 32, 33, 41, 137, 160, 175, 186, 202, 232
Desire, curtain of, 219–220
Detachment, 67
de Vernejoul, Henri, 169
Dharma, 68
Different Drum (Peck), 48
Discipline, 117–118
Disease, stress and, 166–167
Dissonance, 166
Distant healing, 161, 169, 193
Distractions of the human spirit, 131, 149, 151–152
Divine consciousness, 43
Divine paradox, 241–243, 251
Divine Truth, 9, 10
DNA, 188, 189–190, 192, 194
DNA Meditation, 226–227
Donne, John, 147
Doors of perception, 246–247
Dossey, Larry, 58, 66, 68–70, 161, 184, 192, 193
Doubt, 238
Dreams
    insightful, 196, 197
    Jungian analysis of, 43
    precognitive, 195
Dreher, Diane, 75
Drummond, Henry, 82
Dynamic balance principle, 76, *76*

E
Eagle Man (Ed McGaa), 52
Eat, Pray, Love (Gilbert), 140
Eckhart, Meister, 72
Eden, Donna, 165, 176
Ego, 9, 11, 111, 146, 149, 217
    domesticating, 205, 211, 236
    religion and, 104
    soul and, 204–205
Einstein, Albert, 5, 33, 66, 70–72, 80, 88, 208
Embracing the shadow, 236, 245
Emotional well-being, 27, *27*, 177
Emptying process (winter), 139, 140, *141*, 142–145, 149, 154, 155
Energy Ball Meditation, 224–226
Energy medicine, 161, 168–170
Energy system "vitamins," 176–177
Enlightenment, 208–209, 212
Entrainment, 168
Era-II medicine (mind–body), 193
Era-III medicine (mind–body–spirit), 69, 192, 193
Erhmann, Max, 143
Etheric body, *166*
Evolution, 87
Exclusive meditation, 206–207
External relationships, *113*, 115

F
Faith, 17, 102, 112, 135, 237–238, 244, 245
    healing and, 133–134
    love and, 83–84
    rainbows as symbol of, 138
Fear, 10, 12, 217
    as obstacle to love, 83
    replacing with love, 172
    unresolved, 177–179
    veil of, 218
Feminine spirituality, 58–59
Fight-or-flight response, 166
First Nation tribes of Canada, 52, 54
Food and Drug Administration, 161
Forgiveness, 85, 102, 134–135, 230, 244, 245, 254
    anger resolution and, 178
    health and, 158
    sweet, 235–236
Formal-institutionalized individual, *49*, 49–50, 92
Foundation for the Future, 64
Fowler, J., 48
Fox, Matthew, 3–4, 72–74, 89, 232
Francis, Saint, 185

Frankl, Viktor, 15, 77–80, 102, 117
Freud, Sigmund, 42, 79, 87, 205
Fuller, Buckminster, 10, 64, 183, 184

G
Galileo, 30, 31, 35
Gandhi, Mohandas, 20, 39
Gerber, Richard, 165
Gere, Richard, 103
Ghost in the machine, 160, 173
Gibran, Kahlil, 111
Giffords, Gabrielle, 14
Gilbert, Elizabeth, 140
Gill, Jim, 230
Global Family, 64
Global Village, 3
Global warming, 8
Goal setting, logotherapy and, 79
"God Particle," 33
God Theory, The (Haisch), 33
Golden Rule, 83, 84, 115, 136, 171, 240
Goodall, Jane, 31, 103
Gorbachev, Mikhail, 3
Grace, 10–11, 51
Graham, Billy, 6
Gratitude, 237, 254
Great Divide, 5
Greed, 4, 218–219, 231
Green, Alyce, 162
Green, Elmer, 162, 184, 202
Grounding process (spring), 139, 140, *141*, 145–147, 149, 154, 155
Guilt Is the Teacher, Love Is the Lesson (Borysenko), 57

H
Haisch, Bernard, 33
Hallucinogenic drugs, 192
Halo (crown chakra), 173
Harmonious action principle, 76, 76–77
Harmony, 26, 27, 37
Hatha yoga, 9, 169
Havel, Vaclev, 103
Hawking, Stephen, 34
Healing
    curing *vs.*, 164–165
    distant, 161, 169, 193
    prayer and, 134
    spontaneous, 161
Healing Power of Mind, The (Thondup), 172
Healing Words: The Power of Prayer and the Practice of Medicine (Dossey), 69, 161

Health
  human spirituality and, 102
  laughter and, 162
  mechanistic paradigm of, 160
Healthy Pleasures (Ornstein), 241
Heart's Code, The (Pearsall), 186
Hero's journey (Campbell), 62–64,
  94
Hero with a Thousand Faces, The
  (Campbell), 62
Hierarchy of needs (Maslow), *46*,
  46–47
Hinduism, 71, 84
Hippocratic Oath, 45
Hoff, Benjamin, 75
Holistic wellness, 26, 35
Holographic Universe, The (Talbot),
  186
Holons, 88
Holy moments, 186, 187–189, 193,
  197–198
Holy Spirit, 165
Homeostasis, 202
Homolateral pattern, 177
Hopi, 7
Houston, Jean, 80–81, 133, 254
How Then Shall We Live? (Muller),
  116
Hubbard, Barbara Marx, 64–65,
  89
Hubble Space Telescope, 34
Human aura, 165, 170
Human energy field, 165–166,
  166
Human Genome Project, 190
Humanistic psychology, 46
Human potential, personal goals
  and, 79
Human Potential Movement, 80
Human spirit
  health of, 244–245
  mandala of, 123–124, *124*
Human spirituality
  balance and, 230
  defined, 117
  definitions of, 100–101
  divine mystery and, 193
  mystical aspect of, 186
  one source, many names for,
    103
  profiles of, 13–15
  spirits on a human path,
    108–109
  three pillars of, 113–117
  well-being and, 30–31
Humor, 134
Humor therapy, 168, 238
Huxley, Aldous, 88, 101
Hypnosis, 160

I
I Ching, 43
Immune system, positive emotions
  and, 162, 167
Inclusive meditation, 207
Initiation
  hero's journey and, 63, 94
  your mythical journey and, 94
Institute of Noetic Science, 33, 161,
  250
Institutional stage, 49
Integral Institute, 88
Integral theory, 88
Integration, 26, 27, 35
Integrity, 136
  character *vs.*, 13
Internal relationship, *113*,
  114–115
International Society for the Study
  of Subtle Energy and Energy
  Medicine, 170
Intuition, 135
Involution, 87
Islam, 84, 107

J
Jackson, Phil, 103
Jampolsky, Gerold, 82, 83
Jesus of Nazareth, 81–85, 89, 114,
  208, 254
Johnson, Magic, 3
Joint Commission, 163
Joy, 241, 246
Judaism, 84, 107
Judd, Naomi, 3
Jung, Carl Gustav, 10, 42–44, 58,
  62, 70, 71, 87, 102, 113, 114,
  117, 119, 142, 191, 195, 203,
  236, 247, 254

K
Kabbalah, 7
Karma, 171
Keeping the faith, 237–238, 245
Keller, Helen, 80
Kennedy, John F., 84
King, Martin Luther, Jr., 241
Kitchen Table Wisdom (Remen),
  45
Klein, Gerta Weissman, 127
Koran, 66
Krishnamurti, 87
Kriya Yoga, 85
Kübler-Ross, Elisabeth, 27, 29, 30,
  34, 140, 255
Kuhn, Thomas, 192
Kundalini energy, 189, 190–191,
  194

L
Lakota, 7
Lao Tzu, 41, 66, 74–77, 142, 148
Laughter, 162, 238–239,
  245–246
Laziness, obstruction of, 219
Left hemisphere of brain, 209
Lerner, Michael, 44
LeShan, Lawrence, 162, 163
Lewis, C. S., 84, 204
Light, 33, 72
Lightner, Candy, 78
Living your joy, 241, 246
Logotherapy (Frankl), 77, 78
Lou Gehrig's disease, 159
Love, 10, 11, 17, 51, 61, 102
  ascension process and, 191
  conditional, 220–221
  faith and, 83–84
  fear replaced by, 172
  gratitude and, 237
  learning to, 116
  unconditional, 81–85
  Yogananda on, 85–86
Love, Medicine and Miracles
  (Siegel), 146
Lucas, George, 62
Lupus, 158

M
MADD. *See* Mothers Against
  Drunk Driving
Malraux, André, 4
Mandalas
  origin and definition of, 123
  of personal wellness, 35, *36*
  of wellness paradigm, *27*
Mandela, Nelson, 3, 14, 103, 134
Man's Search for Meaning (Frankl),
  15, 77, 78, 117
Mantra, exclusive meditation and,
  207, 210–211
Maslow, Abraham, *46*, 46–48, 64,
  77, 87, 89, 128, 133, 163,
  186, 195, 198
McGaa, Ed (Eagle Man), 52
McLuhan, Marshall, 3
McTaggart, Lynne, 148
Mead, Margaret, 80
Meaningful purpose in life, *113*,
  116–117, 120, 122–123
Mechanistic paradigm, 31, 160
Medicine
  Chinese, 167
  complementary, 163, 168–170,
    173
  new era of, 162–165
  for the soul, 231–232

Medicine wheel (American Indian), 123
  as described by Black Elk, 54–55 54
Meditation, 65, 77, 169, 192
  art of, 202
  checklist, 212–213
  cleansing the mind, 203–204
  defined, 203
  discipline and, 206
  enlightenment and, 208–209
  exclusive, 206–207
  exercises, 213–227
  inclusive, 207
  mindfulness, 207–208
  purpose of, 205
  steps in, 209–211
  ultimately inclusive, 207
Memories, Dreams, Reflections (Jung), 43, 71
Mental body, 166
Mental well-being, 27, 28, 29
Meridians, 166, 167
Merton, Thomas, 82
Metaphor, as language of spirit, 106
Metaphorical mountain, spiritual well-being and, 128–129
Mind–body–spirit healing, 159, 172, 173, 254
Mind–body–spirit medicine, 163
Mindfulness meditation, 202, 207–208
Modern Man in Search of a Soul (Jung), 44
Mother Earth Spirituality, 52, 107
Mother Earth Spirituality (Eagle Man), 52
Mothers Against Drunk Driving, 78
Motivation and Personality (Maslow), 46, 47
Motz, Julie, 165
Moyers, Bill, 62
Muller, Wayne, 116
Multiple personality disorder, 160–161
Muscles of the soul, 132–136, 149, 152–153
Myss, Caroline, 165, 171, 172, 175
Mystical experiences, recording, 194
Mystical spirituality, 184
Mystic-communal stage, 49, 51, 92
Mystics, 55, 59, 71
Myth, meaning of, 61–62, 93–94
Mythic Life, A (Houston), 80

N
Narby, Jeremy, 189, 192
Navajo Indians, 52

Near-death experiences (NDEs), 7, 69
Neihardt, John G., 52
Neuroplasticity, 202
New Dimensions Radio, 64
New Earth, A (Tolle), 8
New Testament, 82
Newton, Isaac, 70, 71
Niebuhr, Reinhold, 237
Nirvana, 171, 192
Nocebos, 161
Nonlocal mind, 69, 70, 192
Norris, Patricia, 162, 163

O
Oglala Sioux (Lakota) tribe, 52
Ó Murchú, Diarmuid, 33
"On Defining Spirit" (Remen), 45
Oneness principle, 75, 76, 148
Open Heart Meditation, 214–216
Optimal well-being, 27
Optimism, 135, 244
Organ transplants, 161–162, 168, 186
Ornish, Dean, 9, 215
Ornstein, Robert, 241
Oslo massacre (2011), 6

P
Patience, 76, 82, 85, 135, 244
Paul (apostle), 148
  letter to the Corinthians, 84–85
Peak experiences, 186, 195, 197–198
Pearsall, Paul, 186
Peck, M. Scott, 48–51, 87, 89, 92, 104, 130, 185, 195
  stages of spiritual growth, 48–51, 49
Perennial philosophy (Huxley), 88, 101
Perfect Health (Chopra), 66
Persistence, 135
Personal cosmology, 74
Personal goals, human potential and, 79
Personal unconscious, 42
Personal value system, 113, 115–116, 119–120, 121–122
Personal wellness, 28
  mandala of, 35, 36
Pert, Candace, 167, 168, 184
Physical body, 166
Physical well-being, 27, 28, 29
Physics, theology and, 70
Pierce, Franklin, 52
Pillar of Mystery, 118
Placebos, 161

Pleasure principle, 241
PNI. See Psychoneuroimmunology
Poirier, Constance, 233
Postdenominational age, 6
Power of Compassion, The (Dalai Lama), 61
Power of Myth, The (Campbell), 63
Prana, 165
Pranayama, 101, 242
Prayer, healing and, 134, 161, 173, 192–193
Pride, mask of, 220
Prodigal Son, 83
Prophet, The (Gibran), 111
Psyche, 101–102
Psychoneuroimmunology, 57, 65, 163, 173, 175
Psychospirituality, 42
Psychotropic drugs, 189, 202

Q
Qi Gong, 161, 169, 170, 193
Quantum Healing (Chopra), 66, 167
Quantum Theology (Ó Murchú), 33

R
Radin, Dean, 33
Rainbow Meditation, 222–224
Rainbows, yellow brick road and, 138–139
Random acts of kindness, 240, 250
Ray, Paul, 5, 18
Reason for Hope (Goodall), 31
Receptivity, to divine insight, 146–147
Recovering the Soul (Dossey), 68, 69
Redford, Robert, 3–4
Reductionist theory, 32, 175
Reiki, 161, 168, 169, 193
Reinventing Medicine (Dossey), 192
Relationships
  connecting process and, 147
  external, 113, 115
  internal, 113, 114–115
  personal and interpersonal, 120
Relativity theory, 70, 71, 72, 208
Relaxation Revolution, The (Benson), 161
Religion, 118
  definitions of, 103–104
  new common ground between science and, 32–34
  spirituality and, 104–105, 105
Religions, Values, and Peak Experiences (Maslow), 47
Remen, Rachel Naomi, 44–46, 89, 114, 157
Resonance, 166, 168

Return home
    hero's journey and, 63–64
    your mythical journey and, 94
Return of the Bird Tribes (Carey),
    60
Right hemisphere of brain, 209
Roadblocks on the spiritual path,
    129, 149–151
Road Less Traveled, The (Peck), 48,
    92, 195
Rolling Thunder (Shoshone sha-
    man), 52
Roth, Ron, 204
Russell, Peter, 2, 3, 5
Russell, Ron, 187
Ryan, Mary Jane, 237

S

Sacred rituals, practice of, 234–235,
    245
Salish tribes, 52
Schweitzer, Albert, 204
Science
    blind spot in, 192
    new common ground between
        religion and, 32–34
Scivias (von Bingen), 56
Screwtape Letters, The (Lewis), 204
Seasons of the soul, 139–149, *141*,
    153–155
Seat of the Soul, The (Zukav), 112
Self-actualization, 46, 47, 48, 77,
    102, 133
Self-help groups, 7
Self-realization, 85
Self-renewal, 233, 254
Selye, Hans, 166
Serenity Prayer, 237
Serpent energy, 190
Service, 45, 239, 240–241, 250
*7 Habits of Highly Effective People,
    The* (Covey), 13
Seven Spiritual Laws of Success, The
    (Chopra), 66–68
Seven Veils Meditation, 217–221
Sex, Ecology, Spirituality (Wilber),
    88
Shadow, theory of, 43
Shamans, 189, 192
    South American, 8
Siegel, Bernie, 146
Simonton, Carl, 162
Skeptical stage, *49*, 50–51, 92
Sobel, David, 241
Soul, 242
    describing, 111–112
    ego and, 204–205
    medicine for, 231–232

muscles of, 132–136, 149,
    152–153
seasons of, 139–149, *141*
spirit and, 109–110
Soul work, defining, 112
Spectrum of consciousness, stages
    in, 87–88
Spectrum of Consciousness, The
    (Wilber), 86, 87
Spell of materialism, 184
Spirit
    breath and, 101–102, 118
    character and, 12–13
    metaphor as language of, 106
    soul and, 109–110
    unhealthy, 9
    use of word in everyday conver-
        sation, 2
Spiritual bankruptcy, 6
Spiritual constipation, 130
Spiritual dormancy, 6, 130, 131
Spiritual guides, 217
Spiritual health, 79, 137
Spiritual hunger, 6, 130
Spirituality
    American Indian, 52, 54–55
    Borysenko's definition of, 58
    feminine, 58–59
    human, profiles of, 13–15
    religion and, 104–105, *105*
    stress and, 12
    use of word, in American lexi-
        con, 2, 3
Spiritual materialism, 8–9
Spiritual path, 254
    choosing, 107–108
    distractions on, 131
    roadblocks on, 129, 149–151
Spiritual potential, 136–137
Spiritual well-being, *27*, 28, 29–30
    integrative model of, *137*
    metaphorical mountain and,
        128–129
Spontaneous healings, 161
"Stages of Faith" (Fowler), 48
Stalking the Wild Pendulum (Ben-
    tov), 71, 191
Starseed: The Third Millennium
    (Carey), 59
Starseed Transmissions, The
    (Carey), 59, 83
Star Wars, 12, 62
Stress, 217
    avoidance and, 129
    complementary medicine and,
        168
    disease and, 166–167
    as global epidemic, 3–4
    lupus and, 158

perspectives on, 110–111
    spirituality and, 12
Stress response, 166
*Structure of Scientific Revolutions,
    The* (Kuhn), 192
Suffering, finding meaning in,
    78–80
Sweet forgiveness, 235–236, 245,
    248
Synchronicity, 43, 195, 197, 254

T

Tagore, Rabindranath, 66, 85
T'ai chi, 77, 168, 170
Talbot, Michael, 186
Taoism, 43, 75, 142, 148
    Golden Rule and, 84
    physics and, 71
Tao of Inner Peace, The (Dreher), 75
Tao of Physics, The (Capra), 71, 148
Tao of Pooh, The (Hoff), 75
Tao Te Ching, 74, 75
Targ, Elizabeth, 193
Tart, Charles, 39, 184
Teachings of Don Juan, The (Cas-
    taneda), 107
Teach Only Love (Jampolsky), 83
Technology, mental distractions
    and, 203
Telecommunications revolution, 8
Teresa of Avila, Saint, 185, 186
Theology, physics and, 70
Therapeutic touch, 161, 168
Thich Nhat Hanh, 207
Thondup, Tulku, 172
Tibet, Chinese invasion of, 7, 60
TM. *See* Transcendental Meditation
Tolerance, 236–237
Tolle, Eckhart, 8
Tragic optimism, 78
Transcendental Meditation, 65,
    161, 207
Transpersonal psychology, 42, 87
Turning Point, The (Capra), 148
24/7 lifestyle, 9

U

Ulfelder, Susan, 170
Ultimately inclusive meditation,
    207
Unconditional love
    Christianity and, 81–85
    compassion in action and, 240
    creative altruism and, 249
    egolessness and, 136
    healing and, 159
    returning to source of, 218
    sweet forgiveness and, 248

Unconscious resistance, 172
Unhealthy spirit, 9
Unified Field theory, 72, 88

V

Values, symbols for, 115
Value system, six core values in, 116
Vatican II, 7
Virgin Mary, apparitions of, 185,
    187
Vision quest, 55, 146
von Bingen, Hildegard, 55–57

W

Waking Up in Time (Russell), 2–3, 5
Walking with a light heart,
    238–239, 245–246
Well-being, human spirituality and,
    30–31

Wellman, Marc, 13
Wellness
    holistic, 26, 35
    in limelight and life cycle, 29–30
Wellness paradigm, 26, 27, 34, 123
WHO. *See* World Health Organiza-
    tion
Why People Don't Heal (Myss), 171
Wilber, Ken, 86–89, 130
Williamson, Marianne, 134
Winfrey, Oprah, 8
Wirkus, Margaret, 224
Wirkus, Mietek, 187, 224
Wisdom keeper, difficult journey
    of, 40
Women of Vision and Action, 64
Women's Journey to God, A (Bory-
    senko), 58, 59
Women's spirituality, 58–59

World Future Society, 64
World Health Organization, 3–4,
    102
Woundology, 171–172
wu wei, 77

Y

Yauch, Adam, 103
Yellow brick road, rainbows and,
    138–139
Yin and yang, 75, 76, 87
Yoga, 77
Yogananda, Paramahansa, 25,
    85–86, 89, 142, 185

Z

Zen meditation, 207
Zip up, 177
Zukav, Gary, 112